Who's Laughing Now?

Who's Laughing Now?

Feminist Tactics in Social Media

Jenny Sundén and Susanna Paasonen

The MIT Press
Cambridge, Massachusetts
London, England

This book was set in ITC Stone Serif Std and ITC Stone Sans Std by New Best-set Typesetters Ltd. Printed and bound in the United States of America.

Library of Congress Cataloging-in-Publication Data

Names: Sundén, Jenny, 1973- author. | Paasonen, Susanna, 1975- author.
Title: Who's laughing now? : feminist tactics in social media / Jenny Sundén and Susanna Paasonen.
Description: Cambridge, Massachusetts : The MIT Press, [2020] | Includes bibliographical references and index.
Identifiers: LCCN 2020004715 | ISBN 9780262044721 (hardcover)
Subjects: LCSH: Internet and women. | Internet and activism. | Feminism. | Social media. | Humor.
Classification: LCC HQ1178 .S86 2020 | DDC 305.42—dc23
LC record available at https://lccn.loc.gov/2020004715

10 9 8 7 6 5 4 3 2 1

To Gittan

Contents

Acknowledgments

Our work for this book started in the spring of 2017 as an article for the *Feminist Media Studies* journal special issue "Online Misogyny." As we greatly enjoyed working on shameless, resistant hags and sluts, we started planning a book project the following autumn as the #MeToo movement first broke. There has been an immediacy to our project, yet its speed has also been a matter of joy and pleasure taken in thinking, writing, and giggling together.

We would like to thank the Faculty of Humanities and the School of History, Culture and Art Studies at the University of Turku, Finland—and Dean Jaakko Suominen, in particular—for supporting our work on this book with a writing retreat grant and Jenny's two-year visiting professorship. We would also like to thank the Department of Media Studies research seminar at Turku and the advanced seminar in gender studies at Södertörn University in Stockholm for comments and suggestions to article drafts leading up to our book. Further, warm thanks for their helpful feedback go to the editors of the *Feminist Media Studies* special issue, Debbie Ging and Eugenia Siapera; to Susanna's coeditors, Kaisu Hynnä-Granberg and Mari Lehto, on a *Social Media + Society* special issue on "Affective Body Politics"; and to the anonymous reviewers for both journals. Two articles that form the basis for chapters 3 and 5, respectively, have been published as "Shameless Hags and Tolerance Whores: Feminist Resistance and the Affective Circuits of Online Hate," *Feminist Media Studies* 18(4) (2018): 643–656, and "Inappropriate Laughter: Affective Homophily and the Unlikely Comedy of #MeToo," *Social Media + Society* (October–December 2019): 1–10.

Last, but certainly not least, thanks to the staff at the MIT Press, most notably Gita Manaktala, for her support and enthusiasm for what is not the most obvious of approaches to feminist social media research, and the authors of the nine manuscript reviews that made us feel very well read.

1 Introduction: What's Laughter Got to Do with It?

Consider this hypothetical scene: Two feminist scholars are having a hotel breakfast in the very beginning of the #MeToo movement in October 2017. "Well, I'm gonna have some more coffee, possibly an orange juice," one of them says. "Me too!," the other replies, making the hashtag symbol up in the air with her fingers. In a split second, both are laughing, helplessly. The more they realize how inappropriate it is to laugh, the harder it becomes not to, and tears are soon running down their cheeks. Starting from this scene of absurd laughter out of place and its contagious energy, this book sets out to investigate feminist tactics of resistance in times of violent online sexism. Online sexism, hate, and harassment aim at silencing subjects coded as female or feminine by resorting to affective mechanisms such as shaming and fear. We are interested in how humor and laughter can help to reroute and reshape these forces and what their affective volatility may add to our understanding of mundane politics. Zooming in on the dynamics of shame, in particular, we further examine the complex ways in which sexuality operates within the affective politics of social media in connection with shame and shaming—and, by extension, the potentialities involved in shamelessness.

In what follows, we move from the markedly nonhumorous #MeToo movement and its ways of rewiring gendered sexual shame to instances where it collides with laughter; to the politics and ethics of commenting on and publishing hateful or otherwise offensive tweets, posts, and messages; to the appropriation of derogatory terminology for resistant ends; and to the tactic of making visible the exclusion of women from the realm of professional expertise and authority within the "Congrats, you have an all male panel!" Tumblr blog. We look into unsolicited vulva pics, consider the possibilities and limitations of satire based on the reversal of gender roles, and argue for the value of absurdity in turning things around. We ask what has given the initiatives we examine their particular affective lift and also scrutinize the conditions and constraints that they both operate in and generate.

Humor and laughter are possibly not the first qualities or tactics to be associated with feminist activism, online or off. The "feminist killjoy" (Ahmed 2010, 2015)—the one who disrupts other people's sense of happiness and refuses to laugh when expected to do so—more commonly embodies feminist tactics in the cultural imaginary. There certainly seems to be equally little to laugh about in the ubiquity of online hate, sexism, and misogyny (Jane 2016; Penny 2013) fueled by toxic masculinity (e.g., Consalvo 2012; Marwick and Caplan 2018; Massanari 2015; Phillips 2015; Salter and Blodgett 2012). As scholarly attention has begun to cluster on online feminist resistance and activism, it has focused on the affective dynamics of anger, rage, and frustration, as exemplified by the high visibility of the #MeToo movement (e.g., Boyle 2019; Chamberlain 2017; Gill and Orgad 2018; Guha, Gajjala, and Stabile 2019; Koivunen, Kyrölä, and Ryberg 2018; Mendes, Ringrose, and Keller, 2019).

At the same time, humor plays a key role in how and where attention clusters on social media, which is increasingly providing platforms and modes for activist mobilization and critique. In this book, we explore feminist initiatives that have grown popular, even viral, and exemplify what Sarah Banet-Weiser (2018, 10), in her discussion of popular feminism, identifies as the imperative of visibility within online attention economy. Here, all kinds of campaigns, from advertising to activism, aim at virality where content—hashtags, posts, images, video clips, animated GIFs, or something else—gains a certain liveliness through its networked sharing, circulation, variation, multiplication, liking, and commenting. *Virality* is descriptive of how content spreads across platforms and geographical terrains in ways that cannot be planned, foreseen, controlled, or achieved by any single individual or group. In the optimized visibility, attention, reach, and volume of redistribution that virality entails, it remains something of a ubiquitous goal. Virality involves affectivity, which Tony D. Sampson (2012, 14) describes as "mesmeric fascinations, passionate interests, and joyful encounters." As discussed in the chapters that follow, the registers of dismay, disgust, anger, and outrage nevertheless play an equally key role in how people engage with social media content, possibly setting it in viral circulation of varying lengths and speeds. Outrage alone involves considerable capacity to set bodies in motion, as the #MeToo movement aptly illustrates.

In addition to the viral logic that guides our general methodological approach, we examine examples that remained emergent without fully trending in order to add diversity and nuance to our analysis. Although our interest is firmly in networked forms of feminism, we are primarily interested not in online feminist spheres, communities, and networks and their histories and activist contexts as such (see Marwick 2019) but in the viral and affective logics of resistant formations that may be more fleeting. Besides the social media examples that are at the heart of the book, we analyze mainstream media coverage in order to map out the broader public visibility and interpretations of contemporary discussions of sexism and harassment.

Throughout the book, laughter operates both as a key theme and as a methodological tool because we have been drawn to examples that attract or repel, entice or annoy us, rather than those leaving us unmoved. It follows that we address viral examples that have pulled us in or simply made us laugh. In the chapters that follow, we explore the role of humor and laughter in rewiring the affective circuits of anger, outrage, shame, and shamelessness that fuel resistant activities. How can laughter be an answer to something as serious as sexism? When is it inappropriate to laugh? Under which terms do feminist tactics of resistance become successfully viral? And how and when may they fall short? Who gets to laugh and about what or whom? And what happens when such relations are flipped or become utterly unclear? *Who's Laughing Now?* sets out to account for feminist tactics at a political moment when laughter is sorely needed.

Feminist online humor certainly exists, but its general visibility is not high (see Rentschler 2015; Rentschler and Thrift 2015; Ringrose and Lawrence 2018). For example, a Google search for feminist memes will result in ample hits on antifeminist memes. Similarly, the results of a search for feminist humor display a range of commentary on humorless feminists (those killjoys). This is by no means a shocking revelation, given the degree to which online humor has been identified as "kicking down" and as being disproportionately leveled at women, queers, and racial others (Kanai 2016; Marwick 2014). Misogyny runs rife on Twitter exchanges and discussion forums where laughter—laughing at and at the expense of someone—is instrumental in the maintenance and reproduction of social relations of power. As Jessica Ringrose and Emilie Lawrence (2018, 686) note, existing research has shown that most online humor is sexist and "working to reinforce and reaffirm notions of gender that are binary and hierarchically opposite." There is an aggressive edge, both sharp and blunt, to much online humor, which trades in sexism, racism, and homophobia and makes downward punches toward socially marginalized and subordinated groups (Lockyer and Pickering 2005). This landscape may come across as gloomy, indeed. Powered by mockery, ridicule, and humiliation, it normalizes misogyny and reinforces male domination (Highfield 2016; Marwick 2013; Massanari 2015; Milner 2014, 2016; Phillips 2015; Phillips and Milner 2017). This, however, is not the whole story, or a book looking at feminist humor in social media, such as this one, would be a redundant project.

Online humor trades in and contributes to networked misogyny that includes persistent, casual sexism; slut-shaming carried out toward women by other women; and alt-right gender ideology and physical violence, celebrated within the so-called incel rebellion of involuntarily celibate men who organize on online platforms and target women with their misogynistic hate (Banet-Weiser 2018). Despite the differences between its articulations and the range of intensities that it entails, "popular misogyny" involves a fantasy of returning women to an imaginary place where they need not be heard, turning back the social clock, and getting back to how things once were (even if these never were). This should not be understood within a simple gender binary as something that men do to women: people of all genders can have strong investments in the status quo or in resistance toward it in ways that fuel and inspire tracking, critiquing, and devaluing the actions of those whose political stances, sexual preferences, or lifestyle choices do not conform to their own. Sexism involves a conservative impulse that points to shortcomings in how the term gets deployed in referring to sticking to, preserving, and conserving things. Conservatism of this kind does not just preserve but actively aims to transform, alter, and influence the social world. It is, in essence, actively regressive. The invitation to "get back to the kitchen," generously offered to women who voice their opinions online (Jane 2014a), would not make sense unless women had not already left the kitchen or were, in fact, never confined to it.

At the same time, much feminist humor trades in popular imageries (advertisements and illustrations) of the 1950s and 1960s that display heterosexual romance, female intimacy, and blissful nuclear family life with clearly assigned gender roles. It adds novel texts to these and, in doing so, practices *détournement* of the situationist kind where objects of popular culture are appropriated for alternative political ends. Like situationists replacing the captions of popular comics with lines from Guy Debord's *The Society of the Spectacle* (a 1967 Marxist critique of consumer culture), feminist humor that is commodified as fridge magnets, postcards, coffee mugs, coasters, and a range of visuals shared online trades in vintage imageries combined with sarcastic, ironic, political, or absurd captions. A Google Image search done at the time of this writing for "feminist humor" resulted in a hit to a Pinterest post with a woman posing in an apron, combined with this caption: "He asked why the house isn't clean since I'm home all day. I asked why we aren't rich since he works all day." Another search hit was to a "retro feminist humor postcard." A man and a woman are holding phones: "Hi honey. What's for dinner tonight?" he asks. "How about a beer served with divorce papers, dear?" she answers.

This attachment of popular feminist humor to the gender imageries of decades past revolves around the institutions of heterosexuality of the white, Western, and middle-class kind: stay-at-home wives, more recently rebranded as "homemakers," are as specific to social class as they are to certain societies over others. This play with the past allows for reimagining it as one rife with snappy, sassy, bitchy, yet glamorous white women resisting patriarchal structures of oppression—and, in doing so, divesting these of their power. Such humor nevertheless remains regressive in the dictionary sense of returning to a former or less developed state, leaving the current moment (as well as the future moment) untouched. This indicates that, in order to be popular on the commodity market of coffee mugs and fridge magnets, feminist humor cannot have too sharp of a political edge. Feminist humor that targets a long-ago status quo is safe in the distance and disconnection that it operates with. The forms of humor addressed in this book, however, emerge in more immaterial, networked exchanges as social exchange, play, and critique. These resistant modes work within and further feed the clickbait media economy of scandal, attention, distraction, and titillation.

Google Image Search results for "feminist humor," May 22, 2019.

Slutty Nordic Positionality

Without giving everything away at the outset, the most successful—in the sense of their visibility and spread—feminist online initiatives prioritize gender differences over other embodied differences and social relations of power. In fact, they tend operate with a firmly binary gender logic reminiscent of feminist activist tactics of the 1970s. This logic unites feminist projects and provides them with much of their popular appeal and resonance while effacing from view other differences and relations that matter. As we argue in chapter 6, there is a certain allure to binary gender in feminist activism, and projects critiquing its operations may get stuck in its logic. For as decades of feminist critique have pointed out, a focus on binary gender—men and women, women and men, over and over again—renders invisible the intersections of diverse identity positions and social relations of power (e.g., Crenshaw 1991; Hird 2000; May 2014; Nash 2008). This, again, regularly involves positioning white women as default subjects of feminism (and beyond) and foregrounding their experiences.

It is therefore unsurprising, albeit dispiriting, that the female subjects to gain the most visibility in the feminist initiatives we explore tend to be white and, for the most part, middle class and heterosexual. On the one hand, sexism comes steeped in and intensely entangled with racism, classism, homophobia, and transphobia in ways that require intersectional analyses. On the other hand, the feminist tactics of resistance that are most broadly discussed and acknowledged—and that may consequently have social impact—seldom foreground intersectionality. As in Banet-Weiser's (2018, 13) discussion of popular feminism, the most high-profile examples are "white, middle-class, cis-gendered, and heterosexual." It follows that an examination of feminist success stories means analyzing the actions and stories of largely white women as well as those of *certain kinds* of white women. This necessitates asking not only who is laughing now but also whose laughter becomes heard and who gets to laugh in the first place.

Perhaps adding insult to injury, our analysis is authored by two white women—firmly middle class, admittedly middle aged, even if not necessarily straight. The first languages with which our white voices speak are Swedish and Finnish, respectively, and this book makes use of what we identify as "slutty Nordic positionality" in unpacking the dynamics of shame, shamelessness, and laughter connected to social media. With our Nordic bent, we contribute to a tradition of situated knowledge production (Haraway 1991) in a field where North American viewpoints tend to masquerade as universal. Since this is a book about social media—and hence the internet—our analysis moves across linguistic and national boundaries, and from one platform to another. Operating with both Nordic and North American examples and initiatives, we are much less interested in doing a comparative analysis than in making use of our own physical and cultural locations as productive analytical reserves. Our point is not that our positionality makes for objectively better knowledge but that there is productivity to integrating Nordic perspectives to debates and initiatives that, networked as they are, are irreverent of geography yet reverberate differently according to political and cultural context.

Our work is informed by Donna Haraway's way of theorizing positionality as a locus of knowledge production and as something by necessity partial, embodied, worldly (not innocent), and situated. According to Haraway (1991, 193), "positioning is . . . the key practice grounding knowledge" because a position indicates how particular forms of power shape particular kinds of knowledge. Although Haraway emphasizes local forms of knowledge production, she does not dwell on the geopolitics of location and the difference an emphasis on the regional may make for knowledge projects. Positionality in feminist research is often a matter of accounting for intersecting identities of, for example, gender, race, sexuality, and class, but more rarely it is a question of considering the epistemological implications of regionality or nationality (Lykke 2004, 74). In a Hawawayian sense, Nordicness, as deployed here, is symbolic and material, fictitious and real. It is a regional formation shaped by strong traditions around social democracy, gender equality, and the welfare state (Mühleisen 2007, 176). In operating with Nordic positionality, we contribute to and diverge from common ways of imagining "Nordicness" as an imagined exclusionary and homogeneous regional identity that helps to sideline linguistic, colonial, and other historical differences (see Dahl, Liljeström, and Manns 2016; Martinsson, Griffin, and Giritli Nygren 2016). In both Sweden and Finland, powerful national imaginaries of being world leading in gender equality coexist with rising nationalism and violent racism—and as the avalanche of testimonies of sexual violence and harassment connected to #MeToo have made evident, painful discrepancies exist between theory and practice when it comes to gender equality.

Both Sweden and Finland are largely Lutheran in their cultural heritage, but they are notably secular in that religious overtones seldom play a vocal role in public and political debates. They are not Puritan when it comes to approaches and attitudes to sexuality and the dynamics of shame associated with it—a point elaborated in chapter 2. As our interests lie in thinking through the redistribution of sexual shame, we use sluttiness as a base note of sorts for a particular feminist attitude and sensibility. In doing so, we foreground the importance of sexual agency, playfulness, and the multiple pleasures that these allow for. Such is the slut who strides confidently through our writing as a vital reminder of how claiming a space for and indulging in pleasure—and laughter—for its own sake is a political act.

Oh, Shame!

According to the *Oxford English Dictionary*, the word *offense* refers to "a breach of a law or rule; an illegal act," "a thing that constitutes a violation of what is judged to be right or natural," "annoyance or resentment brought about by a perceived insult to or disregard for oneself," and "the action of attacking someone or something." These four aspects of offense are in active and rich use on online platforms where trolling and provocation abound and where affective ripples build, grow, and fade as people unwillingly and willingly misunderstand one another, attack each other's persona and stance, and are offended by the comments and reactions of others (e.g., Tagg, Seargeant, and Brown 2017). Offense is readily given and taken in social media, and accusations of being easily offended—as in the title of snowflake associated with millennials—function as offenses in their own right. In social media content policies, offensiveness refers broadly to content that may be experienced as disturbing, such as sexuality, violence, or hate speech. This is in line with how offensiveness is more generally deployed as "the term of choice to flag whatever it is that bothers us so much about hearing an utterance of a slurring term" (Jeshion 2013, 354n4; also Marshall 1991). Many social media platforms ban content deemed offensive, and others tag it as "sensitive," "adult," or "NSFW" (see Paasonen, Jarrett, and Light 2019).

"You should be ashamed" and "Shame on you" are common enough rebukes in networked exchanges grown sharp or sour. As affective addresses, they position the targets of shame as inferior and failed—as people who should engage in self-reflection and critique, hang their heads in shame, and, preferably, apologize for the offense caused. The constant waves of offense rippling across Twitter and Facebook are inseparable from the affective dynamics of shaming involved in mocking, outing, critiquing, challenging, or disagreeing with others. A central focus of this book is on feminist tactics of resistance to shame and shaming (as in instances of slut-shaming), on the operationalizing of acts of shaming (as in publicizing offensive messages sent by others or in ridiculing the actions of others), and on the reworking and rerouting of shame (as in shifting shame from the victims to the perpetrators of sexual violence or as in feminist tactics of moving through shame toward shamelessness). Here, we build on Silvan S. Tomkins's (2008, 200) conceptualization on shame as a strong, negative affect "induced by rejection by others and by self-doubt and self-contempt," which, when increasing in intensity, can grow into a more incapacitating sense of humiliation. At the same time, shame involves the element of surprise and the potentiality to interrupt social hierarchies (Popa 2018).

Shame-humiliation is "the negative affect linked with love and identification" (Tomkins 2008, 636). As such, it is connected to and dependent on interest that becomes ruptured or refused when we are rejected, mocked, or disapproved by those whose recognition, approval, or desire we are seeking out. Shame entails a sense of failure, falling short, and feeling inferior, whether it is connected to failing to meet expectations or to violating a social norm (Tomkins 2008, 648). Shame operates within social relations, tapping into the ways in which one is perceived while also turning inward as one's perception of oneself. There is nevertheless nothing automatic or causal about how shame builds up or fades away. In terms of the affective dynamics and politics that we examine, an attempt to shame does not necessarily stick but may bemuse, whereas a passing comment can unintentionally shame: "If someone expresses contempt for me, I may become angry and counter with contempt for him. The intention of the other to shame me does not necessarily mean I will experience shame" (Tomkins 2008, 370). Shame can linger, layer, and grow into a sense of humiliation; it can be perceived in the much lighter hues of embarrassment; or it can slide by so that others become embarrassed for the one who does not have a sense of shame.

The feminist tactics we address revolve around the dynamics of shame, often in complex ways. Slut-shaming, for example, is a tactic for policing the boundaries of acceptable, appropriately gendered, racialized, and sexualized femininity. This variation of putting women back into their imaginary place not as sexual agents inasmuch as the sexual property of chosen men, such as husbands and partners is countered in initiatives such as Slut-Walks (where women have, since 2011, taken to the streets to protest victim blaming and slut-shaming connected to sexual violence) as well as in more mundane refusals to be confined to its logic (as in the tweeting practices of Stormy Daniels discussed in chapter 4). As such a position of refusal, sluttiness, our chosen positionality, signifies inappropriate or shameless femininity.

The tactics examined in this book are markedly reactive in that they tend to emerge as the means of dealing with offense and injustice: #MeToo reacts to sexual harassment and violence; Instagram projects document, make visible, and comment on online harassment and are reactions to it; the appropriation of terms meant to hurt and shame is reactive in turning their meaning around; and the "Congrats, you have an all male panel!" Tumblr

blog reacts to sexism and the exclusion of women from the realm of expertise. Resistance, as such, entails a refusal to play along, conform to, accept,
or be affected by the state of affairs on offer. Reactivity is a means of turning
tables that allows for forms of parody, satire, and ridicule to emerge. At the
same time, there is a certain passivity at its core, given that reactivity seldom involves queer or otherwise creative world making outside the param-
eters and power dynamics that it comments on and intervenes in. It can
be claimed that such reactivity has been at the root of feminism as a social
movement and social theory arguing for the equal rights for women since
the nineteenth century, when such rights were not available. Although this
is not the whole story, feminism has, throughout its history, responded to
and worked against lack: the lack of rights, of equality, of space, of agency.
And indeed, as Sara Ahmed (2015) argues, feminist critique of sexism is
badly needed, given the persistence of sexism itself.

Our interest in feminist *tactics* is inspired by Michel de Certeau's
(2002/1984) notion of tactics as everyday forms of opposition. We equally
build on Megan Boler's (2008b) understanding of media tactics as interventions in hegemonic structures, whether they are dominant media systems
or systemic forms of sexism. While recognizing the critical importance of
feminist tactics that turn against or provide a wrench in the machinery of
sexist power by lingering close to what is critiqued, we also seek out more
open-ended and unpredictable ways of acting and relating. This is why
we turn to laughter and, more specifically, to absurdity as a means of not
merely turning things around or inside out but disrupting and eschewing
the logic on offer. Such disruptions may be temporary or of the more lingering kind, and the permanence of the traces they leave—or fail to leave—is
impossible to assess in the time of their unfolding. We therefore focus on
their potentiality: the novel combinations, questions, and surprises that
they allow and the possible social and political resonances that they may
set in motion.

This Is Absurd!

According to its *Merriam-Webster* and *OED* definitions, the word *absurd*
translates as "ridiculously unreasonable, unsound, or incongruous," as
"extremely silly or ridiculous," as "having no rational or orderly relationship to human life: meaningless," and as "the state or condition in which

human beings exist in an irrational and meaningless universe." The word *absurdity* is synonymous with "preposterousness, ridiculousness, ludicrousness, . . . idiocy, stupidity, foolishness, folly, silliness, inanity, insanity, as well as unreasonableness, irrationality, illogicality, nonsensicality, pointlessness, senselessness, incongruity." In this sense, absurdity stands as the opposite of reason, rationality, and meaning. This is already encapsulated in its etymological root in the Latin word *absurdus*—"out of tune, uncouth, inappropriate, ridiculous." Following this etymology, humor in absurdist registers plays with whatever is out of harmony with both reason and decency. In her taxonomy of humor, Marta Dynel (2014, 628) sees absurdity as building on untruthfulness and violating "the rules and norms of the real world." For Dynel, absurdity, or nonsense, is distinct from both irony and surrealist humor, with which it is often conflated, in that it does not entail a negative evaluation or reaction toward what is being made fun of. In other words, absurd laughter can take flight toward wherever: there is freedom to its erratic jolts.

Theories of humor tend to be divided into three classic types: incongruity, relief, and superiority (e.g., Meyer 2000; Shifman and Blondheim 2010). Sexist and racist memes, for example, fall into the category of superiority, where the meme creators establish or maintain social hierarchies by laughing at something or someone. At the same time, these memes may also operate through incongruity—namely, the combination of incompatible elements. Relief theory, again, refers to humor as a social pressure valve of sorts that makes it possible for people to decrease tension when feeling baffled, troubled, overwhelmed, or uncomfortable. As Lauren Berlant (2017) points out, theories of humor and laughter also tend to be structured by or play off of binary oppositions such as flipping the switch on dominance and subordination through subversion (Bakhtin 1984/1968), reshaping the repressed through what escapes it and becomes expressed (Freud 1960/1905), or tapping into the pleasant surprise of incongruity and contrast between the expected and the unexpected (Bergson 1999/1911). Berlant (2017, 312–313) thus remarks that "virtually all comedy theorists are structuralists." In relation to these variations that construe comedy as an either/or encounter in which something is turned into something else, escapes something else, or turns out to be something else, her own contribution aims to explore "the *copresence* of structuration and collapse, and its attention to the multiplier effect of comic disturbance" (Berlant 2017, 313, emphasis in original). For us, such comic disturbance of binaries is key, in particular in thinking about the fickleness of affect and its role in humor.

In line with such binary, structuralist logics, many theorists of humor are careful in minutely separating its different shapes and forms from one another into taxonomies where irony and sarcasm, for example, do not touch one another. Elliott Oring (2003, 1) nevertheless characterizes humor in general as the perception of "appropriate incongruity"—as "the perception of an appropriate relationship between categories that would ordinarily be regarded as incongruous" where such incompatibility never fully becomes resolved. Following this line of reasoning, irony, parody, sarcasm, or ridicule—forms of humor and feminist tactics that are examined in the chapters to follow—can all be tinted with the absurd and thereby afford an affective release of laughter (Oring 2003, 18).

In the examples of feminist tactics addressed below, absurdities emerge in diverse combinations with irony, parody, and satire: the ridiculing of the apologies made by men accused of sexual harassment (chapter 3); the ironic appropriations of the pussy-bow blouse as a feminist symbol (chapter 3); the mockery of dick-pic senders and slut-shamers (chapter 4); the alternative parodic world-making practices within the "Shameless Extinction" Facebook event (chapter 5); and finally tips on gaining a fresher complexion by applying yogurt on one's penis, as provided by "Man who has it all," a social media satire "that exposes the absurdity of the patriarchy by turning the tables" along with the cringe-worthy irony of "Congrats, you have an all male panel!" (chapter 6). Although absurd humor can begin from a site of reactivity and negative evaluation, it need not remain confined to it. Rather, by turning things preposterous, ludicrous, and inappropriate, absurd laughter ends up somewhere different. Hence, it makes a good place to start.

Humor does not necessarily amuse, or it can amuse only some people, and not all laughs result from humor. Furthermore, a laugh is not necessarily happy. In his discussion of laughter as an uncensored channel of affective expression, Tomkins (2008, 320) points out that it "may become the prime vehicle of the expression of any and all affects which suffer inhibition. Thus there is the frightened nervous laugh, the dirty laugh of contempt or hostility, the ashamed laugh, the surprised laugh, the laugh of enjoyment, the laugh of excitement and the laugh of distress, the substitute cry." Like shame, the laugh can be a vehicle for contempt

(Tomkins 2008, 367). Laughter is a means of affective expression and, as we argue, allows for active release. In highlighting the unpredictability and factual complexity of laughter, this book explores a range of tactics of intervention, resistance, and mobilization within and beyond Anglo-centric contexts.

Laughter may hold plenty of pleasure and joy but also considerable anxiety, sadness, and anger. Feminist laughter, as we approach it, may consist of everything from the forbidden, smothered giggle to the loud, uncontrollable belly laughter mixed with tears of joy (cf. Parvulescu 2010). Laughter is thus an unreliable force with uncertain outcomes, both affectively and politically. We examine the registers of humor deployed in feminist projects—from irony, parody, and satire to mockery and ridicule—and ask how they relate to seriousness and to the occasional absences of laughter. We also explore the ways these tactics play with the dynamics of public shaming and shamelessness and the ethical reverberations that all this entails. In doing so, we break away from views of humor as either subversive or as reproducing social hierarchies of power, with the aim of providing a more nuanced understanding of how laughter operates and ripples in social media exchanges.

From Sexual Shame to Shameless Hags and Beyond

We initially started planning this book in the fall of 2017, just as the #MeToo movement was gaining momentum and speed. Given the broad cultural visibility of #MeToo as a watershed moment of a kind—identified in markers such as "pre-MeToo" and "post-MeToo" used in discussing instances of sexual harassment and public reactions to them—it is both our chosen place to start and the focus of two chapters. Our analysis focuses not on the tweets or Facebook posts shared under the hashtag but rather on the broader discussions that the movement has given rise to in connection with sexual abuse, violence, pleasure, shame, and agency, as well as the affective politics and publics that all this involves.

In chapter 2, we ask how #MeToo works with and through shame, as well as how heterosexuality—female heterosexuality, in particular—becomes figured within its accounts of harassment, hurt, and abuse in the context of social media. Considering the expressions of distaste toward #MeToo voiced by a group of a hundred French women, we move to addressing continuities and conflicts within histories of feminist activism and analyze the persistent, lingering presence of Puritanism in debates concerning the movement internationally. On the one hand, we argue that shame forms the backbone of #MeToo as a strong affect theory that tints the movement in particular and persistent ways. On the other hand, by working through both Swedish and North American examples, we identify differences in how the scandal of sexual harassment becomes addressed and debated in diverse contexts and how shame becomes differently distributed in the process. Returning back to the question of differences within the category of women, we conclude by asking which differences become highlighted, which ones are effaced, and consequently, what may be the possibilities and limitations of #MeToo.

Taking a different approach to #MeToo, chapter 3 asks what laughter may do to the sharpness of negative affect—of shame and anger—driving the movement. The tone of #MeToo is angry inasmuch as it is serious and engaged with the redistribution of sexual shame. We argue that this dynamic gives rise to what we call "affective homophily," the love of feeling the same that brings people together through networked expressions of similar feeling. Through a discussion of three events—Hannah Gadsby's viral 2018 standup comedy Netflix special, *Nanette*; the nonviral #MeToo musical comedy orchestrated by the feminist comedian, Lauren Maul; and the surprising resonances of humor in the sexual harassment and assault scandal that put the prestigious Swedish Academy in crisis in 2018—we explore the operations of affective homophily and its consequences for feminist humor and activism. We argue for the political importance of affective ambiguity, difference, and dissent in contemporary feminist social media tactics and highlight the risks involved when a movement like #MeToo comes to be organized through expressions and expectations of homogeneous feeling.

Examining public social media responses to hateful or otherwise undesired messaging as a tactic of resistance, chapter 4 first asks what happens when such content crosses the private/public binary. We start with the tactic of shameless retweeting and commenting, as practiced by the adult film star Stormy Daniels, and then consider @assholesonline, Linnéa Claeson's Instagram gallery of hundreds of unsolicited advances and attacks. Second, and moving beyond the unsolicited dick pics that abound in Claeson's gallery, we inquire after the possibilities and uses of the unsolicited pussy pic as a feminist figure of intervention and a source of humor. This may suggest a compulsive repetition of a binary model of gender, but our purpose is to disrupt and in various ways queer the binary genital theater of online harassment and the gendered dynamics of shame and shaming that it entails.

Linguistic appropriation of terms that are meant to hurt and shame is a tested and tried tactic in feminist and queer activism. Digging into Swedish "hags" embodying shameless femininity and feminist solidarity and Finnish "tolerance whores" and "flower-hat aunties" standing for liberal, antiracist values, chapter 5 looks at the intersecting circuits of misogynistic and racist hate and ways of countering them. We attend specifically to the dynamics of shaming and shamelessness connected to linguistic appropriations and the vibrancy of language, as well as the forms of privilege that are tapped into by these appropriations. Because it is not evident that attempts at shaming work as planned or that derogatory labels stick in the ways intended, it is necessary to ask under which conditions labels can be turned around and what effects such rerouting may have.

Chapter 6 tackles the issue and, in fact, the allure of binary gender in feminist social media tactics. The "Congrats, you have an all male panel!" tumblr gained international media attention and something of a viral lift soon after its launch in 2015, making *manel* an academic household word. On the one hand, the tumblr's firmly binary gender logic makes strikingly evident the virility of the "malestream" in how expertise and leadership continue to be articulated and embodied and in how nonmen continue to be excluded from their realm. On the other hand, this logic renders invisible other intersecting variables of difference and axes of power, such as race, language, age, and class. First, we examine the dynamics of embarrassment and the aspects of cringe humor that the tumblr involves, and we then look at the reiteration of binary gender in the Twitter and Facebook satire "Man who has it all," which sets out to turn gender roles and stereotypes around for critical and comic effect.

Finally, we bring our strands of discussion together in the concluding chapter, where we consider the disruptive force of absurdity, the seeming, complex return to 1970s feminist vocabulary and tactics in contemporary projects, and the different ways in which social media platforms feed and support resistant tactics. In analyzing feminist social media tactics on Twitter, Instagram, Tumblr, and Facebook in different chapters, we also consider the rhythms, archival capacities, forms of organization, and social action that these platforms afford or block.

Our title, *Who's Laughing Now?*, foregrounds forms of feminist laughter and the diverse agencies that they involve. As such, it is a means of claiming space in the context of online culture where lulz (amusement derived at another's expense) is a popular sport, beyond the realm of trolling from which the term originates (see Milner 2014; Miltner 2014; Phillips 2015). Starting from a different place of laughter as world making or making the world a more livable place, we are much less interested in what laughter pins down, limits, or suppresses than in what grows with and in it. This book is one example of such potential growth. Returning to the hypothetical example raised in the beginning of our introduction, the process of writing this book results from ample giggles, wet cheeks inspired by random absurdity, and ripples of amusement caused by noticing and mocking our own idiosyncratic ways of phrasing things or from tracking academic conventions more generally. Neither of us suspected that working on topics such as sexual harassment or abuse occurring on online platforms would be particularly fun, yet we have come to realize the importance of embracing laughter—as inappropriate, out of place, or offensive as it may occasionally seem—in collaborative academic work and in feminist lives. Laughter helps to shift and move things, to reframe them, to take distance, and to move up close. It has the power to unsettle, and it can bring pleasure and joy to knowledge production on topics laced with the affective intensities of rage, sadness, shame, and disgust. Our argument is not to do away with these but to see how some of their dynamics may be unmoored in working with and through laughter. We believe firmly in the value and worth of a shameless, irreverent giggle.

2 #MeToo, Outrage, and Sexual Shame

Late in 2017, *Time* magazine named the "the silence breakers" of the #MeToo movement as its Person of the Year. The silence in question concerned sexual harassment and violence against women, and the people pictured in the magazine cover were Susan Fowler, a Silicon Valley engineer; Adama Iwu, a corporate lobbyist; Ashley Judd, a film star; "Isabel Pasqual," a pseudonymous manual laborer; and Taylor Swift, a pop star. Representing different ethnic backgrounds, the women were all dressed in black and faced the camera without smiling. Despite the range of ethnicities, attention was likely to cluster on the white ones, Judd and Swift, due to their already established popular fame.

In October 2017, #MeToo grew into a global, viral Twitter and Facebook campaign with the Harvey Weinstein scandal and soon bled into other social media platforms, national and international news outlets, parliamentary investigations, and forms of retrospective inquiry revisiting accusations of sexual misconduct by powerful men (see Boyle 2019). Sexual harassment became a topic of debate and intervention on an unprecedented, international scale. Ashwini Tambe, writing in the US context, points out that #MeToo's expansive impact may have seemed sudden but was "part of a groundswell in women's activism since the November 2016 elections. The Women's March was the largest globally coordinated public gathering in history. The 3-million strong Facebook group Pantsuit Nation saw hundreds of thousands of posts about experiences of misogyny. . . . The signature affective note running through this political moment is a fierce rage about the election of Donald Trump" (Tambe 2018, 198; also Pellegrini 2018, 263.) Despite its US origins, #MeToo has connected individual personal accounts into a networked entity making visible gendered structures of privilege and sexual violence across cultural, national, and linguistic boundaries. By bringing together under a hashtag these experiences of casual to traumatic harassment, it has allowed for the anecdotal to meet the structural. Following John Protevi (2009), we understand #MeToo as a means of connecting the somatic (the immediately and corporally felt) with the social and of linking personal actions with political activism on a civic level.

Twitter hashtags, as contextual user-generated metadata, unite individual tweets into broader conversations or debates. In doing so, they can give rise to hashtag publics taking shape around a particular theme, topic, or event (Bruns and Burgess 2015). Contingent hashtag publics—of which #MeToo is a prime example—are key to how social activism lives and spreads on Twitter and mobilizes bodies beyond it: they involve transformative, connective, and even contagious potential. By drawing on Zizi Papacharissi's notion of affective publics, we further conceptualize #MeToo as a public formation that is "mobilized and connected, identified, and potentially disconnected through expressions of sentiment" and that supports social change by allowing for the display of affect through personal storytelling (Papacharissi 2016, 308, 311). Affective publics are networked and come together as people tweet, retweet, share, follow, and post. Similarly to the hashtag public of #blacklivesmatter (Jackson 2016; Korn 2015; Rambukkana 2015), #MeToo has continued to vary in its visibility—from its initial high use to periods of slower pace—with peaks in traffic as scandals, protests, and events have unfolded in different parts of the world.

#MeToo has acquired and retained much more public visibility, recognizability, and longevity than most other feminist campaigns against rape culture and the abuse of women internationally (Horeck 2014; Khoja-Moolji 2015). This may be due to how this particular social media movement has come about in multiple streams and threads in a range of languages allowing for a reach that is both global and highly specific in its context and location. Its resonances and applications have not been confined to any specific language group, as was the case with the Tunisian pre-MeToo hashtag, #moi_aussi_j'ai_été_violé ("me too, I have been raped") and the German #outcry that similarly attracted attention to sexual harassment and abuse (Antonakis-Nashif 2015, 110–111). #MeToo quickly gave rise to numerous subhashtags, such as the French #BalanceTonPorc ("Expose/squeal on your pig"), the Finnish #memyös ("#wetoo"), Finnish Swedish #dammenbrister

("#dambursts"), and the many initiatives within a Swedish context, such as #teknisktfel ("#technicalerror"), #tystnadtagning ("#silenceaction"), and #skrattetihalsen ("#laughterinthethroat") that organize local initiatives belonging to specific occupational fields. These diverse subtags all link back to and are used in combination with #MeToo, bringing together accounts of sexual harassment in Indian academia (Chakraborty 2019) with those concerning sexism among Swedish comedians and entwining them into one affective hashtag public. The same horizontal logic is present in the *Time* cover that incorporates pop celebrities, an engineer, a lobbyist, and a manual laborer into a symbolic group figure. This horizontality has allowed personal accounts emerging within #MeToo the same kind of gravity, even as user attention is likely to cluster more on some individuals, tweets, and subtags than on others. This nevertheless also effaces crucial contextual differences between individual articulations of harassment and abuse, while also obscuring the differentials of social privilege among the women contributing to the movement.

#MeToo has gained most visibility through the statements made by successful American white, cisgender female actors of international fame. Unlike the hashtag #SayHerName, which has been used to bring attention to violence faced by both cis- and transgender black women in the United States (Bailey, Jackson, and Welles 2019; Brown et al. 2016; Williams 2015, 2016), it has largely failed to accommodate intersectionality in whose voices become most heard and, consequently, in which voices seem to matter (Tambe 2018, 199–200). As Dubravka Zarkov and Kathy Davis (2018) note, powerful women are at the core of #MeToo, which makes it difficult or risky for many others to speak up. Although the hashtag was coined a decade ago as a slogan by the black feminist activist Tarana Burke as a way to support young women of color who experience and survive sexual abuse (Pellegrini 2018, 262), the origin of the phenomenon was not evident on the *Time* cover (even though Burke was interviewed in the cover story), and broader discussions connected to the movement have repeatedly ignored or downplayed other difference besides gender. Gender tends to be construed as a binary divide structured by heterosexual desire: nothing new here, alas. Clare Hemmings (2018) similarly argues that #MeToo works along the lines of an understanding of sexual violence as experienced through a gender binary, thus undercutting broader coalitions between those who are subject to masculine dominance, including cis women, trans men and trans women, gender-nonconforming subjects, and queer people of color.

At the moment of this writing, the movement has expanded beyond social media to TV news coverage and workplace coffee break conversations as a social phenomenon and a cultural point of reference. Starting out as an avalanche of tweets and posts detailing personal stories of sexual harassment and abuse, #MeToo has since, as a hashtag public, clustered around accounts of hurt, anger, and outrage. It has moved from personal confessionals to a broadly recognizable protest against male domination and silence surrounding sexual harassment. Its feminist tactic involves the redistribution of sexual shame from the victims of sexual harassment to the perpetrators and to the social settings and institutions that have facilitated it.

Zooming in on this affective, networked landscape, we ask how #MeToo works with and through shame, as well as how heterosexuality—particularly female heterosexuality—figures in discussions of harassment, hurt, and abuse. Using the expressions of distaste or even disgust toward #MeToo voiced by a group of a hundred French women as our starting point, we discuss continuities and conflicts within histories of feminist activism and analyze the residual traces or "structures of feeling" (Williams 1977) of Puritanism in debates concerning the movement. We argue that the sticky, lingering quality of shame forms the core of #MeToo as a strong affect theory that bends the movement in specific ways. Working through both Swedish and American examples, we further identify important differences in how the scandal of sexual harassment becomes addressed and debated in diverse contexts and how shame, particularly sexual shame, becomes differently distributed in the process.

Libertines and Puritans

In their open letter published on January 9, 2018, in *Le Monde*, a hundred French women—including the author Catherine Millet and the actor Catherine Deneuve—introduced themselves as "Collectif" and accused the #MeToo movement and its French version, #BalanceTonPorc, of overreaction and hatred of both men and sexuality. The letter argues that the line between rape and awkward flirtation and between the abuse of power and clumsy sexual advances has become blurred and conflated under the hashtags in problematic ways. The undersigned further identify #MeToo as an enemy to sexual freedom that infantilizes women as "children with an adult face, demanding to be protected": "It is the nature of Puritanism to borrow, under the pretense of general good, arguments for the protection of women and their emancipation in order to better confine them in their status as eternal victims, poor little things under the rule of phallocratic demons, as in the good old days of witchcraft" (Collectif 2018).

This critique of a generalized conflation of sexual violence, expressions of sexual interest, and women's amputated sexual agency addresses punitive violence against men accused of harassment, ridicules Swedish plans to establish legal requirements for informed consent prior to sexual intercourse (possibly with the help of an app), and defends the male right to offensiveness as a prerequisite for sexual freedom. The letter also defends the female freedom to engage in practices of pleasure free from shame or stigma, yet insists on casual nonchalance in the face of mundane harassment and disregard toward one's bodily boundaries: "A woman can, during the same day, lead a professional team and enjoy being a man's sex object without being 'a slut' or a vile complicit to patriarchy. She can insist on her salary being equal to that of a man without feeling traumatized by a groper on a subway, even if this is considered an offense. She may even consider it an expression of great sexual misery, or a non-event" (Collectif 2018). The overall dynamic outlined in the letter is firmly that of heterosexual male initiative and female responsiveness—freedom to grope and resilience after being thus groped.

The letter was widely and internationally covered in social media, causing debate on Twitter and in Facebook newsfeeds. Reactions to the letter were quick, broad, and disproportionately focused on Deneuve as its symbolic figurehead—considering that she was one in a group of a hundred. A reaction letter published by a group of French feminists denounced the Collectif as resembling "the embarrassing colleague or tired uncle who doesn't understand what's happening" and as being "apologists for rape." The actor and #MeToo activist Asia Argento more bluntly saw "interiorized misogyny" as having "lobotomized them to the point of no return" (Willsher 2018). The disagreement became framed as generational: younger women accused older ones of being stuck in the temporal fold of 1960s sexual liberation; of being either unable or unwilling to challenge the gendered, classed, and racialized relations of power connected to sexual harassment; and of failing to acknowledge the value of bodily integrity and the lived realities of sexual violence and vulnerability among less privileged women. The generational conflict expanded to a rift between those seen as confined to heteronormative and nonintersectional views of gender and sexuality and those operating in a conceptual framework of multiple, intersecting axes of power and resistance. The Collectif was further accused of knowingly effacing the nuances of #MeToo by conflating rape with random groping for the sake of rhetorical flair.

The *Le Monde* letter insisted on female resilience in the face of subway frottage and unwanted sexual approaches, but the other group of feminists would not have any of this. The incompatibility between these approaches to sexual harassment echoes decades-long feminist debates. In her popular third-wave feminist manifesto, Naomi Wolf (1993, xvii) identified "two different approaches within feminism. One—what I define as 'victim feminism'—casts women as sexually pure and mystically nurturing, and stresses the evil done to these 'good' women as a way to petition for their rights. The other, which I call 'power feminism,' sees women as human beings—sexual, individual, no better or worse than their male counterparts—and lays claim to equality simply because women are entitled to it." In its emphasis on individual strength and success and its general disinterest in structural inequalities, the power feminism of the 1990s broadly associated the second wave, particularly radical feminism, with the victimization of women (see Atmore 1999; Lamb 1999).

In accusing #MeToo of reducing women to victims and infantilizing them as helpless creatures in the process, the Collectif followed a familiar line of argumentation that associates feminist critiques of the eroticization of gender hierarchies with man hating and man bashing (cf. Atmore 1999, 198, 191). In doing so, the letter signers also explicitly cast #MeToo as Puritan, as joyless, and as incompatible with the sexual freedoms that their own letter defends. Meanwhile, younger #MeToo activists accused the Collectif of being outdated and naive. All this points out the degree to which the waves of feminism—the first wave of liberal feminism, the second wave of radical feminism, the third wave of intersectional and queer feminist critique, and the fourth wave of social media–driven activism—fail to be contained in a linear account of generation. As we discuss throughout this book, contemporary feminist social media projects tap into tactics that were deployed in previous decades, making evident the need to conceptualize feminist activism in terms of continuities and variations rather than clashes and gaps—despite the narrative attractions that the latter model holds in both its linear clarity and drama.

The Collectif accused the #MeToo movement of Puritanism while the reactions to the *Le Monde* letter accused the group of obsolete and male-biased libertine ideals that help to bolster straight male privilege and hegemony. By defending the right of men to grope women and to act inappropriately, the letter aligned itself with the much-critiqued logic of sexual liberation as being connected to male initiative and female availability, yet without insisting on equal agency or freedom for the partners involved or considering the matter beyond heterosexual encounters. Sexual freedom emerges in the letter as a concept connected to the so-called sexual revolution of the 1960s and 1970s that set out to resist Puritan sexual norms but that is not compatible with the insistence on women's right to bodily integrity—as in the freedom not to be groped against one's will. This friction between claims for sexual freedom and bodily integrity and the diversity of the actors involved in these encounters is nevertheless too complex to be reduced to a binary opposition between French libertinism and American Puritanism, to neo-Puritan tendencies shaping the landscape of feminist politics via networked social media campaigns, or to intergenerational miscommunication.

Lingering Puritanism

Collectif's letter was far from being the only incident where #MeToo has been accused of "man-hating puritanism" (Nyren 2018) or mob justice against men who become deemed guilty by virtue of accusation. The trope of Puritanism, as deployed in this context, gestures less toward the sixteenth- and seventeenth-century reformist movement within the Church of England than to the cultural legacy of the Puritans who settled in New England in the first part of the seventeenth century. As the journalist Rockwell Stensrud (2015) explains, "Massachusetts Puritans set the intellectual tone of the country for three centuries. They branded the land with the Protestant Ethic. They introduced New England to a lingering burden of guilt and existential angst. . . . They established towns around Boston and forged a theocracy of magistrates and Congregational clergymen to control the growing population." This legacy has been seen as particularly resistant to sexual expression and experimentation outside the framework of heterosexual matrimony. Silvan Tomkins (2008, 660) goes as far as to argue that "in puritanism, one hates pleasure and life."

Critiquing the applications of Puritanism in discussions surrounding #MeToo, theologian James Eglington (2018) argues that although the movement has brought the concept back into public consciousness, "it has done so within a culture where knowledge of Puritanism largely depends on H. L. Mencken's claim that Puritanism is 'the haunting fear that someone, somewhere, may be happy.' . . . In the present day, the idea of the Puritan functions as a kind of bogeyman—the fanatical killjoy witch-burner of a dim and distant past—and has little to do with the Puritans of history." This is undoubtedly true. Puritans occupy a rhetorical position similar to what Sara Ahmed identifies as feminist killjoys—those who refuse to laugh when expected and to enjoy the things they are supposed to enjoy and who, in doing so, opt out from reciprocal networks of happiness (Ahmed 2010, 17, 69). In critiques squared against #MeToo, the two figures partly blend into one figure: the fantastic Puritan feminist killjoy lacks a sense of humor, is filled with rage, and feels categorical disdain or even hatred toward heterosexual men—as in Collectif's complaint.

It can nevertheless be argued that Puritanism remains more than a rhetorical figure deployed for the purposes of ahistorical critique. We propose that residual Puritanism lingers in American public attitudes toward sexuality and that its presence is felt, for example, in how sexual content is filtered and flagged out from social media as categorically risky and unsafe. Meanwhile, there is more lenience toward diverse forms of violence and hate (see Paasonen, Jarrett, and Light 2019, 40–41, 141–144). Following Raymond Williams (1977, 132–133), Puritanism can be understood a residual structure of feeling that orients "impulse, restraint, and tone; specifically affective elements of consciousness and relationships" and generates specific forms of sociability. Residual structures of feeling linger, possibly unnoticed yet attuning the rhythms of contemporary culture: "The residual, by definition, has been effectively formed in the past, but it is still active in the cultural process, not only and often not at all as an element of the past, but as an effective element of the present" (Williams 1977, 122). Although residual elements are detached from dominant culture, their effect depends on their having been incorporated into it. The residual remains actively present through "reinterpretation, dilution, projection, discriminating inclusion and exclusion" (Williams 1977, 123), which it does passively as reverbs and emphases of the kind that can be identified in American sex scandals. As a residual structure of feeling, Puritanism shapes culturally specific attitudes toward sexuality and bodily display.

According to Kathleen Verduin (1983, 223), seventeenth-century Puritan clergy treated sexuality "with wariness, distaste, even horror, as a virtual invitation to damnation." In Puritan sermons, marital sex was haunted by "inexpressible uncleannesses," and discussions on sexual offenses were driven by the "fear of punishment, often unspeakable punishment" (Verduin 1983, 225–226). Here, the fall of Sodom remained a frequent reference point warning against the dangers of sensuous excess. Furthermore, the "remedy for the sins of the flesh enumerated and condemned in Puritan sermons was unambiguously a matter increased control . . . against that nature that struggled for expression" (Verduin 1983, 231–232). Such a combination of distaste, unease, fear, and the imperative of control connected to sexuality may have been a dominant structure of feeling during the early project of establishing the principles and values of American culture, and it may have since grown residual in the sense of being largely unnoticed yet continuing to impact understandings of sexuality (see Fessenden et al. 2001).

George Shulman (2004, 172), for example, argues that the self-control required in Puritanism translates as "hysteria about nonprocreative, nonmarital, and nonconventional sexual practices," which remain to be positioned as problematic as such. In addition to feeding the logic of sex scandals where the scandal may well be sex itself, rather than the fact that it is nonconsensual or otherwise steeped in the abuse of social relations of power, Puritan residue remains present in the preference for abstinence-only programs over comprehensive sex education in schools—which are unsupported by existing data on sexual health, made on moral grounds, and preferred by the current US government. All this involves no small degrees of ambiguity, given that the United States is probably the largest global producer of pornography, as well as the hub of multiple and diverse sexual cultures. Addressing the seeming paradox between "extraordinary ascendance of conservative sexual moralizing in this most sexualized of societies," Arlene Stein (2006, 3) identifies it with an affective economy of shame where shaming operates as a tool for controlling those seen to be out of line.

Oh, Scandal, Oh, Disgust!

As the prime catalyst for #MeToo, the Weinstein scandal rendered visible the abuse of female actors within Hollywood, as well as the misuse
of power by some of the industry's key movers and shakers. The incident
was a scandal in the essential sense of the term: a public event where the
audience is invited to witness norms of appropriate behavior being trans-
gressed and to judge the issue for themselves. Independent of whether the
issue at stake concerns sexual or financial misconduct (or both), scandal
reveals the behavior of individuals and communities, subjecting them to
public evaluation and debate (Adut 2008). A scandal involves publicness on
two interconnected levels. First, the perpetrator, or the accused, has to be a
public figure of some standing. Domestic violence or sexual abuse committed by a random person—a nobody—toward someone equally unknown
does not qualify as newsworthy, let alone as a scandal. Second, scandal
becomes a scandal only when it is a media event shared with an unspecified
public, making it a topic of general, shared consumption and judgment.
Within the avalanche of narratives of sexual abuse, coercion, and violence
shared under the #MeToo hashtag, attention has clustered on scandals
involving famous men and women (also Salter 2019).

Within the Weinstein scandal, the unacceptable behavior of a highly
privileged and influential man was shown as being supported and enabled
by a network of colleagues and employees committed to a code of silence.
The media coverage of the affair nevertheless framed it equally, if not more
explicitly, as a sex scandal through the disclosure of salacious details of
events taking place behind closed doors—including an assault victim's
account of Weinstein masturbating onto a potted plant and his former
employee's description of semen-dotted sofas and his use of erectile dys-
function medication (see Gill and Orgad 2018). Public commentary notably often focused on the physical figure of Weinstein, whom the radio host,
Howard Stern, soon identified as a "big, fat guy," whom "no girl on the
planet . . . wants to see . . . naked" and become aroused by the sight. The
British tabloid *The Mirror* covered exposés from Weinstein's former chauf-
feur, according to whom the movie producer was known as "the Pig" due
to his "sweaty and grunting" manner (Duff 2017). Online reader comments
to articles on the scandal were rife with victim blaming but equally with
articulations of distaste toward Weinstein's physical appearance: "The only

sound 'signal' that an ugly pig like Harvey Weinstein should expect from a woman is DISGUST," a *Variety* reader stated. In the February 2020 trial in New York that resulted in Weinstein receiving a 23-year prison sentence, a witness described his body as being not only hairy but as having "moles on his rolls, a disgusting looking penis"—photos of which were then offered to the jury for contemplation (NZ Herald 2020; Schwartz 2020). All this facilitated Weinstein being singled out as a monstrous predator whose physique is as disgusting as his actions. Numerous victims of Weinstein reported their respective feelings of shame and disgust following the assaults. Although the publicness of the scandal helped lift some of these feelings of shame, commenters resorted to shaming Weinstein not merely for his actions but for his bodily appearance. It can even be argued that the two circuits of shame intermeshed within the logics of body shaming, as exemplified in memes depicting Weinstein as Jabba the Hut.

The overall setup of the scandal is both similar to and strikingly different from the Swedish coverage of Jean-Claude Arnault, known as the "Kulturprofilen" (the cultural personage), who was accused of sexual harassment and rape and was protected by members of the cultural elite despite several

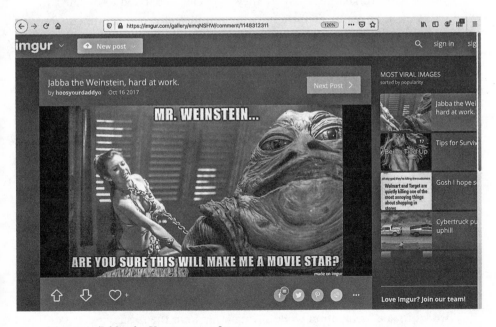

Weinstein/Jabba the Hut meme on Imgur

complaints. Following the outbreak of #MeToo internationally, eighteen women in Sweden came forth in the leading national newspaper, *Dagens Nyheter*, accusing Arnault—a high-profile power player in Stockholm's literary circles with close ties to the Swedish Academy known internationally for awarding the Nobel Prize in literature—of more than two decades of sexual assault and harassment (Gustavsson 2018). Arnault is married to Katarina Frostenson, a poet and also a member of the Academy, and the two have since 1989 run the private cultural club, Forum.

The article opens by setting the scene: The epicenter of Swedish high culture has had the same address for thirty years—a below-ground Stockholm club (Forum) that is a legendary stage for literary readings, academic talks, dance, jazz, classical music, and theater. Its windowless rooms have gathered Nobel laureates, international composers, Sweden's most prominent authors, actors, artists, and academics, as well as numerous young talents from prestigious schools of literary composition, music, and art. Forum has for the most part been run by public funds from the City of Stockholm, the Swedish Arts Council (Kulturrådet), and the Swedish Academy. Forum also takes center stage in the narratives of the eighteen women, some of whom have worked there (where they were always referred to as "girls"). Other charged places in their stories are Academy-owned apartments in Stockholm and Paris.

The scandal came to reveal a tangle of decades of systematic sexual abuse and abuse of academy finances, cronyism, nepotism, and leaked secrets, held together by a deep-seated code of silence within an old boys' network. Media coverage of the scandal zoomed in less on the details of Arnault's behavior and more on the networks of privilege and silence that made it possible. The coverage, as broad as it was, did not dwell on Arnault's persona, character, or physical appearance, and the trickle of salacious details remained modest. Sexism, rather than sex, and social structures of power and inequality were the key foci—even if the original stories of the eighteen women in *Dagens Nyheter* involved violent and explicit sexual details. Swedish discussions highlighted the ways in which sex, sexism, and misogyny become entwined in abusive male heterosexual conduct within tightly knit social networks of silence. This conflation of sex with sexism in public debates has worked to contextualize sexual assault within a broader framework of male domination while shying away from the specificity of these offenses.

Sweden is the Nordic country where #MeToo has had the broadest impact, with sixty-five separate initiatives demanding change in their respective work sectors. In a country that prides itself of having a feminist government, including a feminist foreign policy, #MeToo made previous cracks in the idea of Swedish gender equality run deep indeed (Måwe 2018). #MeToo has rendered visible inequalities across the professional and educational strata in ways that have undone some key assumptions concerning the level of gender equality in the country and within the Nordic region more broadly. Although fully unpacking the differences that may matter in public debates concerning sex, sexuality, and gender in the United States and the Nordic countries is well beyond the scope and aims of this book, such contextual differences matter in #MeToo's international reverberations because they connect to the redistribution of sexual shame and the diverse politics that can emerge from this. So let us try.

As we point out in the introduction, the Nordic countries are largely Lutheran in their cultural outlook but not Puritan in the sense of highlighting sexual restraint, control, and governance. The emphasis on abstinence and restraint over information on sexual health in the US context is in stark contrast with the educational policies within the Nordic countries, of which Sweden was the first country to introduce compulsory public sex education in schools in 1955—a development covered in a *Time* magazine article, "Sin in Sweden," the same year. Together with successful cultural exports such as Ingmar Bergman's *The Summer with Monika* (1953), this development helped to propel an image of Sweden as a promiscuous secular nation lacking in moral fiber (see Paasonen 2017). And yet this so called Swedish sin may be everything but perverse (or slutty), but rather steeped in ideas of good, healthy sex. The Swedish model of good sex vibrates with gender equality and involves, according to Don Kulick (2005, 208), "socially approved, mutually satisfying sexual relations between two (and only two) consenting adults or young adults who are more or less sociological equals."

The principles of sex education in the Nordic countries are based on sexual rights (e.g., Helén and Yesilova 2006). In this framework, healthy sexuality is active, consensual, *good for you*, and something that all people should have a right to. The model of healthy sexuality is certainly rife with norms in itself, haunted by notions of normalcy connected to the concepts of health and healthiness, yet this relative healthiness or unhealthiness, goodness or badness of things is based on the quality of sexual activity rather than on the fact of sexual activity itself. This liberal framework may not result in lives led free of sexual shame under the pale skies of white summer nights, yet it has tangible effects on how sexuality and sex are approached on social and personal levels—bringing us back to the positionality of the Nordic slut as our point of identification. The weight of sexual shame may be differently distributed in these two contexts, which can explain some of the differences in how scandals connected to #MeToo have unfolded in Sweden and United States.

For those standing accused within #MeToo, reactions have ranged from apology to denial, from confession to sharp counterattack. Weinstein alone has deployed all four tactics against his various accusers, and Arnault has denied any wrongdoing, despite being similarly sentenced and imprisoned for rape. As Susan Wise Bauer (2008, 2) notes in her analysis of American sex scandals, an apology does not equal a confession, and being sorry is not an admission of fault, wrongdoing, or sin. An apology therefore carries much less weight and is more ephemeral in its focus, whereas a confession involves taking moral responsibility (Bauer, 2008, 3). According to Bauer (2008, 27), at early American Puritan revivals, believers and congregations—and not merely those converting—publicly confessed their sins and repented them. She tracks this culture of confession as moving from encounters between sinners and God to more horizontal encounters of "public groveling" necessary for those caught in sex scandals to redeem themselves and to find forgiveness. The example of Bill Clinton—his public confession and broad popularity following a sex scandal—serves here as a key example.

No full confession has been forthcoming from Weinstein, who consequently cannot be absolved. Following the outbreak of the scandal, Weinstein, similarly to actor Kevin Spacey, who also was caught in a harassment scandal, sought help for sex addiction. Since addiction implies being in the power of forces beyond one's control, this admission helped to position Weinstein as a subject who has limited potential to modulate his own actions—and hence as someone who is, to a degree, helpless. The scandal unfolded gradually as disclosures made by over eighty female actors and employees, woven together into recognizable, repetitive patterns. These disclosures, both in the form of tweets and interviews, functioned as calls for public witnessing and judgment (see also Rentschler 2017).

Expressions of outrage within #MeToo have included moralizing, being scandalized, being angry, being disgusted, and all combinations thereof. Disgust has oscillated from the visceral (as in articulations of disgust toward Weinstein's body) to the moral (as in distaste toward his actions). In fact, the two forms of disgust intermesh in the coverage of the Weinstein scandal to the degree of becoming impossible to tell apart, marking him out as abject (see Kelly 2011). William Ian Miller (1997, 181) argues that articulations of disgust are central to moral judgment in that "the disgust idiom puts the body behind our words, pledges it as security to make our words something more than *mere* words." The visceral gravity of disgust anchors moral judgments in indisputable, embodied immediacy. As Michael Warner (2000, 4) points out, moral disgust can involve ethics and general principles of acceptable and unacceptable behavior, but it may equally be about moralizing that dwells in other people's shame and takes pleasure from it. Moral outrage and disgust, as fed by the logic of scandal, may then be steeped in titillation as such.

The increased nuance of detail and pattern that news items afforded into Weinstein's demeanor came with a titillating edge by promising to fill in the gaps and to shed light on places where no daylight had shone before. In their discussion of sex scandals, Paul Apostolidis and Juliet A. Williams (2004, 5–6) argue that absorption within them comes tinted with shame. In other words, rather than merely sticking to the accused, shame leaks due to the guilty pleasures afforded by the scandal itself. This stickiness, or mirroring effect, renders the position of a smug outsider impossible. Understood in this vein, sex scandals close their audiences, which are the public witnesses required for the circuit on confession, into their embrace, implicating them in their questionable pleasures and tinting these with shame.

Further, while the sharpness of anger, shame, and disgust may seem unequivocal in their force, different affective qualities intermesh, bleeding into and amplifying one another. For those following #MeToo scandals, shame may amplify disgust, and both may amplify pleasure, just as shame may cancel out any tingle of emergent interest or joy. Disgust may give rise to laughter as well as to rage, and outrage may well titillate. Our point here is that the dynamics of shame remain sticky in ways that are not easily confined to those being shamed or humiliated as objects of disgust.

Shame Lingers and Sets in Motion

We suggest that shame, in its multiple circulation and reworking—even more than anger or outrage—comprises the affective backbone of #MeToo. The affective intensity of anger takes the shape of sharp spikes, whereas shame sticks to and remains in the body in a different way. As Rachel Kuo (2019, 174) points out, "anger mobilizes political subjectivities by producing affective frames that shape politics," yet it is both laborious and tiresome to sustain anger. Anger is a powerful and draining force that moves bodies into action while exhausting them, yet it lacks the persistence of shame, which works the body at a tenaciously lingering frequency. It is in this sense that we propose shame to operate as the affective backbone of #MeToo. Shame occupies the position of strong affect theory that is supported by the Judeo-Christian legacy linking sex with shame, sin, and guilt, of which Puritan articulations are but one variation. Eve Kosofsky Sedgwick (2003, 134) points out that, for Tomkins, what characterizes strong theory is not "how well it avoids negative affect or finds positive affect, but the size and topology of the domain that it organizes." It then follows that an affect theory can grow stronger through the amplifying of shame into humiliation rather than by the offering of releases from it. A strong theory eats away at affective complexity in an engulfing manner: "The stronger the shame theory, the more expensive it is for the person who holds it" and the more often the person "misrecognizes, imagines, sees, or seizes upon— shame" (Sedgwick and Frank 1995, 21). A strong affect theory amplifies the qualities of sensation involved. If one sees #MeToo as operating with the strong affect theory of shame, then the redistribution and reorientation of shame occurring within it will fail to disrupt or even disturb its overall logic. Rather than helping to lift the sense of shame brought forth by sexual assault or associated with sexuality more expansively, a strong affect theory further solidifies such connections.

It is possible to fail in the eyes of others, in one's own eyes, as well as in the eyes of some more abstract entity, such as a deity. Shame, guilt, embarrassment, and the desire to want friends and family not to find out, along with concerns about confidentiality and a fear of not being believed, have been identified as key barriers to reporting sexual assault, independent of a person's gender (Sable et al. 2006). Furthermore, shame, in connection with self-blame, disgust, and anger regularly follows experiences of sexual assault, potentially limiting ways of acting in the world and feeding traumatic stress (see Resick and Schnike 1992, 749; Vidal and Petrak 2007). The circulation and redistribution of shame in #MeToo sets into motion and possibly alleviates the shame caused by sexual assault by breaking the assumed silence around it, by rendering it shared and even structural as threads in a social pattern, and by shaming the perpetrators through disclosures in social media. Shaming can shift to humiliation or move along a more ambivalent route steeped in ironic mockery. The shame involved in experiences of sexual harassment then moves outward toward other people and the ways that one may become perceived by them, and it travels inward as shame connected to one's own sense of self. The intensities of shame and anger, self-blame, and disgust may well pull people into opposite directions, both eating away at their sense of self and galvanizing them toward action.

Shame, for Tomkins, involves interest or desire growing unavailable through a perceived sense of failure and is hence couched in disappointment, whereas disgust is a reaction toward an offensive object that one wants to take distance from or to remove from sight altogether (Tomkins 1995a, 84). The affective intensity of disgust draws some of its force from a sense of uncomfortable proximity or exposure to something with the potential to defile (Kolnai 2004; Probyn 2000, 131). A victim of sexual assault can carry such an internalized sense of defilement, which can also turn into self-disgust steeped in shame. Given the complex entanglement of affective intensities involved in sexual harassment and assault, however, shame cannot be isolated or locked into any specific trajectories. And although shame regularly follows and haunts recovery from sexual assault, its presence should not be assumed by default: shame may well remain vacant or become displaced by rage, while its entanglement with disgust may feed an ambivalent sense of horizons of future possibility.

Within #MeToo, the circuits of shame glue together the experiences of sexual assault victims, the shame of perpetrators exposed, and the shame woven into the pleasures that scandal affords for those who witness it. They extend to attempts to alleviate the shame experienced and to reorient it by exposing the actions of others and by rendering events subject to sharing and public witnessing. Shaming and countershaming, such as that squared against Weinstein in social media, recalibrates the economy of shame without disrupting its presence as strong theory. Sally R. Munt

(2007, 2–3) further identifies shame as contagious in how the intensities of envy, hate, contempt, humiliation, and disgust readily stick to it. In the affective circuits of #MeToo, shame in its various shapes and forms sticks to and amplifies the overall dynamic of anger, rage, and disgust and, in doing so, both galvanizes the movement and tunes it to the frequencies of negative affect.

Heterosexual Resentment

In December 2017, some months into the #MeToo movement, Kristen Roupenian's short story "Cat Person" was published in *The New Yorker*, went viral, and soon gained the author a seven-figure book contract. The story is about an awkward budding romance and even more awkward sexual encounter between a twenty-year-old woman and a man assumedly in his thirties. "Cat Person" is rich in nuance as it describes the gaps between fantasy and lived experience, moments of miscommunication and misreading, and the elusiveness of sexual pleasure for the female partner. Analyzing its success, the journalist Olga Khazan (2017) identified it as "a viral short story for the #MeToo moment" that "seems to resonate with countless women" by "revealing the lengths women go to in order to manage men's feelings, and the shaming they often suffer nonetheless."

The story, often described as an account of bad sex, is not about sexual harassment but about the uneasy boundaries of bodily comfort and the difficulty of leaving an unpleasant situation once it has been consented to or even sought out. Eva Illouz (2014) deploys the notion of resonance to the ways literary works gain success by tapping into structures of feeling. As Williams (1977, 133–134) notes, emergent structures of feeling, in particular—more than residual and dominant ones—are ephemeral and possibly difficult to translate into language even if acutely felt. For a text to resonate, it needs to be "able not only to address a social experience that is not adequately understood, named, or categorized but also to 'frame' it in adequately explanatory ways" (Illouz 2014, 23). What resonates strikes a chord and, in doing so, makes it possible to articulate things that are otherwise hard to express. For its part, the viral resonance of "Cat Person" in connection with #MeToo gestures toward the female discontent and resentment felt toward the dynamics of heterosexuality beyond explicit instances of harassment and abuse.

In January 2018, Katie Way's *Babe* blog post—"I went on a date with Aziz Ansari. It turned into one of the worst nights of my life"—gained a similarly viral lift. The post describes a date between Grace, a twenty-three-year old photographer, and the comedian Aziz Ansari, then in his mid-thirties, and the unsatisfactory sexual encounter that ensued (see Salter 2019). Similarly to "Cat Person," the account is rife in signs of reticence going unnoticed and female pleasure remaining inaccessible in heterosexual encounters. The fact that Ansari's comedic work has been focused on romantic hetero-sexual relations in an era of smartphones added fuel to the fire because he presents himself as aware of gendered power discrepancies. The post was broadly discussed in social media, and as Caitlin Flanagan (2018) points out, young women in particular seemed to find it "frighteningly and infu-riatingly similar to crushing experiences of their own." Unlike the ficti-tious "Cat Person," this account of a date gone wrong identified the man in question, who had some celebrity status. Although no accusations of abuse were leveled against Ansari, the sexual encounter was described in tones of pressure, violation, and lack of consent. Addressing the post's popular resonance, Flanagan (2018) sees it as exemplary of #MeToo gone into over-drive in equating dissatisfactory dates with sexual violence and undermin-ing female sexual agency in the process:

> I thought it would take a little longer for the hit squad of privileged young white women to open fire on brown-skinned men. I had assumed that on the basis of intersectionality and all that, they'd stay laser focused on college-educated white men for another few months. But we're at warp speed now, and the revolu-tion—in many ways so good and so important—is starting to sweep up all sorts of people into its conflagration: the monstrous, the cruel, and the simply unlucky. Apparently there is a whole country full of young women who don't know how to call a cab, and who have spent a lot of time picking out pretty outfits for dates they hoped would be nights to remember. They're angry and temporarily power-ful, and last night they destroyed a man who didn't deserve it.

Flanagan's dismayed account zooms in on the ambivalent presence and absence of intersectionality within #MeToo, which is structured on and animated by a white binary gender dynamic. The wide attention that both "Cat Person" and Way's blog post gained speaks of the perceived ambivalence of female sexual agency, which, connected to the dualistic framework of female victims and male aggressors, helps to render hetero-sexuality into a site of shame, hurt, and trauma. Within this site, female sexual pleasure is elusive at best, and heterosexual men are either unable or unwilling to acknowledge gestures of reticence. As argued above, the horizontal logic of #MeToo's affective hashtag public levels the experiential differences between singular accounts linked to it. On the one hand, this evening out can efface distinctions between assault and bad sex, between aggressors and inconsiderate partners, and between victims and those regretting the choices they have made. On the other hand, this can, as Sophie Hindes and Bianca Fileborn (2019) suggest, help to make evident the ambiguity of grey zones connected to consent in heterosex in general: "Harm minimization tactics, societal expectations and pressures, and normative ideas around sex and gender roles mean it is not always possible to make clear distinctions between pressurized sex, coercive sex and rape. Thus, the discursive scripting of 'normal' heterosex and sexual violence overlap, creating ambiguous experiences that do not fit neatly into the available discourse of sex, or sexual violence" (Hindes and Fileborn 2019, 5).

If, as we propose, sexuality and heterosexuality, in particular, emerge as a site of shame, hurt, and trauma within #MeToo, what avenues does it open up and close down for thinking about female sexual agency? Furthermore, what broader figure or understanding of sexuality can be construed from all this? Both "Cat Person" and the *Babe* blog post address the elusiveness of consent in how it gets or does not get expressed, interpreted, or rerouted in heterosexual encounters. Female agency comes across as markedly passive: the male partner is left to take a role that leads and guides the action, and when this action takes unwanted turns, there seems little for women to do about it. In this sense, both accounts reproduce a normative, conservative binary between aggressive or even predatory male sexual desire and its passive, vulnerable feminine recipients (Hindes and Fileborn 2019, 4; Ringrose and Lawrence 2018, 697). Expressions of active female sexual desire, preference, and initiative remain strikingly absent from these zeitgeist narratives to the degree that pleasure and any sense of lightness, experimentation, and playfulness connected to sexuality evaporate from view. Heterosexual dating culture and casual sex then come across as glum, indeed: structured by female passivity and male activity and haunted by dysfunctional communication between the parties involved. This construction comes steeped in sexual shame, even if diluted into awkwardness, and a looming edge of disappointment, displeasure, and possible trauma.

Speaking Bitterness

The feminist tactic of #MeToo involves a decisive redistribution of shame from the victims to the perpetrators and to the bystanders who knew but remained silent. #MeToo breaks the silence and presumed privacy surrounding sexual harassment and reworks the circuits of sexual shame and shaming by calling out aggressors and by inviting others to witness personal accounts. The movement's affective dynamics are driven by outrage over the ubiquity and mundaneness of sexual harassment, the inability of institutions and corporations to respond to reports of abuse, and the tendency not to believe the harassed and instead to undermine their credibility. The affective dynamics of shame and outrage of #MeToo circulate around and stick to women as victims and survivors of sexual violence, and they unfold both in the streams of tweets that make use of the hashtag and in the ways the media cover male celebrities accused of harassment.

The social media posts comprising the hashtag public of #MeToo have made evident things that women have experienced and survived, with more or less trauma. Here, the movement follows a longer "assimilation of feminist politics to the discourse of victimization," which, as Judith Butler (1997, 9) notes, operates with a binary, heteronormative gender model. This conceptual framing shifts focus onto and calls out the behavior of predatory men, and in doing so, it shifts the focus away from women's reactions to instances of harassment. At the same time, the framing of victims and survivors taps into the registers of vulnerability, hurt, and pain in unequivocally negative registers of affect that further resonate with ways of understanding the experiences and practices of heterosexual women.

In its feminist tactics, #MeToo broadly follows the women's liberation movement of the 1960s and 1970s, which made it possible to "discuss painful relationships, sexual abuse, and experiences of powerlessness that were before kept private, speaking for the first time about taboo subjects and mobilizing a public expression of feelings against a culture of shame" (Stein 2006, 10). Taking cue from the late 1960s feminist slogan "The personal is political," #MeToo joins personal stories into a larger whole and, like many previous feminist social media practices and hashtag projects before it, facilitates a surge of consciousness raising connected to sexuality, violence, and sexism (see Boyle 2019; Clark 2016; Gunn 2015; Mendes, Ringrose, and Keller, 2019; Rentschler 2017; Wood 2008). Consciousness raising, however, was not invented by second-wave feminists but draws both on revolutionary practices of "speaking bitterness," as introduced by the Chinese communist party, as well as on the black radical practice of "telling it like it is" as a way of bluntly calling out racism. Lisa Rofel (2007, 49) traces the drama of speaking bitterness (*suku*)—from its origin as a narrative genre deployed as a form of revolutionary organizing in China in the 1940s and 1950s to its use during the Cultural Revolution in the 1960s—as a means of encouraging oppressed groups "to tell stories of bitterness they had eaten under the previous system." Feminists similarly shared intimate and painful experiences of sexism and male domination as a mode of knowledge production and a foundation for activism in processes of consciousness raising. As these stories kept accumulating, they contributed to an elevation of a feminist consciousness, a collective process of becoming a feminist subject by arriving at a realization that you are not alone.

Through stories of discrimination, harassment, and violence, feminist consciousness raising pinpointed a shift in perspective from the individual to the systemic, hereby linking them together (Hanisch 1970). bell hooks (2015/1984, 161) nevertheless argues that although it makes visible how sexism works and how it relates to male domination, "Feminist consciousness-raising has not significantly pushed women in the direction of revolutionary politics." In other words, personal shared testimonies have not necessarily been mobilized toward social transformation, rendering the exercise meaningful on a personal and group level yet—following Protevi's (2009) formulation of affective politics—without extending to the societal. Furthermore, as Caitlin Gunn (2015, 24) argues, second-wave consciousness-raising groups not merely excluded but silenced, dismissed, and belittled women of color, even treating them with violence. Gunn sees such racism as being "echoed in the reactions of many white feminists to the consciousness-raising efforts of women of color on Twitter" (Gunn 2015, 24). This critique can be extended to the politics and aesthetics of #MeToo that embrace the category of women in its heterogeneity and yet remain partial in the voices, bodies, and experiences that are foregrounded (Bailey, Jackson and Welles 2019; Gill and Orgad 2018, 1319).

It remains impossible and even unnecessary to judge what revolutionary potentialities #MeToo may hold. The reverberation of second-wave feminist practices within #MeToo is nonetheless noteworthy, as they echo the once radical notion that women should be believed. That this may still seem like a radical notion is suggested in the broad uses of the hashtag #ibelieveyou, which quickly surfaced in response to #MeToo. It is of course a beautiful thing to be trusted, yet #ibelieveyou manages simultaneously to undermine the trust in the original stories as seemingly requiring an external stamp of approval. The fact that #ibelieveyou gathered many men in support of the #MeToo storytellers was no coincidence.

Obvious differences are at play between previous practices of consciousness raising and the circulation and sharing of personal stories within #MeToo. Making the personal political within the framework of #MeToo may come closer to the Maoist mode of speaking bitterness than to the process of a becoming conscious as a feminist subject, which by necessity assumes a previous position of not knowing—or even one of relative ignorance. To speak one's bitterness, whether coinciding with second-wave feminism or with #MeToo, makes storytelling a critical part of revolutionary practices by putting things in motion through the repetition and circulation of certain narratives. The telling of these stories has moved from personal networks in private or semi-private spaces to those of affective, networked publics. This move from living-room meetings to social media platforms makes the personal political in a more obviously public sense, given that the circulation of stories takes place globally for an audience of which men are also part—as in the broad distribution of the Aziz Ansari story.

Temporalities of Transformation

Papacharissi (2016, 314) points out that affective publics allow for connective but not necessarily collective action of the kind that is necessary for achieving social change (also Stache 2015, 163). In other words, the sharing of stories and the temporary formation of bonds through articulations of sentiment—as in speaking bitterness—do not in any direct or automatic way translate as political action or transformational force. As "public formations that are textually rendered into being through emotive expressions that spread virally through networked crowds," affective publics operate and have an impact on semiotic and symbolic levels (Papacharissi 2016, 320). The power they can attain is of a liminal, transient nature, while their speeds are not necessarily compatible with the much slower rhythm and tempo of social transformation (Papacharissi 2016, 321):

These platforms amplify voice and visibility, and along with those, they amplify our expectations. The speed, the spreadability of information frequently, wraps us up in expectations that just because a story about a movement unfolded and spread quickly through social media, it should be followed by immediate political, legislative, systemic change. When that does not occur, we blame social media and assert that they have no political impact, all the time failing to realize the fallacy in our reasoning. It is not social media that have misled us, it is our own expectations that have let us down.

Change is gradual. Revolutions may spark instantaneously, but their impact is not instant; it unfolds over time, and for good reason. Revolutions are meaningless unless they are long. They have to be long to acquire meaning. Understanding social media as structures of feeling, as soft structure of storytelling, permits us to examine them as soft structures of meaning-making practices that may be revolutionary.

#MeToo operates within such a conundrum where its effect is constantly being questioned: Is the #MeToo movement over? What has it changed? It is much to ask that a hashtag public both render evident and transform gendered relations of power steeped in institutional practices and social norms. Long-term effects can be evaluated only in the course of time, yet this does not mean that the movement's potential should be undermined or underestimated. Protevi (2009) schematizes the body politic of affective mobilization as involving three levels—personal, group, and civic—through which singular experiences become enjoined as affective dynamics driving social change. On a personal level, a somatic body politic becomes registered as "patterns and triggers of bodily action and reaction," while on a compositional group level, "we see short-term events of concrete social perception and action, forming eventual bodies politic, or perhaps less barbarically named, social encounters" (Protevi 2009, xii). On the third, social level of political physiology, this mobilization involves "a body politic in the classical sense, what we will call a civic body politic: the patterns and triggers of institutional action" (Protevi 2009, xii). Considered on these terms, #MeToo currently operates on all three levels, depending on the specific context and location where it is being debated. A civic body politics is the slowest of the three to form, and it may fail to form if the affective energy cutting through the somatic to the social fades or becomes redistributed.

A certain conflation of specificities, registers, and contexts comes inbuilt in #MeToo, comprised as it is of thousands of independent tweets and posts connecting events both casual and profoundly traumatic under the same hashtag as forms of similar, shared forms of experience. To the degree that #MeToo is focused on women's experiences of sexual harassment and sexual assault enacted by men, many events—a case of violent rape on one continent, extended childhood abuse on another, unsolicited dick pics and pedestrian name calling on a third—are thread together as nodes and patterns of a broader social fabric of gendered power abuse. This fabric—whether identified as patriarchy or phallocracy—renders the personal political while gaining solidity, gravity, unity, and expansiveness in the process. The logic, in sum, is that of generalization where differences and singularities are effaced from view. The political force of affective hashtag publics therefore comes with the risk of losing sight of granularities of nuance, scale, and context connected to violations against sexual and bodily autonomy.

#MeToo operates within and performs a gender binary that leaves little room for the diversity of experiences narrated by people differently gendered, classed, raced, and sexualized. The very rhetorical strength of #MeToo is therefore also its key weakness—and as discussed in the chapters that follow, feminist humor and resistance online routinely resort to such antagonistic and exclusionary gender binaries (Ringrose and Lawrence 2018). Similarly to second-wave feminist politics, #MeToo can be critiqued for homogenizing both the category of women and the category of women's experiences in ways that severely limit the movement's potentiality for social change. Such homogenization haunts #MeToo in how a feminist movement, yet again, takes shape at the expense of questioning the hierarchical formations of binary gender, whiteness, and social class. Given the disproportionate ways in which black cis- and transgender women in the United States face sexual and other forms of violence (Williams 2015, 2016) or the high figures of harassment and bullying experienced by LGBTQI+ youth internationally (e.g., Mitchell et al. 2014), the degree to which public attention within #MeToo clusters on the experiences of white, middle-class heterosexual women is both problematic and emblematic of the broader social relations of power at play. All this remains connected to the clickbait attention economy of social media—and that of contemporary media culture more broadly—where the profit principles of media companies drive attention toward certain objects, such as the bodies of famous men and women and the gossip and scandals connected to them.

Outrage of the kind that fuels #MeToo is forceful in animating bodies into action, yet it is also an affective intensity that consumes these bodies and that requires much energy to retain. This creates obvious challenges to the temporality of #MeToo and the degree to which its connective practice keeps people collectively engaged in order to give rise to a civic body politic. As we discuss in more detail in the following chapter, the formation of negative affect, like the strong affect theory of shame that we identify as central to #MeToo, seems to repel lightness or humor of the kind that would afford a release or a temporary lift from outrage and disgust. Shame truncates ways of operating in the world and relating to others. For Tomkins, shame-humiliation reduces the positive affects of interest-excitement and enjoyment-joy while not blocking them entirely. Shame both sets boundaries to positive affect and attunes ways of being and relating to others. Considering feminist tactics of resistance, which is the general focus of this book, it is then necessary to ask what shamelessness, laughter, and joy can afford and engender in the context of #MeToo. How may positive affect, in such a framework, increase the capacity of bodies to act and, indeed, to exist? And what would there be to laugh about?

3   Affective Homophily and the Unlikely Comedy of #MeToo

As argued in the previous chapter, #MeToo is energized by articulations of anger, hurt, and outrage and is driven by the dynamics of shame. Steeped in negative affect, its affective body politics are as serious as the claims to bodily integrity and gender equality that the movement makes. This dynamic gives rise to what in this chapter we term *affective homophily* that brings people together through expressions of similar feeling. Humor and #MeToo may seem mutually exclusive, beyond the kind of sexist humor that underpins misogynist culture and in relation to which women become the objects of ridicule or those who just "don't get it." It is the kind of humor that turns feminists into humorless killjoys, the ones refusing to laugh with others and thus to laugh at themselves.

Although playfulness, humor, and laughter can even feel impossible to connect with the sharpness of negative affect that experiences of sexual harassment, violence, and abuse entail, feminist and other political movements have long used humor, laughter, and parody as forms of resistance and even subversion in coping with or providing relief from oppression and violence (e.g., Bonello et al. 2018; Gilbert 2004; Krefting 2014; Sanders 1995). Considering this legacy of laughing at power, humor may provide a breathing space of sorts where the pressing heaviness of sexual harassment and abuse of power become momentarily lighter to bear. As Judith Butler (1999, xxviii) persuasively argues, "Laughter in the face of serious categories is indispensable for feminism. Without a doubt, feminism continues to require its own forms of serious play." We thus find it important to explore the unexpected spaces of laughter in contexts where playfulness and humor seem unlikely, out of place, or even inappropriate.

In this chapter, we investigate the ambiguous affective dynamics of humor when it makes its way into the #MeToo debate. Our inquiry comes in three vignettes. In the first of these, we deploy *Nanette*—Hannah Gadsby's critically acclaimed 2018 Netflix live-comedy performance—as our entry to explore the interconnections of humor, seriousness, and trauma. *Nanette* resonated powerfully in queer and feminist settings but also attracted a much broader audience of reviewers and journalists and countless shares and likes in social media. In contrast to Gadsby's understanding of humor and the format of stand-up comedy as something that short-circuits her (and by extension, her audience's) possibilities of reworking and understanding hurt and trauma, we argue for other ways of thinking about the affective unpredictability of laughter as it intersects with and operates through feminist politics and registers of vulnerability.

Our second vignette examines the online #MeToo musical comedy "The Louis CK Apology . . . Set to Music" orchestrated by the feminist comedian Lauren Maul, who riffs on apologies made by male celebrities accused of sexual harassment. Her playful songs and animated videos render the apologies, as well as the men performing them, subjects of ridicule by pointing out their acute shortcomings. These two vignettes make it possible for us to consider how the dynamics of shame and outrage that are connected to #MeToo become reworked and rerouted through laughter in the realm of comedy.

Our third and final vignette opens the door to irony and its inherent ambivalence in a social media campaign. In considering the unexpected pockets of humor within the #MeToo scandal that ripped apart the Swedish Academy and put the Nobel Prize in literature on hold, we explore the emergence of carnivalesque comedy in the unruly performances of Sara Danius, then the permanent secretary of the Academy, as well as the feminist uses of irony in the appropriation of her trademark pussy-bow blouse (a strikingly conservative blouse named after the practice of tying ribbons around the necks of pussycats) as an ambiguous feminist symbol shared through social media selfies as a form of support and protest.

Our three strands of investigation move from the affective homophily of seriousness, anger, and shame to the more volatile feminist terrain of ridicule, irony, and absurdity. They map out ripples of feminist laughter (or the lack thereof) connected to #MeToo and the interventions that they afford or perform. Taken together, our case studies allow us to argue for the political importance of affective ambiguity, difference, and dissent in contemporary feminist social media tactics and to highlight the risks involved when a movement like #MeToo closes ranks around expressions of homogeneous feeling—not only of shame and rage but equally of love.

Nanette, or, the Viral Warmth of Affective Homophily

Nanette, a queer and feminist stand-up comedy performance by the Australian comedian Hannah Gadsby, was released as a Netflix special in June 2018, and it went viral almost overnight. It generated an explosion of shares in social media feeds that proclaimed the life-changing qualities of the show and was further propelled by highly positive reviews in established media outlets. Gadsby's performance was considered "remarkable" (*Washington Post*), "groundbreaking" (*Slate*), "soul-affirming" yet also "comedy-destroying" (*New York Times*), as well as daring "to dream of a different future—for ourselves and for comedy" (*The Guardian*). Fellow comedians also were generous with their praise. Jenny Yang, known for her viral videos and political satire, tweeted that "This one's gonna linger for a while and will influence a whole generation of comedians. If I don't change how I do comedy after seeing her special, why even?" In her tweet, Aparna Nancherla found the show to be "one of the most incredible, powerful, wrenching pieces of comedy and art I have ever seen."

The first half of *Nanette* is a clever yet conventional queer stand-up comedy set that leaves plenty of space for laughter for audiences of diverse sexual orientations and gender identifications. Gadsby tells stories about growing up "a little bit lesbian" in rural, conservative Tasmania. In a knowing play at the straight and male-dominated world of comedy, she asks, "What sort of comedian can't even make the lesbians laugh?" "Every comedian ever," she answers: "The only people who don't think it's funny are us lezzies, but we've gotta laugh, because if we don't—proves the point!" The joke wittily uses a marginal position for laughter while also positioning the (hypothetical) lesbian in the audience as someone uncomfortable with laughing along at her own expense.

But it is the second part of *Nanette* that gives the show its viral edge. It basically consists of a rebuttal of stand-up comedy or a deconstruction of how a joke is structured, with a buildup requiring a certain amount of affective tension and a punch line that releases this tension through laughter. Gadsby tells the story of how, as a child, her very existence created tension and how she learned to use humor to turn things around. She argues that jokes need tension to function, yet they also cut off stories or, more precisely, do away with the traumatic weight of personal stories in order to generate laughter. For her, comedy cannot embrace or work productively alongside trauma because it short-circuits the very space in which it could be processed. Laughter affords no such space, the audience learns, and here *Nanette* leaves comedy behind in order to relay painful, violent stories of moving through a homophobic, sexist world as a butch lesbian—stories that had previously been cut short in the interest of laughter. Having built a career based on self-deprecating humor, Gadsby states that she is quitting comedy because she no longer wants to relieve her audience of the kind of tension people like her create ("it's not humility, it's humiliation").

In the second half of *Nanette*, Gadsby is angry. No longer wanting to use herself as the butt of her own jokes or to make the audience feel good while being complicit in the structures of homophobia and sexism, she replaces the tension and release afforded by laughter with anger. Rather than ending here, she nevertheless soon denounces anger as toxic in the tensions it generates and fuels. Something that in one moment appears to open up a space for queer rage in the middle of a stand-up comedy set is quickly transformed into a speech on the need for civility and mutual respect. In one of the few critical analyses of *Nanette*, Peter Moskowitz (2018) argues that "in order to convey her trauma, Gadsby dismisses all of comedy, the uses of queer anger, and the entire premise of self-deprecation as inadequate."

The rapid and wide circulation of *Nanette* in the summer of 2018 testifies to how affective intensities may travel, amplify, and resonate through social media and give rise to networked events. As forces and intensities that operate beyond capture, comprehension, and control, affect does not settle as an object of knowledge to be grasped and dissected. To the extent that affect is anything, it is unpredictable, volatile, in motion, and never still as it connects and separates bodies, impacts their capacities to act and relate, and transforms them in the process. There nevertheless seems to be something in the affective events of social media that works against this very instability by pushing affected, networked bodies to sense things strongly in similar ways and by generating waves of affective uniformity resistant to ambivalence in how things become sensed and made sense of.

The registers of feeling connected to *Nanette* proved rich and manifold— from anger to anxiety, shame, sadness, joy, and even love. Audiences loved the show, and they loved Gadsby. And those who did not pretty much remained silent, unwilling to risk the underbelly of this love that can protect its objects of affection from critique with sharp flames of resentment, othering, and anger. In investigating how social media is shaping the production and consumption of comedy, Rebecca Krefting and Rebecca Baruc (2015) argue that social media networks make for a sort of homophilic tribalism among like-minded comedy fans, which impacts both the makeup of audiences and the content of comedy made. They therefore warn against any hasty celebratory analyses of social media as having the power to confront social hierarchies. The uniformly warm virality of *Nanette*, in turn, emphasizes the affective dimensions of homophily and similarity that allow for intensity while resisting dissent.

Homophily—love of the same—is a classic sociological concept and an attempt to understand the formation of friendships based on similarity of values (Lazarsfeld and Merton 1954). It was coined in tandem with *heterophily*, or love of the different, which added complexity and an analytical openness to how sameness and difference operate in the formation, maintenance, and rupturing of social ties. More recently, homophily has been broadly used in accounting for how people bond in social media networks and how these networks algorithmically reinforce similarity. As "similarity breeds connection" (McPherson et al. 2001) and "like-minded people tend to listen to like-minded people online" (Papacharissi 2016, 309), homophily becomes something that both drives and shapes social media connectivity among birds of a feather that prefer to flock together.

Homophily is, on the one hand, an issue of user preference—a gathering of the like-minded rather than an engagement in constant conflict and debate. On the other hand, the issue is even more centrally one of algorithmic design and agency in the sense that social media platforms (such as the market leader, Facebook) feed users with content that they are presumed to like on the basis of its similarity with their previously expressed preferences in the form of follows, likes, and shares. This then leads to similarity of opinion (discussed as "filter bubbles" and "echo chambers") that repel divergent views and intensify bonds of mutual feeling within them (see Chun 2018, 60–61). As bubbles and echo chambers feed fragmentation and division in political debate, they have been seen to play a key role in the current polarization of politics in the United States and beyond (e.g., Flaxman, Goel, and Rao 2016; Groshek and Koc-Michalska 2017). As Wendy

Hui Kyong Chun points out in an interview with Martina Leeker (2017, 79, emphasis in the original), homophily has become an intrinsic yet problematic part of network algorithms as the easiest way to grasp how connections take shape and linger: "Homophily *is* segregation. It assumes that love is love of the same, that you would naturally love to be around people like yourself, so therefore, segregation is natural."

With *Nanette*, such homophilic logics of love and sameness have contributed to what we identify as "affective homophily"—the love of *feeling* the same. Considerations of affect add an important dimension to the discussion of homophily based on shared values, opinions, or identities in that they draw attention to the bonding power of networked affect. With *Nanette*, the contagious qualities of laughter are tamed by a networked logic of homophily, according to which similarity underpins connection but also affection. Here, love becomes a love of feeling in the same way as others or even a love of feeling love in the same way. And if you feel differently, you do not belong, for you do not love—or you do not love quite right. If you feel differently, you may even be a bad feminist or a bad queer, given that such politics of sentiment (and sentimentality) are formed around feeling good together in the midst of everything that is bad. It is a matter of being similarly touched and feeling hope through touching similarity. Affective homophily brings bodies together through feeling, pulls them apart in instances of conflicting feeling, and in doing so, drives the emergence of affective publics.

Standup Tragedy, or, Take Me Seriously: I'm Not Laughing

Although humor involves "a capacity to hold together a greater variety of manifestly clashing or ambiguous affects" (Berlant and Ngai 2017, 239), the affective resonances of *Nanette* seemed more distinct. In transgressing some boundaries and leaving others intact, comedy can be helpful in sketching out the bounds of an "us" through the contagious force of affective homophily. Gadsby herself states that "anger, much like laughter, can connect a room like nothing else," yet she also claims that she no longer has an interest in uniting her audience in this way ("I just need my story heard"). Writing for *Slate*, Andrew Kahn (2018) claims that it is precisely this move from stand-up comedy to "stand-up tragedy" and the reluctance to unite an audience that makes *Nanette* radical. Yet the affective homophily of viral online warmth and affection spun tightly around the show indicates that its audience was indeed united—perhaps not primarily by laughter but by love, tears, and joy. We argue that such an affective shift from unpredictable laughter and justified queer anger to heartfelt, teary love and respect may not make queer feminist comedy more radical but less so. *Nanette* turns seriousness into a queer-feminist protest, a plea to be taken seriously in a way that is incompatible with laughter. This not only makes it impossible to use humor and laughter as a way of dealing with hurt and trauma: it also makes comedy much smaller than it needs to be.

It is this seriousness, connected with rage in the face of discrimination and violence, that afforded *Nanette* with a position as the comedy show of the #MeToo era (e.g., Boyd 2018; Donegan 2018; Dry 2018; Gajanan 2018; Scherer 2018). In other words, the show's affective registers found harmonious resonance in those of the #MeToo movement. Furthermore, how *Nanette* is situated in the intersection of *lesbian* feminist comedy and politics also does things to Gadsby's claim to seriousness. Jennifer Reed (2011) points out that feminist scholarship on women's performances of humor often operates within the frame of binary gender and heteronormativity. The focus tends to be on how women's humor is different from men's, on whether it reproduces gendered subject/object relations, and on whether it can be used subversively for feminist ends. Defined according to these terms, feminist humor necessarily takes shape in relation to men in a binary "battle of the sexes." While having a clear investment in a critique of male power and domination, *Nanette* also has an obvious lesbian component that disconnects it from men and heterosexuality (but perhaps less so from masculinity). Such disconnect may afford more freedom than heterosexual comedy scripts (see Krefting 2014).

Historically, women's need to be taken seriously in public spaces has made them seem unlikely to be comedians or to have any sense of humor at all (see Barreca 1988; Boyle 2015; Finney 1994; Gray 1994). Defiant laughter has been a productive political counterstrategy for marginalized groups using charged humor to turn tears and anger into laughter—African American humor playing with racism, rude gay and queer high camp, and even Holocaust jokes told within Jewish families (e.g., Gilbert 2004; Krefting 2014; Moskowitz 2018). Caught in binary understandings of both gender and humor, according to which women rarely are funny or taken seriously, the space for funny women comes across as differently limited.

For a butch lesbian stand-up comedian, there may be additional things at stake that make laughter risky or difficult. As Don Kulick (2014) shows, stereotyping positions marginal groups diversely in relation to laughter and seriousness. For example, gay men are associated with sharp wit and edgy humor, whereas lesbians—much like feminists and women in general—are perceived of as humorless creatures devoid of joy. Kulick traces the root causes of "the humorless lesbian" and argues that it is not merely that lesbians are women and therefore dominated by men but also that (stereotypical) lesbians embody yet fail to perform masculinity. In a reference to Jack Halberstam's (1998, 234) take on dominant understandings of masculinity as essentially nonperformative and natural—as opposed to femininity, which "reeks of the artificial"—Kulick holds that the nontheatricality of masculinity makes it difficult to laugh at, except for when it fails. According to this logic, the masculine lesbian is bound to fail and as such becomes something to laugh at rather than someone who laughs (other than at herself). Since Gadsby no longer wants to contribute to this logic in *Nanette*, seriousness may be her only resort.

To turn to seriousness as the last resort for feminist and queer humor in connection with #MeToo is also to subscribe to a particular understanding of how feminist politics and vulnerability relate, or fail to relate, to humor and laughter. As pointed out above, *Nanette* has been heralded as the comedy of the #MeToo era precisely because it does not aim to be funny, to make people laugh, or to offer the release of humor but rather sets out to abandon and even destroy the format of stand-up comedy. The forging of some connections, such as those between politics and seriousness, at the expense of others may also speak of how laughter is understood and how it operates affectively. Indeed, as Anna Lundberg (2008) argues with respect to contemporary cultures of laughter, the comic and the serious tend to intermingle in unpredictable ways, yet these cultural forms are simultaneously hierarchically differentiated in ways that make the comic into something that the serious is *not* (that is, superficial, unimportant, irrelevant).

Much theorization of humor and laughter sidelines their affective unpredictability. In a variation of the "pressure valve" theory of humor, laughter to Gadsby functions as a release of affective tension that simultaneously helps to efface social tensions, hierarchies, and violence from view. As such, laughter connects the bodies of a live audience with those who consume the show online and who afford momentary solace from how social norms make these bodies tense and vulnerable. This is not the only way for laughter to work. In the affective force and intense relationality that it may entail, laughter is unpredictable in both how it feels and in what it does, and hence it is resistant to or even disruptive of affective homophily. Laughter may release tension but equally build it up. Are you laughing at me, with me, or both? Laughter can be comforting yet uncomfortable, both freeing and opening things up and painfully closing them down.

"The Louis CK Apology . . . Set to Music," or, Sorry, Not Sorry

If enabling the affective power of outrage and anger has lent #MeToo much of its initial political lift, then affective homophily has helped to extend the movement's momentum beyond October 2017. Although it is energizing, the negative affective charge of #MeToo repulses different kinds of intensities and modes of engagement. We argue that humor can, particularly in its irreverent and inappropriate forms, create spaces for an affective lift where the weight of trauma temporarily lightens and where shame becomes much less solid as it meets the unruly ripples of laughter. Laughter can set things into motion, and in doing so, it complicates and possibly disturbs the affective homophily that organizes affective publics.

At the same time, affective homophily presses bodies to move and laugh in similar ways because it is encapsulated in considerations of what gets to count as "good" feminist comedy and which comedy becomes recognized (through social media likes, shares, and comments) as central to affective publics. In an attempt to disentangle feminist humor, ethics, and politics, Danielle Bobker (2017) uses the so-called sex wars between antipornography feminists and sex-positive feminists of the 1980s as her catalyst, arguing that sexuality and humor are not merely analogous but overlapping: "Both are understood to be culturally coded but with powerful bases in the body. Like sex, laughter has historically been considered an unruly instinct." Bobker points out the double standard that regulates both sex and laughter and the fact that both have, in paradoxical ways, been imagined as things that men need to persuade "respectable" and implicitly heterosexual women to do, while at the same time being something that the inappropriate woman excessively wants. In parallel to Gayle Rubin's (1984, 282) critique of the cultural need "to draw and maintain an imaginary line between good and bad sex," Bobker (2017) wishes to complicate the distinction between good and bad (feminist) humor precisely because feminist politics are saturated by justified anger and outrage. "If we get used to approaching jokes with trepidation, expecting offense, how might that wariness affect our political movements?," she asks.

In the wake of #MeToo, it may have become trickier than ever to know when to laugh—or even if to laugh—at jokes that play at gender, power, and sexism. It is not always easy to tell which jokes merely manifest sexism and which manage to make fun of it. And what happens to humor that takes shape in such close proximity to painful realities that laughter may never happen? In a discussion of the ambivalence of comedy, Lauren Berlant and Sianne Ngai (2017, 233) point out that the pleasure of comedy partly arises from its ability to do away with anxiety but that it equally produces anxiety, "risking transgression, flirting with displeasure, or just confusing things in a way that both intensifies and impedes pleasure." What a collective "we" find funny is contextual in highly volatile ways since what appears funny mixes with what is not so funny, perhaps conflating the two. *Nanette* may balance precisely on this tipping point between laughter (in the first half) and the absence thereof (in the second). The absence of laughter is nevertheless tightly scripted in ways that empty out the comedy turned tragedy of ambivalence and the potentiality of risky transgressiveness.

Some of the redistribution of shame that is connected to the affective publics of #MeToo becomes evident in how the terrain of rape jokes has been shifting as some male comedians accused of harassment now find themselves at the receiving end of the joke. Known for his dark and shock humor, the award-winning comedian Louis C.K. made a public apology admitting to sexual misconduct in November 2017. The apology may at first glance seem to contain both admission of wrongdoing and remorse. It opens in the following way: "These stories are true. At the time, I said to myself that what I did was okay because I never showed a woman my dick without asking first, which is also true. But what I learned later in life, too late, is that when you have power over another person, asking them to look at your dick isn't a question. It's a predicament for them. The power I had over these women is that they admired me. And I wielded that power irresponsibly. I have been remorseful of my actions. And I've tried to learn from them." The apology nevertheless lacked the word "sorry" while repeatedly emphasizing how admired he was, also by the women who did not consent to his masturbatory performativity. The question of consent here is curious because he did ask, but he also admitted that these women did not have much choice in the matter and were effectively overpowered by him. With respect to the Twitter apology made by Kevin Spacey, Suzanne Marie Enck (2018, 81) argues that although these statements are framed as apologies of sorts, they also repeat the logics of rape culture. Jeffrey Di Leo (2018, 2) suggests that such apologies, post-#MeToo, are in fact no apologies at all: "in saying that they are 'sorry' if their actions have caused any offense, they are in fact expressing dismay that they have to make this '(non-apology) apology' to the accuser." In hindsight, given how C.K. has continued telling rape jokes, the "apology" comes across as hollow.

This nonapology apology was turned into musical entertainment by the filmmaker Lauren Maul in a video clip uploaded in Vimeo on November 21, 2017. "The Louis CK Apology . . . Set to Music" consists of Maul singing the comedian's apology in a somewhat infantilizing vein, combined with an animated DIY mise-en-scène where cutouts of Louis C.K. shed glittery tears and articulate his apology with sticky notes and speech bubbles. The song's chorus plays up the statement's least believable line for comic effect: "I never showed a woman my dick without asking first." The Louis C.K. video can be seen as intervening with the misogynistic overtones of comedy discourse by making the comedian a laughing stock (see Elrick 2016, 266). Ridiculing the apology and the man who made it, the video operates within the scene of shaming and yet simultaneously disrupts it through its absurdist and playful aesthetic choices. This is not a scene heavy with sticky shame but rather a light and distanced one where a man who has admitted to sexual harassment becomes a cartoon figure that, as a cutout, literally lacks depth. The light treatment of a heavy topic makes the video traffic in a light seriousness of sorts, rendering the serious unserious or trivial and as such laughable (cf. Reilly 2015).

The aesthetic choice of cutouts in "The Louis CK Apology . . . Set to Music" reverberates with the weightlessness of his apology that did not extend to the word "sorry." The clip is one in a series of videos made by Maul titled "Apologies from Men," which is available on Vimeo and as an audio album from iTunes, Google Play, and Amazon. Similar in their execution, the videos star men equally caught in the dynamics of #MeToo, from "Kevin Spacey's Apology: THE REMIX" to "Sorrow & Regret: The Matt Lauer Apology," "Humbly Apologize by Russell Simmons," "A Short Apology by Dustin Hoffman," "The Culture Then by Harvey Weinstein," "I Do Not

Believe by Charlie Rose," "Pizza Dough Cinnamon Rolls Recipe by Mario
Batali," as well as an instrumental song, "The Men Who Have Not Apolo-
gized," a video somewhat similar to that of the 1985 "We Are the World."
Here, the cutout figures of Bill Cosby, Woody Allen, Donald Trump, and
other men accused of sexual misconduct are wearing headphones as they
approach a microphone one by one, yet they always meander back again,
unable to break into song. The musical score is cinematic, dramatic, and
somber.

In contrast to the viral popularity of *Nanette*, "Apologies from Men"
largely flew under the radar. The Louis C.K. video attracted a modest seven
thousand views and twelve likes on Vimeo within the ten first months following its release. Despite being crafted as spreadable media that is connected to the viral energy of #MeToo and therefore is to be expansively
shared and enjoyed, Maul's particular form of ridicule found little resonance
among social media users. It might be that this comedy was perceived as

being not funny or as treating its topic without enough sincerity. Considered in relation to shame and rage that organize feeling while contributing to affective homophily, the particular frivolousness of Maul's videos disconnects them from the affective public of #MeToo. Maul's videos focus on the men in question, framed by an absurdist aesthetic as objects of ridicule. By making fun of the apologies, which fail to apologize and remain concerned with saving male face, the distanced, playful, and stylized videos veer away from the personal: there is no play with shame or trauma, and any anger expressed remains indirect at best.

Gittan, or, Unruly, Absurd Laughter

Sara Danius, a Swedish literary scholar and author who until April 2018 was the first female head of the Swedish Academy, launched a legal investigation into the actions of Jean-Claude Arnault after he was publicly accused of sexual harassment and abuse (see chapter 2). She was eventually forced to leave her post because of the Academy's handling of Arnault. The crisis then spiraled rapidly as other members resigned in protest and as public trust in and respect for the work of the Academy plummeted, leading to the Nobel Prize in literature in 2018 being put on hold. The scandal and its repercussions quickly made its way into international media reporting. The *New York Times* article "In Nobel Scandal, a Man Is Accused of Sexual Misconduct. A Woman Takes the Fall" notes the "stunning causality" between Danius's forced exit and the reveal of sexual abuse (Anderson 2018). The article also quotes a professor of Nordic literature, Ebba Witt-Brattström (who was once married to the former head of the Academy, Horace Engdahl): "What they did was orchestrate a palace revolution, a coup to get rid of her, because she's too headstrong. . . . A headstrong woman is not what they are used to in the Swedish Academy." There is a lot of secrecy around Danius's exit, but it is reasonable to argue that her gender and both powerful and playful leadership style did not help her case.

Let us introduce Gittan P. Jönsson, Danius's self-crafted alter ego. Unlike Danius—who brought an unprecedented elegance to the Academy with her signature designer pussy-bow blouses, pencil skirts, and high heels—the virtual Gittan was a blonde Valkyrie with big, lacquered, helmet-like hair, and sensible shoes, sporting the same handbag as Margaret Thatcher. In an interview on Swedish television with the journalist Anna Hedemo for the show *Min sanning* (*My Truth*), Danius switched to Gittan. The audience learned that Gittan is head of the fictive Skånska forskningsrådet (Skåne Research Foundation), speaks with a broad southern Swedish accent, has a clear interest in the Öresund Bridge connecting Sweden and Denmark, and is fascinated by all things "continental." When Danius was in the Academy, Gittan apparently made appearances several times a week, becoming something of a regular. In interviews with the Swedish media, Danius describes Gittan as loud, slightly obnoxious, and an unstoppable steamroller who came to dominate dinners with members of the Academy and broke into formal functions. This kind of absurdist humor—as embodied by a relentless, fictitious *nineteenth* lifetime member of the Swedish Academy—did not work for everybody within the formal, male-dominated context. One anonymous Academy source admitted that although surprise appearances by someone more outspoken than Danius herself (although this person was still Danius) were fun at first, they grew confusing when taking notes (Börjesson and Skoglund 2018). What do you write exactly, when Danius becomes Gittan? Who is actually speaking?

Without missing a beat, Danius summarized the current political moment on Swedish television, hinting at the connections between Gittan and the social media uprising of #MeToo: "It could use some more Gittan, this me too-discussion!" To state that #MeToo needs more Gittan could mean a number of things: that we can all use an alter ego now and again; that someone loud and fearless could speak for us when we ourselves run out of steam; that debates on sexual assault and harassment could use some absurdist, situational humor that allows for seeing things differently; or that #MeToo could, for all its gravity and experiential sharpness, perhaps paradoxically use a good laugh.

Theories of humor and laughter tend to shuttle between examining laughter as temporary relief from social norms and expectations and considering laughter as a subversive force that opens up spaces of rebellion against normalcy (Palmer 1994). Viewed in the framework of Mikhail Bakhtin's (1984/1968) notion of the carnivalesque where laughter is a disruptive force related to the underworld of society and, as such, primarily linked to transformation and potential subversion, Danius's performances as Gittan shook up an exclusive cultural institution by transgressing bounds of normalcy that are tensely regulated by a particular form of official seriousness steeped in culturally elitist masculinity. Not surprisingly, Bakhtin has a number of scholarly feminist allies who find in his work alternative and liberating articulations of laughter, as well as those framing the female body as something other than constantly risking exposure, exploitation, shaming, and ridicule (e.g., Isaak 1996; Lundberg 2008; Rowe 1995; Russo 1994). In theorizing the feminist potential of laughter via Bakhtin, Kathleen Rowe (1995) pictures the figure of "the unruly woman" as someone who interferes in male-dominated spaces by taking up too much space, being too loud, and laughing too hard and who unsettles the lines of heteronormative femininity. Stemming from Hélène Cixous's (1975) "the laugh of Medusa" that is at once joyful and disruptive, as well as from Bakhtin's (1984/1968, 25) grinning, senile pregnant hags, Rowe's (1995, 10) unruly woman is "an ambivalent figure of female outrageousness and transgression with roots in the narrative forms of comedy and the social practices of the carnival." Although Danius may have posed a challenge to the Swedish Academy already as herself, Gittan's outrageous, rule-breaking performativity was an appeal to laughter in an effort to undermine male norms and authority.

Rowe argues that the unruly woman holds a potential for feminist appropriation because her home is comedy within an imaginary of excess and inversion where (for a time, at least) the world can be turned upside down. It is an overturn created by women who turn themselves into spectacles for their own (and others') enjoyment. Following Rowe, unruly women bring release, joy, and pleasure in doing so—yet they may equally produce anxiety, fear, and anger. Due to the affective power and relationality of laughter, its outcomes are always unpredictable (Kyrölä 2010). Rowe is careful to point out that the figure of the unruly woman is not inherently radical but rather deeply ambivalent and as such open to competing appropriations and interpretations. Such ambivalence may well have played a part in Danius's downfall. The unruly woman may evoke delight but also unease, fear, and loathing in the men she dominates. Gittan was perhaps loudly calling for male retribution. What is more, Bakhtin's carnival was never merely subversive but also conservative in that carnivalesque laughter and spectacles may help sustain or even reaffirm the status quo. Unruliness may help claim or create spaces of rule breaking while precisely reifying normalcy. In this sense, Gittan ultimately helped underscore how so-called good women look, sound, and behave. The carnival becomes a momentary release from a suppressive reality that ultimately remains the same.

In theorizing theatricality and performativity through a feminist lens, Mary Russo (1994) understands the female transgressor as spectacle in public, male-dominated spaces as someone at once marginalized and threateningly unruly. "Making a spectacle out of oneself," she argues, is a specifically female danger linked to the risk of exposure (Russo 1994, 53). Such inadvertent stepping into the limelight involves liberatory potential, yet it is bound to emerge as "out of turn—too young or too old, to early or too late" (Russo 1994, 53). For Danius to step into the limelight and take the lead within the Swedish Academy was deemed to be "out of turn" and "too early." Moreover, Danius was not afraid of making a rather stunning spectacle out of herself by showing a snappy fashion sense, wearing glamorous designer gowns, or portraying Gittan, her relentless, colorful sidekick. Deliberately turning oneself into a spectacle comes across as a rather explosive possibility tugging at the edges of dangerous exposure and attention. At the 2018 Nobel Price award ceremony, Danius arrived dressed in a voluminous, orange Valentino dress matched with an equally striking shocking-pink cape by the same designer. Sitting by herself in the center front row among the Academy fellows dressed in much darker and sober hues, Danius took up space—for there was much garment—while her chosen color scheme alone made her presence impossible to miss. Without saying a word, she was extremely loud. The performance, which soon found its way to social media commentary, points to both the force of unruly gender spectacle and to the paradoxical political potential of Danius's designer wardrobe indicative of class privilege.

Pussy Bows, or, Selfie Solidarity

To rewind: social media reactions to Sara Danius's exit from the Swedish Academy were immediate. On April 13, 2018, the day after she stepped down, Twitter, Facebook, and Instagram exploded with feminist support and solidarity, primarily gathered around hashtags such as #knytblus ("pussy-bow blouse"), #knytblusforsara ("pussy-bow blouse for Sara"), and #backagittan ("support Gittan"). Her signature pussy-bow blouse went viral as small armies of cis women, trans women, and some cis men, including high-level politicians and one of the defected Swedish Academy members, sported blouses with neck bows in her honor and as a symbolic protest against male power structures and sexual violence. People also took to the

← **Tweet**

Jonna Sima   ⌄
@jonnasima

Wow Sara Danius Nobel-kreation!! Svenska Akademien i dagens skick förtjänar inte henne.

Translate Tweet

Sara Danius at the 2018 Nobel Price award ceremony. Tweet by journalist Jonna Sima reads, "Wow Sara Danius's Nobel creation!! The Swedish Academy in its current shape does not deserve her."

streets in a #knytblusmanifestation at Stortorget in Stockholm (as well as in other Swedish cities) outside of Börshuset, where the Academy convenes on Thursdays, loudly demanding the resignation of its entire membership. According to Danius, she started wearing the pussy-bow blouse—a garment vibrant enough to evoke strong emotions—as a joke with her students, yet over time, she came to acquire quite a few of them (Strömquist, 2015). According to *Vogue*, "Whether or not Danius wore her bows with irony, her supporters wear them earnestly" (Borrelli-Persson, 2018). Of this we are less certain. Why should we grant Danius ambivalence in her pussy-bow wearing but not extend the same to her supporters? Would it not take a fair amount of irony and humor to transform the conservative pussy-bow blouse into a symbol of feminist solidarity and transformation?

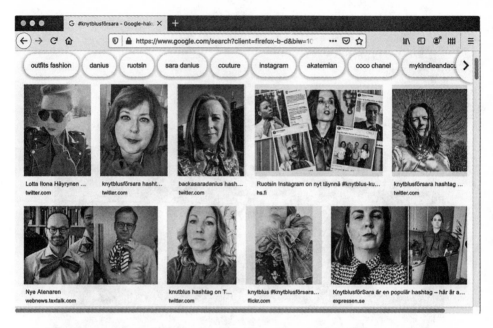

Google Image Search results for #knytblusförsara.

The pussy-bow blouse is a loaded garment, its ribbons tightly tying together questions of gender, class, and race. It has made its way into fashion and politics in waves, perhaps most iconically worn by Margaret Thatcher in the 1980s when she found it softened her appearance. More recently, Melania Trump wore a hot pink Gucci pussy-bow blouse to the second 2016 presidential debate, which much to journalistic delight was interpreted in juxtaposition with her husband's infamous statement to grab women "by the pussy." To fashion journalist Susanne Ljung (2018), the pussy bow is nothing short of ingenious in simultaneously concealing and accentuating the body of the wearer. It hides the skin while giving the personality plenty of leeway. Ljung traces the garment historically to the "cravats" worn by Croatian soldiers in the service of the French army during the reign of Louis XIV. Their unusual, picturesque scarves piqued the Parisian curiosity, and the flamboyant masculine forerunner of the pussy bow was born.

Nonetheless, as far as feminist symbols go, it is admittedly an odd choice. Apart from being a central component of Thatcher's power suit, it signals femininity as at once innocent and modest, and yet it works with girly, silky flirtatiousness. While helping to power-dress legions of professional women in the 1970s and 1980s, it was always a paradoxical garb, holding together things that did not easily stay together. As fashion scholar Philip Warkander puts it, due to its seemingly impossible combination of femininity and professionalism, the pussy-bow blouse has been ridiculed as a strange and almost "unreasonable" garment (in Lejon 2018). In other words, the pussy bow reeks of the absurd.

The pussy-bow blouse is equally unreasonable as a symbol of feminist solidarity. The trending of the #knytblus hashtag performed a humorous, ironic spin and opened up a political space afforded by the fundamental ambiguity of the garment itself. Because many of those gathering around the hashtag did not own an actual pussy-bow blouse and never would have considered wearing one, instead they tied a scarf or a tie around the neck of a regular blouse. The affective ambiguity of the garment makes it ripe for this kind of ironic appropriation and playfulness. Irony literally translates as expressing the opposite of what is meant for critical, comical effect. Linda Hutcheon (1994) nevertheless argues that irony is different from other modes of expression because of its "edge." This edge is social and political but also something that can put people on edge. For Hutcheon (1994, 35), irony is slanted toward the unsaid, and in leaving out more than it states, irony's ambiguity makes for affective edginess.

Read through the lens of irony, the pussy-bow blouse sets the scene for an affective relationality entailing a disruptive force between expression and understanding that is rife with possibilities to misunderstand and to misinterpret. Judgments were passed in connection with the #knytblus hashtag on the emotional and political positionality involved in the possibly ironic gesture, while some questioned whether it could be understood as ironic at all. Was the hashtag about detachment or involvement? Was it an example of distanced and self-centered "slacktivism" or a passionate feminist statement? The hashtag came animated with such nervous edginess involving both delight and anger. Delight came from those involved in the playfulness of the moment and its juxtaposition of rather incongruous images and fantasies. Anger came from those who skimmed over the ironic openings and went for a more sincere reading of the incompatibility of upper-class attributes and radical symbolism or of aesthetics and politics more generally. As the Academy member Göran Malmqvist put it in an interview with Swedish national public radio: "It has been claimed in the press that [Danius] has renewed the Academy, but I have no idea what it is that she has done. I would love to hear comments on this, but there are none. Which renewal is it that Danius has contributed to? A scarf!?" (Lille, 2018.) As Hutcheon (1994, 118, 171) argues, it is difficult to operate with theories of intentionality when discussing irony, given that the intended audience may not be the actual one and that it may reject the irony or even find it inappropriate or downright offensive.

#knytblus shuttled in intricate ways between bodies and digital networks as well as between aesthetics and politics, affectively entangling the somatic with the political in rather fleeting affective assemblages where homophily was not constant. The main bulk of #knytblus posts consisted of selfies taken by mainly cisgender women in ribboned blouses, wearing bright red lipstick without even a hint of a smile, grounding a form of activism reminiscent of what Theresa M. Senft (2008, 98) calls "networked reflective solidarity," a kind of political affiliation that stems from recognition of being "one of us." A similar point is made by Lena Gemzöe (2018) in noting that Swedish feminist pussy-bow solidarity builds on contingent and coalitional identity politics. Within the temporal logic of rapidly flaring spikes of affectivity and visuality that hashtag publics involve, #knytblus heightened the similarities of these selfies at the expense of their differences, due to which oppositional hashtags such as #vågavägraknytblus ("dare to resist the pussy bow") never quite took off. Despite its appeal, #knytblus's edge of irony remained rife with affective dissonance and uncomfortable feeling because not everyone was convinced of the capacity of the pussy-bow blouse to move from conservative political registers to feminist ones.

Activism has always been a site for mobilizing bodies, affect, and a sense of connection (see Karatzogianni 2012; Kennelly 2014; Knudsen and Stage 2012). What the term *affective activism* does, specifically, is to facilitate research on activism organized in other ways than through the representational paradigm of identity politics premised on shared qualities. For Katherine Johnson (2015, 288), "affective activism is used to note a practice that offers the potential for surprising or hopeful connections across identity differences." Affective activism helps in thinking through how bodies become mobilized and moved from one state to another in possibly surprising ways, in different rhythms, and through diverse temporalities. In its ironic openness, #knytblus certainly afforded contradictory affects, making bodies and their politics move and shift in unpredictable directions. The erratic features of affective activism and political mobilization resonate with Clare

Hemmings's (2012) notion of "affective dissonance"—of feeling uncomfortable (rather than emphatic)—as a possible starting point for transnational feminism. Feminist solidarity does not need to build on sameness, homophily, or even agreement. Uncomfortable, dissonant, and conflicting feelings may equally mobilize bodies and move them into action.

Despite its playful and ironic potentials, the pussy bow holds classed as well as racialized connotations by primarily assembling white upper-class femininity. And Danius was also a representative of the white cultural elite. Tensions in terms of class and race were not lost in the discussion of the #knytblus hashtag. Cecilia Persson (2018) argues that not everybody can identify with an expensively clad cultural elite: "To sign a feminist contract around a pussy-bow blouse is also to cement a class society and its inequalities even further." Persson points out how pussy-bow feminism forms a feminist "we" with sensitivity to power structures based on gender, while at the same time displaying class blindness. For who is continuously excluded from the seemingly homogeneous "we" of pussy-bow feminism? Are some forms of discrimination or gendered injustice more important than others? A catwalk appearance by Danius at Stockholm Fashion Week 2018—sporting a limited edition black silk pussy-bow blouse adorned with red women's movement's symbols designed by herself—did not ease these tensions. This makes evident that pussy-bow feminism holds together a range of differences and contradictions, combining humor with dead seriousness in unpredictable ways and rubbing against the call of affective homophily in doing so. At the same time, given its attachment to social class and particular feminine performance styles, the pussy bow renders visible a much broader tension apparent within #MeToo. No matter how powerfully the movement makes visible the relations of power and gender, its binary logic focusing on male perpetrators and female victims obscures the complex differences in how sexual abuse and harassment press differently on different bodies.

What Laughter Does

Anger mobilizes affective publics and fuels social change, but it also wears bodies down: constant anger is simply exhausting. Meanwhile, the kind of redistribution of shame carried out in the context of #MeToo comes with a heavy stickiness that never quite releases the bodies involved in it from its grasp. As we have suggested above, laughter facilitates affective release that energizes bodies by increasing their capacities to act. Laughter and humor are, therefore, as crucial to affective publics as are expressions of outrage and fury: all these intensities of feeling set bodies into motion, transform their capacities to act, and help in connecting the somatic with the social (cf. Protevi 2009). The fact that *Nanette*, heralded as *the* comedy of the #MeToo era, wishes to destroy comedy and refuses to laugh speaks volumes of how the role of humor is perceived in this particular context.

Refusing this commitment to seriousness, this chapter has aimed to expand considerations of humor and its affective potentiality by focusing on instances of ironic affiliation, mockery, and irreverent laughter that displace some of the weight of anger and shame connected to the affective publics of #MeToo. As we have argued, the affective body politics of laughter are nevertheless ambivalent by definition as ripples of amusement often fail to catch on and as jokes may easily result in others not registering them or taking offense. Laughter disrupts the strong affect theory of shame and outrage that drives #MeToo, but rather than dismantling any of its force, it enables momentary releases in instances of proximity steeped in pleasure that increase bodily sense of liveliness and, ultimately, makes lives more livable.

As we also suggest, there is a seductive quality to networked affective homophily—a love of feeling the same—that permeates digital connectivity and gives shape to affective publics. This may have serious ramifications for how feminist politics emerge in the wake of #MeToo. As sexual violence is certainly no laughing matter, there is an investment not only in seriousness, anger, and outrage but also in shared sentiments of love, tears, joy, and compassion. The viral warmth of *Nanette*, as comfort in stressful and discomforting times, provides such affective unity and community. At the same time, it makes it virtually impossible to accommodate affective differences in how sexism is being resisted and combatted. The affective homophily of #MeToo in its emphasis on similarity and sameness has very little room for difference—and, by extension, for intersectional critique. This love of feeling the same effaces differences in feeling and other gendered, classed, and racialized differences. The tribalism of #MeToo has powerfully consolidated a critique of sexism in connection with men's sexual violence against women, yet a mostly straight, mostly middle-class, mostly white norm is inherent in how the movement plays out in European and North American contexts. This dynamic foregrounding and focusing on the experiences of white straight women is not exceptional in hashtag campaigns against sexism (see Antonakis-Nashif 2015, 105), yet it frames out ways of feeling and relating differently that may stem from being differently positioned. In other words, if you embody a more marginal position than those bodies populating the core of the #MeToo movement, you may feel differently about the weepy feel-good-ness around *Nanette*, for example.

In her discussion of white privilege and what she terms "white fragility," Robin DiAngelo (2011, 2018) argues that white people live in a world that protects them from race-based stress. This protectedness creates a particular kind of white racial comfort in relation to which it takes very little for racial stress to arise. For DiAngelo (2011, 54), white fragility is a mode in relation to which even the smallest amount of race-based stress becomes impossible to bear, triggering a range of defenses, including "the outward display of emotions such as anger, fear, and guilt, and behaviors such as argumentation, silence, and leaving the stress-inducing situation." These emotions, in turn, reinforce white racial balance or stability. Public displays of white fragility are, in this sense, public displays of privilege that do not entail examinations or challenges of that very privilege. *Nanette* performs a similar display in how it connects with a form of straight fragility in its audience moved to tears through displays of sadness and queer rage. The audience is reminded of the homophobic and transphobic violence aimed at certain bodies but also instantly released from the stress that this may have caused. The aftermath is loving, and the comfort of privilege restored.

We find it essential to argue for the importance of "affective heterophily"— the love of feeling the different or of feeling differently—which opens up a much needed space for a multitude of voices and bodies, for affective ambiguity, and for a multitude of ways of connecting politically through how things feel. Put differently, affective heterophily forms the basis of an urgent intersectional critique of #MeToo, which brings together affect, digital technologies, and embodied differences. Affective homophily is likely to give rise to airless spaces within which inappropriate laughter is seen as too disruptive and risky. Within #MeToo, laughter may be interpreted as disrespectful and offensive and by extension as a failure to express appropriate sentiments of love or outrage. In this sense, affective homophily powerfully segregates networked bodies by shrinking the very space where not only opinions but also feelings may diverge yet come together. In its unpredictability, vibrancy, and volatility, absurd humor is one means to resist the love of feeling the same that aligns people and joins them in affective publics. This matters, for if networked feminist politics operate through filter bubbles premised on sameness or generate affective intensity through similarity, the necessary spaces of friction, difference, and dissent shrink from view. And we need spaces to breathe.

4 Countershame, Startle, and the Unsolicited Pussy Pic

"No one gives a flying fuck what you have to say cunt," comments a Twitter user "Doberman_Dad" on a tweet by the adult film performer Stormy Daniels. "You sure seem to care, Mr. Doggie Fucker," she tartly replies, pointing to both his engagement with her online activities and the multiple meanings that his user name involves. Mundane as such, this exchange had over four hundred of Daniels's followers joining in to mock Doberman_Dad and articulate their support for her. In other words, we have here a failed attempt at online bullying and shaming where a comment meant to silence is countered with a chorus of voices ridiculing the attempt.

A discussion on humor and feminist resistance in social media would be lacking without analysis of tactics for countering harassment, abuse, and shaming. Tackling this and moving further below the belt, this chapter examines slut-shaming (also addressed in chapter 5), tactics for outing and shaming harassment occurring via dick pics, and the diverse, intricate functions that the less common phenomenon of pussy pics can serve. We open with a discussion of one of the most immediately recognizable feminist social media tactics—the public and sometimes nonconsensual recirculation and commenting of hateful, disturbing, or otherwise undesired social media messaging. Rendering harassment visible is a widespread, successful, and to a degree risky feminist tactic. It is used widely at, for example, the @everydaysexism Twitter account "documenting experiences of sexism, harassment and assault" and at tumblrs and Instagram projects that make public the abusive flow of social media backchannel messaging.

Examples remain abundant, but we focus on two. In the aftermath of the disclosures of her sexual encounter with Donald Trump and the attempts to silence her on the matter in the interest of his presidential campaign,

Daniels has been an object of broad media interest and vitriolic personal attacks, developing a unique tweeting style in response (as already sampled above). Our second example brings in some Nordic flavor through Linnéa Claeson's Instagram account @assholesonline, a gallery of hundreds of unsolicited advances paired with Claeson's responses to insults or abuse and confrontations with the senders.

We then move to examine what seems to be the stuff of legend—the unsolicited pussy pic—starting out with one attempt at turning the tables on the widespread phenomenon of unsolicited dick pics. The Los Angeles–based writer Kerry Quinn (2015) decided to send preemptive "vagina pics" to a number of men on the dating app Bumble to, "in [her] own twist on revenge porn," let them have a taste of their own medicine. The experiment failed in the sense that the men did not respond in the way she expected them to. The failure highlighted how acts of sending and receiving unsolicited pictures of one's genitals are caught up in a heterosexual imaginary that determines what such surprise appearances might mean and how they might feel. At the same time, this does not foreclose other ways in which such images may travel, affectively as well as symbolically. We investigate such ambivalences in the traffic in genital pics to open up feminist analysis and critique on a topic that is currently overdetermined by an interpretative framework of heterosexism and violence.

Finally, we expand our focus on feminist tactics of creative pussy-pic making as forms of intervention in the culturally pervasive dick-pic culture, by evoking genealogies of feminist "cunt art" and its activist uses. Our main example in this section consists of the work and social media presence of feminist artist Stephanie Sarley, particularly her sassy, absurdist pictorial treatment of vulvas on Instagram. Her work has generated a wide range of reactions, from enthusiastic praise and fan love to shock, disgust, and aggression. As an echo of feminist 1970s gynocentric art, this is a digital instantiation gone viral, right at the intersection of copyright infringement, harassment, and platform politics that strike down hard on content that is deemed sexually suggestive.

Rerouting Hate

Online hate aims at silencing those it targets. As the Gamergate movement made evident, beginning in August 2014, online hate campaigns targeted against women and other others online make use of slurs and rape and death threats, can be highly organized, and can efficiently bar contributions in online publics. In different combinations and variations, hate sticks with a sharp racist edge to nonwhite bodies, with a homophobic edge to nonstraight bodies, and with a trans-phobic edge to trans bodies. Pointing out the conceptual limitations of euphemisms such as *offensiveness* in tackling hostile and hyperbolic misogyny, Emma Alice Jane (2014a, 559) identifies this misogyny as "gendered e-bile" involving "a distinctive semiotic flavour." E-bile may grow vitriolic, vary in its intensities, or remain something of a persistent hum, yet its misogynistic tones remain clear in how it targets bodies marked as female, too feminine, inappropriately feminine, or not feminine enough (Jane 2014b, 2016). Although femininity in these discussions is at risk of being something that belongs to or marks merely female bodies, we find it vital to make a distinction between the two because femininity, rather than femaleness, often gets the most heat. So trans and gay male femininities, for example, also need to be part of the consideration. The default mode of femininity is failure. You are bound to perform it incorrectly or improperly (see Skeggs 1997; Sundén 2015), yet the retribution for such slipups can be severe.

The retweeting of hateful tweets and the publishing of private social media messages are probably the best-known tactics for countering online hate and harassment by rendering them objects of public witnessing, engagement, and debate. The whistleblower, activist (and trans woman) Chelsea Manning was long known to retweet her haters with comments such as "We got this" and with additional rainbow, heart, and unicorn emojis. This was a means to make visible both the style and volume of hateful commentary and to frame it as something for her followers to relate to and possibly react to. Retweeting, especially when practiced by a social media influencer such as Manning, greatly amplifies the visibility and reach of individual tweets and, in this sense, potentially amps up the affective reverberations of hate. This, again, may inspire novel attacks. When hateful messaging is continuous, daily, and voluminous, its force may grow too heavy, making it easiest to leave the platform in question—as Manning temporarily did in February 2019. Since hateful messaging aims at silencing, this tactic of self-preservation is perfectly aligned with the aims or goals of such campaigns.

At the same time, retweeting dislodges the tweets from their original dynamics of communication and serves them as different kinds of messages (cf. Sadowski 2016). Reframing thus makes it possible to undo the premise of shame involved in being the recipient of such communication. To the degree that harassment (such as being called an idiot, fat, or a whore or facing rape threats) is also a tactic of shaming, visibility makes it possible to turn the tables by shaming the shamer. Given our interest in the dynamics of shame, shaming, and shamelessness that cuts through this book, the retweeting practices of Stormy Daniels (the stage name of Stephanie Clifford) are particularly pertinent. After entering the adult film industry in the early 2000s, Daniels has had a highly successful career in the industry as a performer, director, and producer. In 2010, she launched a bid for the US Senate as a Republican in Louisiana, following a grassroot campaign that encouraged her to run against Republican Senator David Vitter, who was accused of belonging to a prostitution ring. Reacting to news that the Republican National Committee had reimbursed its members for their expenses at a topless, bondage-themed nightclub called Voyeur, Daniels announced that, despite having long been a registered Democrat, "I cannot help but recognize that over time my libertarian values regarding both money and sex and the legal use of one for the other is now best espoused by the Republican Party" (Condon 2010).

Daniels was no newcomer to either political debate or ironic rhetoric when news of her nondisclosure agreement with Donald Trump's lawyer, Michael Cohen, became public in 2017. The following year, Daniels launched a strip tour titled "Make America Horny Again" and published an autobiographical book, *Full Disclosure*, detailing her interactions with Trump and the attempts to silence her, all to much media attention. Daniels has been on Twitter since 2009, but after she became the most searched-for porn star of 2018 on Pornhub, the leading porn video aggregator site, her followers increased to one million. Her Instagram account, with some 287,000 followers, focuses mainly on promotional materials, news coverage, and photos of Daniels at work and at leisure, with occasional live events, such as one during Trump's 2019 State of the Union address. "If you're looking for anything even remotely worth watching tonight at 9 pm EST, I will be folding laundry in my underwear for 8 minutes on Instagram live," Daniels announced on Twitter, gaining an audience of around 100,000 viewers.

In addition to posting largely promotional materials on her Twitter account, Daniels makes sharp rebukes to hateful tweets. In many cases, the

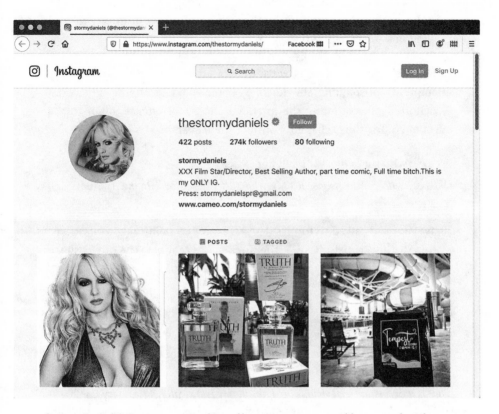

Stormy Daniels's Instagram page, https://www.instagram.com/thestormydaniels.

original tweets sent to her have been removed or the tweeters' accounts deactivated or suspended, leaving Daniels' responses—or burns—as the last words:

Really? I think it's epic and I'm proud that I'm still able to have my career. What is REALLY sad is another woman using ageism in a (failed) attempt to shame another woman. I haven't even reached my sexual peak. Watch out world! (January 10, 2019)

News to me. My STD test (every 14 days for over a decade) says I am 100% clean of ALL diseases. Let's see yours? (January 17, 2019)

I am not cheap! Ha ha! And I don't judge people based on religion but I do judge people based on their grammar and spelling. I am confident that you are actually the ignorant one. (January 20, 2019)

I think you meant "whore" and . . . you do know how birth control and
condoms work, right?? (Please say yes) (January 21, 2019)

Daniels' tweeting style is witty and often ironic. Impervious to any
attempts at slut-shaming, she ridicules people who take offense at her work
or actions while rerouting the intended circuits of offense, often to the
effect of ending the exchange. Consider these examples:

Ok lady who sucks dicks for a living

Ok! Boy, who poorly tweets at lady who sucks dicks for a living. (January 20,
2019)

I have met and talked to topless dancers before in political conversations,
this Stormy Daniels, has not the intelligence of a nat. The others spoke
to had more intelligence, and understood people. Stormy is as dumb
and sand.

It's spelled "gnat" and "as sand" . . . this one was too easy. (January 21, 2019)

tell me this, how are you always spewing nonsense? I mean rumor has it
you're mouth is always full and the spewing your doing is because you
don't swallow!

That is a disgusting and vicious lie! I absolutely DO swallow! (January 23, 2019)

Worn out porn horse. Are you still yapping. Man

*What kind of porn have you been watching? Your whole tweet is confusing and . . .
well . . . I won't judge on your fetishes.* (January 23, 2019)

WTH, when did they start giving out trash of the year awards?

Years ago. I have an entire trophy case of them. Pretty awesome! (January 28,
2019)

Routinely attracting thousands of likes and lively participation among
Daniels's followers, these exchanges open up as social theater of sorts,
one that she has expanded to comedy club performances (Marks 2020).
Daniels's rhetorical tactics include deliberately misunderstanding people's
intent, critiquing their grammar, and using *slut* as a point of proud self-
identification. Her tactic of slut pride ignores views of sex work as offensive and as violating moral norms and instead pokes fun at the offense,
annoyance, and resentment of the people who claim to consider it as such.

Meanwhile, she performs offense at not being identified as a slut of the correct, high caliber, turning the dynamics of shaming around and serving this as entertainment for other tweeters to participate in. We develop our discussion of shamelessness as a feminist social media tactic further in chapter 5, but argue that Daniels has developed and mastered her own variation of it.

Daniels's embrace of shameless, active, and advanced sluttiness involves a detachment from the label of victim, and she has separated her complaints concerning Trump from those voiced within the #MeToo movement: "I have NEVER compared myself to rape victim or been a part of #metoo. I've been very vocal about both" (January 12, 2019). "Victim of what? I've been VERY vocal about just the opposite and how it's not even a #metoo thing. I stood up for myself INSTEAD of being a victim" (January 28 2019). In an interview with *The Cut*, one year into #MeToo, Daniels similarly denied connections to the movement: "I'm not a victim. It's really annoying. It takes power away from the people who've been assaulted or raped or sexual-harassed by their boss." After arguing against overly expansive and generalizing labels of harassment and victimhood, she continued to describe the pleasure she gets from Twitter traffic: "They'll be like, 'Whore.' And I'm like, 'Yes?' I mean, I guess I feel the most powerful when someone tries to take my power or belittle me or insult me and it doesn't work. I've sort of taken all their power away from *them*" (Nuzzi 2018).

All this seems to make it more than easy to identify Daniels a contemporary feminist hero figure, but she is swift to refuse the label, arguing that she is no feminist because her primary interest is not helping women and because gender should not matter: "What's between somebody's legs. I used to be really annoyed that people would be like, 'Oh, Stormy Daniels is the best female director.' And I'd be like, 'What does my vagina have to do with it? She hasn't directed shit.' . . . I feel sorry for men right now. It's not a good climate to have a penis" (Nuzzi 2018). Daniels's concern is explicitly about social power, but rather than framing the issue in terms of gender, the key lens of #MeToo, she foregrounds sex instead. Her lack of allegiance to #MeToo—or, in her view, feminism—does not mean that she approves of rape culture but rather expresses her disinterest in the gendered relations of power within which rape culture and slut-shaming emerge.

All this needs to be considered in the context of debates on pornography, the primary professional field through which Daniels has gained her public status. According to a popular damaged-goods hypothesis, women end up having careers in porn as result of childhood abuse and trauma rather than through knowing choice, and they are under the power of the male-dominated adult industry during their careers. Although this myth has been debunked in empirical inquiry (see Griffiths et al. 2013), it continues to hold much power and is efficient in downplaying the agency and experiences of the women involved. The damaged-goods hypothesis remains key to feminist antipornography critiques that position female adult performers as victims who are to be exploited. Daniels's firm refusal of victimhood means refusing the damaged goods label and political alignment with those who might label her thus. Meanwhile, she remains highly vocal in sex worker rights activism (see Marks 2020).

Slut-shaming is not practiced by male users alone but is widely deployed by women toward other women (Miller 2014), although this is rarely fully accounted for in feminist discussions. Such gender dynamics in the affective economy of shame highlight how the nexus of sex, power, and agency may be differently put to use by women as a way of controlling other women, their bodies, and their sexuality. Lewis Webb (2015) argues that women have always been complicit in slut-shaming (from ancient Rome to the age of the internet) because shaming other women for their sexual behavior comes with its own set of benefits. If sex is seen as a power source with limited access (for straight men), then (straight) women who are deemed promiscuous and more than willingly giving "it" away would distort the power balance, undermining the power of other women. To call out such promiscuous women on their slutty behavior rebalances the scale and restores the order in which sex functions as proper hard currency (see also Dragotto, Giomi, and Melchiorre 2020).

Considering the volume of insulting tweets hurled at Daniels by users identifying as female, some of which have been quoted above, it is not surprising that she refuses to align her interests along the axis of binary gender in the general service of womanhood. Hers is a sexual politics that builds on strategic gendered body performances (as exemplified by her extensive pornographic work) but has no patience with mapping out agency in terms of gender binaries. This politics is paradoxical inasmuch as it is provocative, and it implies a narrow understanding of feminism. The possibilities that its shamelessness affords should not, however, be ignored.

Outing the Dicks

Daniels is likely to remain as unfazed by unsolicited dick pics as she is by attempts at slut-shaming. Dick pics nevertheless remain the most recurrent symbol of gendered online harassment—indicating interest and desire in the form of unsolicited sexual advances as well as symbolizing phallic male aggression and toxic masculinity in connection with rape threats. Unwanted dick pics are ubiquitous in both hook-up apps and social media backchannels. Attempts at fighting dick pics and the affective intensities of shame connected to receiving them are a dominant theme in media coverage of women's resistant social media tactics. Reports abound of turning the tables by publishing dick pics and sometimes ridiculing their senders, some of these reports growing viral through shares and likes (Paasonen, Light, and Jarrett 2019). Meanwhile, projects such as the Instagram-based Bye Felipe, which since 2014 has focused on "calling out dudes who turn hostile when rejected or ignored," remain popular.

The rationale of Bye Felipe, which, at the time of this writing, had 496,000 followers, is simple: participants share screen grabs of unwanted private dating app and social media exchanges without the knowledge of the communication partners in order to reveal their hostile, sexist, and offensive behavior. These screen grabs may come with or without the user names and profile pictures attached. According to a repeating dynamic, when men's sexual advances are not returned or acknowledged fast enough or not at all, the senders turn to body-shaming, slut-shaming, and other dismissive behavior, fueled by what Frances Shaw (2016) identifies as a sense of straight male sexual entitlement that is vulnerable to challenge and is both volatile and predictable in the speed with which it shifts to hostility. Similar feminist projects have been addressed as critical witnessing and resistance through strategies of ridicule, mockery, humiliation, and public shaming (Vitis and Gilmour 2016). By making assumedly private exchanges public, countershaming detaches the messaging from the personal—that is, from being about the individual woman in question—and helps to frame these exchanges as an issue of gendered routines and hierarchies.

The platform is key in terms of the degree of assumed publicness involved. A public tweet is intended and performed for an audience, lending a particular dynamic to Daniels's gleeful social theater that integrates the original tweeters in its loops. Meanwhile, dick pics or insults sent as WhatsApp, Facebook Messenger, or Twitter direct messages operate with the premise of backchanneling. Since these are not meant for public consumption on any feed, posting them on Instagram means turning the tables through the refusal of privacy. This is a simple tactic of outing. Many social media platforms have archival functions in that the data posted remains present unless specifically removed, and a sender cannot remove personal messages received by another. Meanwhile, Snapchat is built on the principle of transience: chats disappear once they have been seen, affording a temporal sense of flashing.

Independent of the platform, messages can be saved as screen grabs, stored with the aid of additional software, and recycled across platforms for sharing in ways impossible for the senders to control. There is no cause to believe that an unsolicited dick pic could not enter social circulation under terms other than those set by the sender. This, however, does not efface the ethical questions connected to shaming and the nonconsensual recirculation of dick pics as feminist tactics of resistance. Outing can be gleeful in the joy that shaming affords. Especially when the posts outed grow viral without having been anonymized, the repercussions for the men involved can be considerable and long-term, given the tenacity with which the data circulates and remains available (van der Nagel 2016). Someone's name and face may be connected to and haunted by a dick pic incident in top Google search results for years and years to come.

Linnéa Claeson, a Swedish handball player, human rights activist, and law student, has published a gallery of hundreds of unsolicited messages on her Instagram account @assholesonline, which, at the time of this writing, had 278,000 followers. The earliest posts date to 2014 and involve diverse comments and invitations that grow increasingly aggressive with her lack of response, such as "Wanna blow me?" / "Please" / ???? / Respond bitch / Respond bitch!," accompanied by Claeson's complaint to her followers, "It's hard out here for a bitch" (March 13, 2014). Claeson's Instagram selections soon expanded to include dick pics, and those posts started to include responses from Claeson, who framed the exchanges into dialogues of sort. Ranging in content that includes random come-ons, dick pics, and explicit expressions of hate, @assholesonline is a public documentation of unsolicited feedback from strangers, much of it with Claeson's snappy responses and the ensuing exchanges attached.

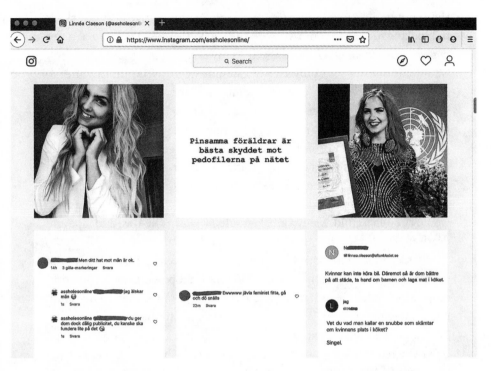

Excerpt from Linnéa Claeson's Instagram account, https://www.instagram.com/ assholesonline.

Sporting a striking, rainbow-colored hairstyle, Claeson has written on her childhood experiences of online sexual grooming and abuse and engages in activism well beyond social media as a celebrity figure. As Claeson has become known for her vocal defense of feminist, queer, and antiracist politics, the messages she publishes have shifted to address, dismiss, and ridicule her and her assumed hatred of men—although uninvited sexual approaches also remain constant. In clear contrast to the gender dynamics involved in Stormy Daniels's Twitter feed, no instances of female-presenting users dismissing or aiming to shame Claeson appear on her Instagram account. Meanwhile, her feminist stance clearly functions as a red flag for many men—whose responses may consist of simply an unsolicited dick pic.

Claeson's rebukes can be harsh, but her response style is often gentle, if not kind: "You are so blooooody tedious, whining, and pathetic" is encountered with "And still you hang around post after post. Maybe you like me a little in secret? ;)," Her manner can be pedagogical and patient, as when she counters a critique of her wearing sexually provocative outfits if she is not looking for sexual company with this reply: "Because I want to be a free person, a free woman with free access to my body, identity, and sexuality. I want to be free to express myself without judging looks. I want to be free to choose to fuck or not to fuck when I want, with whom I want, on my terms. I want to be a whole person. Erotic or not erotic. Sexy and ugly. That's the reason." Claeson gets political and serious, and yet her responses share some of the witty and surprising qualities of Daniels's tweeting style. Her rebukes are often funny, which is a central component of their popularity. A hostile message can be countered with the wish that the sender will step daily on a Lego block, or a sender will be accused of being unkind, as one would chasten a child. Many verbal assaults, sexual come-ons, and rape and death threats come without any commentary at all.

In order to comply with Instagram's content policy of banning nudity or sexual content, Claeson has placed emojis on top of dick pics. The earliest posts included the full name and profile image of the man in question, but in more recent ones, last names and profile photos have been removed. This implies a transformation in the ethical framing of the project, which otherwise remains coherent in its focus and goals. The men in question are still identified as "assholes" in accordance to the account's title, yet partial anonymity means that, rather than being specifically identified as and shamed for being assholes, they become representatives of broader, structural issues. Launched the same year as Bye Felipe, @assholesonline bears considerable similarity to it while also being distinct in that the exchanges it documents have taken place outside hookup apps or dating platforms. The posts are drawn from email and private social media traffic of the unsolicited kind, affording the project a different kind of resonance as documentation of sexual desire, gendered aggression, resentment, and hate.

We would like to highlight the importance of a contextual take on dick pics and the notion of harassment that is used to encompass all kinds of unwanted or unpleasant advances. This makes it possible to obscure differences between the contexts and platforms where harassment occurs, as well as to efface nuances that this involves. As we have suggested in chapter 2, the hashtag #MeToo both makes visible the ubiquity and volume of sexual harassment and violence and helps to obscure differences between groping and rape, cat-calling and abuse. The quickness and sharpness with which offense is given and taken in social media similarly helps affect flare high, effacing contextual gradation. An offer to lick someone's anus, for example, although possibly experienced as offensive, means something quite different when delivered on a hook-up app where people are looking for sexual partners than it does in a professional email exchange or in a random private message, such as those shared by Claeson. Although one may not wish to receive a dick pic as a prequel to hooking up, it is not altogether outlandish for the outcome of sexual self-shooting practices to be shared on an app like Tinder, given the motivations and purposes of its use. Treating all unsolicited dick pics horizontally as signs of male violence and offense, without paying adequate attention to contextual detail, obscures the possible ambiguities and diverse intentions involved.

Since November 2019, Claeson has been accused of fabricating and exaggerating instances of sexual harassment, particularly those of the physical kind. Because her career as a social media influencer is underpinned by the experiences she documents and shares, she has been critiqued for building a cult of personality based on inaccurate and partly nonfactual accounts of harassment in a context where factual examples do not gain similar publicity and for undermining a broader feminist project in the process (Gustafsson 2019; Roslund 2019). Accusations of fabrication have been leveled at Claeson by feminist journalists, by predominantly male far-right antifeminist Twitter users, and by the leftist podcast "Haveristerna." According to these critiques, the dick pics she claims to have received actually have been harvested from online porn sites and hook-up apps such as Grindr and hence are not real instances of harassment. Here, the investigation takes a turn toward the absurd. We can envision straight men trolling through gay sites and apps in search of a matching penis and comparing image backgrounds to identify the country where just this kind of a bathroom might exist. Aiming to question the veracity of an antiracist and feminist public figure, this homosocial fieldwork does, after all, necessitate careful and expansive close visual analysis. Although it is entirely possible to send a dick pic to someone without the pic in question being that of one's actual dick—but, let us say, sourced from the rich image file masses of the internet—authenticity operates here as a broader guarantee and proof of trustworthiness.

In an answer to her critics, Claeson (2019) apologizes for not being clear enough about her work methods as well as her overall objective of creating feminist comedy. She does edit messages and conversations from other platforms and formats so that they fit the image logic of Instagram. For this reason, she has also translated messages into English and sometimes has published the same content twice. Despite critiques concerning the high volume of instances of sexual harassment, online as well as off, she argues that @assholesonline was never a site for displaying sexual harassment targeted only at herself but that it also has functioned partly as an aggregator where she posts conversations and examples that other women have sent her. Regarding the physical advances from men, she persistently stands her ground and refers to documented legal procedures and court cases involving the more difficult ones. In an earlier newspaper chronicle about how dick pics have more to do with power than with sex, she puts the phenomenon of repeat or duplicate dick pics in a comic light. It indeed seems to be the case that different men have used the same dick pics in their unsolicited correspondence and hence have unwittingly, much to her amusement, displayed "the same taste in dicks" (Claeson 2017). Claeson emphasizes that her feminist project always has entailed comedy and humor as weapons for fighting sexism: "This is my shield. This is my self-defense. A willy satire, a penis parody, and cock comedy" (Claeson 2017). This cock comedy comes with its own share of what we might call dick-splaining—for, once again, the question of "truth" seems to hinge on the dicks being presented in a believable manner.

A Feminist Dating App?

As a straight single woman living in Los Angeles and frequenting dating apps, Kerry Quinn had her fair share of unsolicited dick pics interloping into her everyday life. To interfere in a dynamic in which men become the insistent senders and women the reluctant recipients of dick pics, she wanted to reverse the order of operations: "What would guys do if I turned the tables and sent them an unexpected vagina pic?" (Quinn 2015). In her experiment, Quinn decided to not use images of her own private parts, which seemed far too intimate. Following the general trend of ethical laxness connected to the sharing of identifying data in repurposing private messages for public consumption through a feminist lens, Quinn did not comment on the ethics of using a picture of someone else's body part or on the ethics of rendering parts of the men's responses public, although these were, to some extent, anonymized in the article she published on the experiment. Profile names were included, and profile pictures and those parts of the exchange that were (supposedly) too graphic were blurred.

She went online to find, as she put it, "the perfect vagina pic. . . . I searched the Interwebs, and after extensive research I have to give props to straight guys and lesbians—vaginas are like fingerprints except you really don't know what you're going to get. After a lot of 'Whoa!'s and 'Oh my!'s I found a vagina that somewhat matched mine (correct skin tone!) and seemed 'cute'" (Quinn 2015). Armed with this new "cute" vagina avatar, which in actual fact most likely was a picture of a vulva (the pictures in the article have been blurred, so we cannot be sure but can make an educated guess), she proceeded to send forty men surprise "vagina pics" on the dating app Bumble.

The choice of Bumble was no coincidence. Bumble allows for image transfers as part of the platform rather than via text messaging, which keeps the interaction safe in a way that interplay involving phone numbers does not. Founded by Whitney Wolfe Herd, also a cofounder of Tinder, Bumble has come to brand itself as a "feminist dating app" (e.g., Lott-Lavigna 2015) that both empowers and protects women. On Bumble, women in straight configurations need to make the first move, nudity is forbidden, and kindness a company motto. In an attempt to challenge the dynamics of straight dating games, Bumble has women taking the lead, makes it easy to report harassment, and has banned male users for fat-shaming and for calling women "gold-digging whores" (Bennett 2017; Tait 2017). To Wolfe Herd, having women initiate contact encourages a more assertive attitude, but also makes men "calm down" (Tait 2017).

As a dating app designed to counteract sexism and abuse, Bumble figures feminism and heterosexual relationality in highly specific ways along the lines of gender, sexual agency, and safety. Caitlin MacLeod and Victoria McArthur (2018, 11–12) argue that gender on Bumble is binary and static because participants have only one option for selecting their gender. Rena Bivens and Anna Shah Hoque (2018, 445, 455) further point out that Bumble optimizes control and safety for cisgender straight women at the expense of other users. Its sense of safety is connected to the absence of both nudity and harassment and to an assumption that straight masculinity includes overt sexuality and aggression. In other words, because the platform's main concern is the safety and protection of its straight female users, men are positioned as potential sexual harassers and compulsive dick-pic senders. Although women get to be proactive, this involves a limited, fully clothed form of agency: within Bumble's logic, following the ban on nudity, female sexuality and female sexual agency in fact become oxymorons. Women get to make the first move as long as they comply with the norm of white, bourgeois, demure femininity. Quinn's choice of Bumble for her experiment makes sense because image transfers are safely part of the platform dynamics and women making the first move is a design feature. But Wolfe Herd probably did not foresee that her platform and her work for eradicating dick pics by designing for "active" women, kindness, and decency could be used as a hotbed for a wave of unsolicited vulva pics and, in a sense, a more sex-positive feminism.

Quinn opened up the experiment with a few flirtatious lines and then hit the receivers with the "v-pic." She received not the shock and appall she expected but detailed sexual descriptions of what the receivers wanted to do with her lady bits, so she amped up her game by sending the v-pic right after initial hellos. When this did not seem to make anybody uneasy either, she then simply sent the v-pic instead of a hello as soon as she matched with someone. Not even this changed the rhythm of the interaction or appeared to throw anybody off. Men seemed more than willing to continue the exchange. Three of the men who got a v-pic as a conversation starter did not respond, but nobody unmatched with Quinn (which regularly had been her own strategy when receiving unwanted dick pics). Out of the forty men visually proposed, thirty-seven wanted to meet up. Quinn ended up not meeting with anybody because "how do you come back from a level of pseudo-intimacy generated by a fake body part?" (Quinn 2015). She admits, however, that she felt oddly empowered when men were tripping over themselves to meet her and when many of them genuinely seemed to like vulva pics.

Taken by Startled Surprise

Kerry Quinn's experiment failed in the sense that the men who received the images did not respond in the way she expected. She had hoped that the images would come across as being as invasive as the dick pics she had received. Instead, these exchanges turned out to have their own sense of humor. According to Quinn, by far the most common response was sexually explicit, such as "my tongue needs to be there asap." Tapping into a different repertoire, one man quite ingeniously replied with a picture of a dog looking all alert, whereas another became more of an art critic by claiming that "Lighting is a little off." The most out-of-tune response was probably the one from a man who wrote to Quinn as if she was an old school friend: "Nice. Let's catch up some time" (Quinn 2015). She does not seem to notice or acknowledge the unmistakably enthusiastic and happy tone of many of the responses, such as "Oh wow wasn't expecting that haha what do you do in LA?," "Best girl I matched with on Bumble so far," and "You just took my productivity at the office to zero." Or consider this exchange in the form of a compliment, testifying to the scarcity of the unsolicited vulva pic phenomenon:

Man: "I bet the rest of you looks equally as good. Maybe better"

Quinn: "you made me blush" "Do girls usually send vagina pics?"

Man: "I've gotten one before. So no lol"

In considering such seemingly pleasant and sudden interruptions in focus and attention, Silvan Tomkins (2008) writes about the neutral affective dynamic of "surprise-startle," which covers everything from mild surprise to a more intense form of startle. Surprise-startle is, for Tomkins, a general interrupter to an ongoing activity triggered by a sudden, brief stimulus. An unsolicited vulva pic can certainly cause such an interruption in the fabric of everyday life of the men who receive them as something that, all of a sudden, demands attention. Surprise-startle is a "resetting affect" that orients the body by swiftly demanding a shift in attention or focus: "It is ancillary to every other affect since it orients the individual to turn his attention away from one thing to another. Whether, having been interrupted, the individual will respond with interest, or fear, or joy, or distress, or disgust, or shame or anger will depend on the nature of the interrupting stimulus and on the interpretation given to it" (Tomkins 2008, 273).

Surprise-startle is thus always dependent on what the interruption involves (a firecracker or a vulva pic?), on how the interruption feels, and on what it means. It can evoke positive or negative affects or combinations thereof, and it entails a moment of openness as such. Surprise-startle functions as a reset button of sorts, something that clears body and mind of whatever the engagement might have been only a short moment earlier. "You just took my productivity at the office to zero" can be understood as such a reset when the surprising appearance of a stranger's vulva inserts itself into the rhythm of office life, calling for a sudden change of attention from, say, spreadsheets to the promise of sexual encounters. Its surprise appearance may certainly have reset or short-circuited the current activities of the recipients as a form of bodily reorientation and shift in focus generating a stream of sexual fantasies and scenarios.

As readers of Quinn's piece, we are not too surprised (or startled). The only truly surprising part in Quinn's story might be her own surprise at the reactions she received—the ways that these men replied in kind to her overtly sexual opening. The "failure" of the experiment thus draws attention to the affective economy in which unsolicited genital pics tend to move and make sense within straight settings—an economy where gender and heteronormal desires shape what the appearance of a stranger's genitals on one's phone might mean and how that might feel (see Paasonen, Light, and Jarrett 2019). The expressions of enthusiasm and excitement of these men are clearly not in line with how someone would respond to an attempt to shame or sexually harass. Nonetheless, in covering Quinn's experiment for the *Washington Post*, Britni de la Cretaz (2015) points out that "When women send unsolicited naked pictures, it isn't revenge—it's harassment," arguing for the need for women to hold themselves to a higher standard. She continues, "When photos of penises are sent without being requested, they are not consensual and sending them is an electronic form of sexual violence. Unexpected vulva photos are no different." This categorical statement is somewhat nonsensical in the context of Quinn's experiment, given the responses of joy and excitement from the men allegedly subjected to sexual violence. Although receiving an unrequested genital picture can certainly constitute a form of sexual violence, our point is that it also can be experienced as something else. As Tomkins points out, surprise-startle is a neutral affect that can tilt any odd way.

Any object can be linked to any affect, and vice versa: the autonomy of affect means that there is no general causality to how a certain object, such as a dick pic or a vulva pic, becomes sensed and made sense of (Tomkins 1995b, 54–55). In other words, the affect or meaning produced through a dick pic (or vulva pic) exchange does not reside in the object or in the bodies that are momentarily tied together through these digital transactions. How these images feel and what they mean are questions of relation because particular pictures are produced, consumed, and felt in encounters with particular bodies. Most of the public discussion of unsolicited nudes is pervasively straight in that it excludes pictorial transactions between trans and queer bodies, such as the playful use of dildo pics between queer women and other nonmen or the steamy dick-pic sharing between gay men (on dick pics in dating practices among men who have sex with men, see Paasonen, Light, and Jarrett 2019). Yet so-called straight image practices also hold more complexity than crude gender binaries such as active and passive can comfortably embrace.

In the popular imagination, the unsolicited dick pic seems to occupy a sliding scale between sexual violence and harassment at one end and milder forms of inconvenience or irritation at the other. A lion's share of feminist analyses focus on unwanted dick pics as a form of sexual exposure that makes women feel victimized and violated (Hayes and Dragiewicz 2018; Powell and Henry 2017; Salter 2015; Vitis and Gilmour 2016). Strange penises that pop up on one's phone can indeed have a distinctly violent, abusive feel to them. At the same time, the affective edge of the dick pic makes for volatility and unpredictability in the encounter. What one person finds highly offensive and invasive, another may find arousing, silly, ridiculous, funny, or simply unbearably boring in its repetitiveness (Waling and Pym 2019). And conversely, even if a common response among straight men to receiving surprise vulva pictures is one of joyful surprise at being sexually propositioned in such a way, there will be other ways of feeling and reacting.

Pussy Pics and Cunt Art

The relative scarcity and rarity of the surprise pussy pic sent between strangers becomes obvious in online searches for its occurrence, even when these searches are careful, creative, and deep. Since pussy pictures are a pornographic leitmotif, there is no shortage of them online and they—like the even more ubiquitous tit pic—are routinely shared in sexting practices. But finding evidence or traces of image practices involving women and other pussy-bearers snapping pictures for unsolicited image-sharing purposes is a case apart. One witty testimony to the rare existence of uninvited pussy pics can be found in a 2015 tweet from the Tumblr-born DIY porn performer and film maker Vex Ashley (with 100,000 followers on Instagram and 50,000 on Twitter): "I just got my first unsolicited pussy pic in my inbox (with added bonus butthole) so I guess . . . it is a thing?" The tweet engendered a range of crafty responses (April 25, 2016):

"i send those . . . a lot but usually its because I need a job"

"bonus butthole" is AMAZING! haha"

"What happened to my dichotomic world? The borders of gender behaviours are blurry now"

"I. . . . I got one too and I'm very very confused. A sea of dicks and all of sudden . . . Is it the same pussy? Is it a new thing?"

"definitely a thing. little less common tho"

"those are as rare as mew"

"rare but I've had one or two :p"

As part of playful exchanges in "a sea of dicks," the surprise pussy pic has the potential to interrupt simple views of gender and heteronormal desire, as well as to provide a kind of resistance to dominant understandings of these image-sharing practices as merely a matter of sexual harassment and abuse. Nearly all of the replies to Ashley's tweet were sent from female-presenting Twitter accounts, most of which were part of similar circles of sex workers, DIY porn makers, and queer kinksters. Admittedly, such a milieu of sex positivity would be a relatively safe space for sending and experimenting with surprise pussy pics—yet these did not seem to be particularly common or clearly recognizable as "a thing," even here.

To the extent that sending pussy pictures is an expression of "female" desire—either within straight configurations or in lesbian, queer, and trans networks of desire between women and other pussy bearers—the relative absence of the phenomenon has everything to do with how such desires are virtually nonexistent in the cultural imagination. Elizabeth Grosz (1995) has formulated a critique (which sadly still holds) of the conventional understanding of desire along the lines of a Freudian ontology of lack. According to this logic, desire figures intimately as part of a heterosexualized binary arrangement where men are active, desiring subjects and women are passive objects of desire, which renders impossible the sexual autonomy or agency of women (a figuration also examined in chapter 2). Desire expressed as a form of lack or negativity is a desire for what is unobtainable because it can work only if it remains unfulfilled. The more you want it, the more you cannot have enough of it.

Furthermore, if desire, following Sigmund Freud, can be only masculine, this makes the notion of female desire a contradiction in terms. The only way in which "she" can be understood as a desiring subject is if she abandons her femininity and instead desires as a man. Grosz seeks to reverse the terms of this sexual equation by thinking women as desiring subjects and also to find a way for thinking something even more unthinkable—desire between women (cf. Sundén 2012). If women can figure as subjects of desire within a heterosexual dynamic only with great difficulty, imagine how hard it would be to think of desires that circumvent the male subject altogether and play out between women and other nonmen, such as in the circulation of unsolicited (but perhaps rarely unwanted) pussy pics.

For Grosz, the term *lesbian* does not disappear in order to become queer, and it does not include trans. Yet with respect to experimental vulvacious social media practices, it is vital to expand the discussion not only beyond heterosexual exchanges but also beyond subjects assigned female at birth. In other words, the discussion needs to include everyone with a pussy, all of whom do not belong to the category of "women."

As a feminist reverb of sorts in and through 1970s feminist "cunt art," vulvas seem to enjoy something of a revival in current feminist artistic and activist practices and their intersections with social media platforms. The pink "pussy hats" that became the viral symbol of feminist resistance (of primarily white, cisgender women) within the international #womensmarch and the rallying cry "pussy grabs back" (to counter Donald Trump's infamous 2005 statement that he could "grab 'em by the pussy," which aired in 2016 during his presidential campaign) indicate how female genitalia continue to both shape the anatomy of contemporary sexism (Boryczka 2017) and provide grounds for reappropriation and resistance (Bore, Graefer, and Kilby 2017). As a battleground for both controlling and taking control over female-encoded sexuality and desire, depictions of vulvas retain their affective charge and ability shock and provoke, attract and entice.

As Amelia Jones (2012, 180) points out in her discussion of feminist cunt art, "In spite of 40 years of feminist anti-essentialist critique, the cunt won't disappear. Clearly the image of the female sex is working in ways not fully comprehended or encompassed by the critical dismissal of such practices as essentializing or self-fetishizing. The cunt explodes the frames of critical analysis. . . . For younger generations the 'snatch' still speaks." By tending to how cunt art by Judy Chicago, Miriam Shapiro, Faith Wilding, and others has persistently been immobilized by particular essentialist and binary understandings of gender, sexuality, desire, and anatomy, Jones traces more unexpected flows of desires and shifting modes of identification in this work and its contemporary reverberations. Alexandra Kokoli (2016, 134) takes this line of reasoning a step further by arguing that "the quest for a visual vernacular for women's genitalia" is not automatically discriminatory of people identifying as nonbinary or transgender, the point being to open up a multiplicity of bodies "by challenging phallic monism."

In revisiting the 1970s and the time when feminist artists reclaimed and made use of the cunt in various ways, two perhaps surprising themes emerge. First, in the minds of the artists, these art practices had little to do with actual cunts. Second, the risk of essentialism was present from the beginning, fostering analytical disconnections between the biological and the political. Vulva-shaped forms provided artists with what Chicago referred to as "central core-imagery" (which she fleshed out ceramically as plate settings in her epic collaborative installation *The Dinner Party* from 1974 to 1979), and their swirling labiaesque folds framed both clitoral and orificial action. Yet, cunt art was considerably more political and cultural than biological in its references (Broude and Garrard 1994; Kokoli 2016).

Following the logic of synecdoche, the (body) part came to signify the whole in that a particularly fleshy metaphor contributed to ways of revisiting and rectifying the politics connected to female bodies and sexualities, not as sites of patriarchal oppression but as opportunities for feminist interventions (cf. Jones 1996, 22). Essentialism was imminent from the start, threatening to collapse female anatomy into biological destiny, and Chicago and others used the shape of the vulva as "a metaphor for an assertive female identity" (Chicago 1996, 6). Such artistic modes involved their own sense of humor. In the parodic sexual comedy, *Cock and Cunt Play* (1972), Chicago and her students made visible the ridiculousness in how gender is inscribed in human anatomy. Dressed in black leotards equipped with a giant pink vulva and a huge satin penis, respectively, the actors moved from the kitchen sink ("a cock means you don't wash dishes") to the bedroom, the play ending rather darkly with a self-castrating scene where "he" ripped off his penis and beat "she" to death for demanding sexual pleasure.

The claim that the vulva in cunt art has little to do with actual vulvas also needs to be understood in a context where close-up representations of female genitalia had only recently begun to be included in mainstream porn. Working with vulvacious shapes while claiming to stay clear of sex could therefore also express fear of having these depictions of female sexual anatomy appropriated and dominated anew by phallic desires. But the longer you dwell in the archives of cunt art, the more difficult it becomes to think that it has nothing to do with cunts. Kokoli (2016, 136) makes a similar observation in considering today's visitors to the Brooklyn Museum (which permanently houses Chicago's *The Dinner Party*): "Unless the work is approached historically and in full awareness of its context in feminist art practice, would the contemporary viewer see 'central core-imagery' and a struggle against the invisibility of women's (always embodied) experience, or rather glistening, idealized and vaguely appetizing vaginas on a plate?" (Kokoli 2016, 136). While taking into account the risk involved in letting cunt art be about cunts at the time, it is nevertheless possible to think that 1970s cunt art was in fact *at least a little bit* about cunts.

Inappropriate Content

By building on particular bodily morphologies, which may or may not belong to female-identified bodies and speak of heterosexual flows of desire, artistic vulvas in digital formats are no less provocative than their feminist forerunners. One particularly vibrant example of twenty-first-century cunt art as a volatile site of affective intensity is the work of the feminist artist Stephanie Sarley, who has an Instagram following of 435,000. Sarley's art consists of playful takes on female sexuality—with a particular penchant for the pussy itself. This has repeatedly led to her Instagram account being disabled for not following the service's community guidelines and then being restored. She is particularly known for a series of videos in which she is fingering pieces of juicy fruit resembling vulvas, leading the *New York Magazine*'s art critic Jerry Saltz leave the comment "You. Are. Genius" when a video in which she is working an especially ripe blood orange went viral on YouTube (e.g., Frank 2016).

Judging from the hot stream of comments on Sarley's Instagram photos, videos, and drawings, her work gives rise to a wide range of reactions from fan love, laughter, and bemused arousal to offense, shock, and repulsion. As in the case of Stormy Daniels, Sarley has noticed that many young women feel the need to voice their disgust online (Sisley 2016). Such expressions of disgust at the sight of sexually provocative art could, again, be understood as a form of female slut-shaming, one building on a causal link of sorts between the artwork as slutty and, consequently, the artist as slut. Sarley's

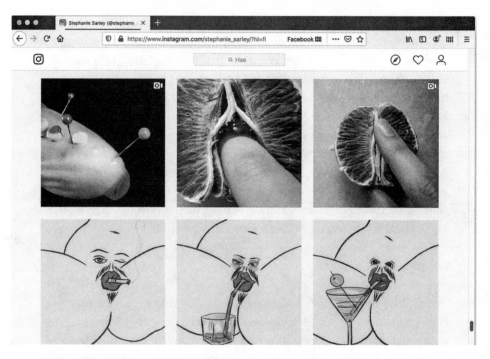

Excerpt from Stephanie Sarley's Instagram account, https://www.instagram.com/
stephanie_sarley.

work has been subject to copyright infringement as meme accounts regularly recirculate her videos with unauthorized edits and no credits attached. This process has involved notable harassment when those who are using her videos and pictures attempt to discredit or shame her and particularly when she has tried to fight back and enforce her copyright (see Lefebvre 2016).

Her fruit fingering has also proven to be sexually charged to the point where it has repeatedly become censored due to Instagram's ban on sexual content. According to the service's community standards, no nudity is allowed. "This includes photos, videos, and some digitally-created content that show sexual intercourse, genitals, and close-ups of fully-nude buttocks. It also includes some photos of female nipples, but photos of post-mastectomy scarring and women actively breastfeeding are allowed. Nudity in photos of paintings and sculptures is OK, too." The regulations have gradually tightened, and in April 2019, Instagram made a move to demote "inappropriate" content that may not even violate community guidelines. Although the platform has yet to explain what is meant by such borderline inappropriateness, the examples it gives are posts deemed sexually suggestive (which by appearing less on the Explore and hashtag pages remain invisible to the broader community). Back in 2016 when Sarley's work went viral, Instagram's content moderation was similarly both strict and vague: "You may not post nude, partially nude, or sexually suggestive photos." Users can react to images they see as violating the guidelines by reporting offenses for content moderators to review. In an online climate involving high intensities of offense and ever more rigid forms of content moderation connected to sexuality, even artistic renderings of fruit can become forbidden. At the same time, reports of harassment on the platform and beyond may go ignored.

Sarley's cheeky anthropomorphic drawings of vulvas in the series "Crotch Monsters," published on Instagram similarly to her vulva-like fruit, involve explicit potential to insert themselves into or otherwise challenge ubiquitous dick-pic culture (cf. DiDomizio 2016; Frank 2016). Rife with absurdist humor, these pussies are embellished with faces and lips that smoke, sip stiff drinks though straws, and eat spaghetti. These minimalist drawings consist of a few well-placed black lines adorned with some color to bring out the makeup on the faces. Sometimes the eyes get a bit of eye shadow, the brows are plucked and stenciled, and the red pouting lips hold a cigarette or a straw. The smoking pussy has one of "her" eyes closed, as if leisurely taking a deep drag on the cigarette. Although these "faces" surely belong to bodies with pussies, the ways in which the pubic hair masquerades as moustaches and beards make the question of gender complex. Rather than letting the vulva straightforwardly become the face of a "woman," Sarley's "Crotch Monsters" are rather instances of queer drag in their juxtaposition of makeup and facial hair. These queer queens exude a lazy laidback-ness of not giving a fuck, indulging as they do in all kinds of oral pleasures. The smoking pussy is then aptly titled, "Fuck it."

As the smoking pussy winks at its audience, it may also be winking at previous generations of feminist artists who had a passion for cunty shapes and forms, but it does so without pretending to be otherwise. This cunt art is clearly about cunts and (once again) about making space for their political, sexual, and affective power. Yet by flirting with queer drag, they more readily open up for analyses across bodies and genders. These drawings are rather upbeat and cheerful in their humorous approach, but they come with a darker, existential edge that comments on the simultaneous sexualization and policing of (bodies with) cunts. These cunts are shameless.

Absurdism below the Belt

Returning to the question of feminist absurdist humor that frames this book, Stephanie Sarley's "Crotch Monsters" are certainly in humorous discord with reason, a (non)sensical breakdown with bodily logics and with the idea of appropriate sites or loci of human subjectivity. They are apparently also unseemly: the links to them kept breaking during the time of our analysis ("Sorry, this page isn't available. The link you followed may be broken, or the page may have been removed," Instagram advised). Although Sarley's videos and stills of fruit fingering may have been subject to harsher censorship in being repeatedly reported as being indecently out of tune with the service's content policy, even her comical vulva drawings seem incongruous with the platform's community standards.

As a platform for feminist cunt art and visual experimentation connected to vulvas, Instagram is volatile indeed. After Tumblr's ban of nudity and adult content in December 2018—preceded by eleven years during which the service became known for the lively presence of sexual subcultures, erotic art, pornographic content, and queer world building—the spaces for the sharing of sexual content, even in more indirect and suggestive forms, have grown ever more narrow on social media. As sexual content and communication are marked out as offensive and unsafe, they are also labeled as lacking in value and importance. Through content policies, Puritan echoes associating sex with risk and shame influence the visual practices of social media users on a global scale.

Our feminist absurdism traffics in the unreasonable, the illogical, and the inappropriate. Its material is quite dark, which in this chapter takes the shape of online hate and harassment, on one hand, and shaming or censorship of female sexuality and agency, on the other. Despite this darkness or rather because of it, its tone is considerably lighter. In his treatment of absurdist humor, Will Noonan (2014) highlights it as being concerned with a refusal of meaning, often understood to be split in two: rational or logical absurdism on one hand and existential absurdism on the other. The rational absurd is concerned with a logical breakdown exemplified in the technique *reductio ad absurdum* (in which a logical proposition is led to a ridiculous or impossible conclusion), whereas the existential absurd deals with the absurdity and meaninglessness of human existence (often related to French existential philosophy and the postwar theater of the absurd). Following this division, Noonan (2014, 1) holds that the rational absurd tends toward lighthearted playfulness and that the existential absurd has a darker bend. Although such distinctions between playful nonsense and the absurdity of human existence can be useful to differentiate, say, Lewis Carroll and Albert Camus, they are much less productive for our understanding of feminist absurdist humor.

Defining humor is notoriously risky, yet we find in our examples of feminist absurdism—whether these consist of witty recirculations of offense or drawings of smoking pussies with beards—a compound of the lighthearted and the darkly existential. Put differently, the utmost absurd or surreal qualities of everyday life for women and other nonmen provide a sounding board for (seemingly) lighter forms of humor that combine the illogical with the indecent. In this sense, "absurdist humor can in fact help bring out the brighter side of the lack of meaning it highlights" (Noonan 2014, 4). Feminist absurdist humor has a lightness to it yet remains grounded in something considerably heavier—a paradox that forms a tactic for dealing with a ludicrous reality (cf. Massanari 2019).

In this chapter, Stormy Daniels, Linnéa Claeson, Kelly Quinn, and Stephanie Sarley provide us with rather delightful responses to the absurdity of online sexism and sexual harassment. They put a serious spin on attempts at slut-shaming along the lines of shamelessness, strategies that for Daniels and Sarley were partly responses to slut-shaming by other women. Sex and power are intricately linked, and yet explaining the slut-shaming of women by women as merely a question of safeguarding the power of straight female sexuality sidesteps how pleasure and agency may figure in notions of sluts and sluttiness. As Nishant Shah (2015) points out, "The slut is a verb—to slut, or to be slutty, indicates that there is an action and agency embedded in 'slutty' bodies. A slut is also a noun—a name—and thus reduced to nothing but a static object which, in its naming, is robbed of its agency." The distinction between subjecthood and objectness may be less than clear, but female slut-shaming could be a tactic of immobilizing other women's sexual agency and, by deferring onto another such sticky labeling, could allow people to avoid being labeled as such themselves. As becomes apparent in Daniels's exchanges as well as in Sarley's "Crotch Monsters," such ways of being rendered into the object of the slut are everything but stable as these objects may be rather witty agents that fight back.

We have showcased a number of feminist strategies and humorous interventions in an otherwise pervasive dick-pic culture. When a load of unsolicited vulva pics is sent out, even as part of an experiment, something happens to the affective economy in which these images circulate: the happy excitement of the recipients indicates that something in the balance has shifted. The sudden appearance of an image of a man's genitals may be a surprise yet not surprising or serendipitous, in that its arrival is rather to be expected within the framework of heterosexual dating apps. The truly startling surprise arises when the dense traffic in dick pics is disrupted by a different set of images, creating an unexpected opening in the heterosexual choreographies of flirting, hooking up, and dating. By moving from Quinn's experiment to Sarley's art, we followed images of the pussy (as it were) and a logic of surprise, virality, and also censorship. Through this journey, it became possible to disentangle questions of harassment and platform politics that strike down hard on content deemed "sexually suggestive" and also to think through how such charged scenes are currently underpinned by very particular notions of gender, (hetero)sexual agency, and desire.

5 Shameless Hags, Tolerance Whores, and the Vibrancy of Language

Exploring the dynamics of online hate, particularly the intersections of sexism and racism, this chapter focuses on linguistic appropriation and shamelessness as networked feminist countertactics where words intended to wound are turned around through humorous, playful interventions. In doing so, we work through Nordic examples and contexts of online misogyny, hate, shaming, and feminist resistance. Our Swedish examples involve an affective reclaiming of the term *hagga* (hag), which has come to embody shameless femininity and feminist solidarity, as well as the Facebook event *Skamlös utsläckning* (shameless extinction), which used the hag as a source of collective imagination and humorous inspiration for a feminist social media movement of nonmen. Our Finnish examples revolve around the appropriation of the derisive terms *kukkahattutäti* (flower-hat auntie) and *suvakkihuora* (tolerance whore) by women who defend multiculturalism and counter the rise of nationalist anti-immigration activism.

In what follows, we ask how verbal denominators contribute to affective intensities on online platforms—how they stick and fail to stick onto bodies (Ahmed 2004), what spaces of critical intervention they may allow, and how they feed into discussions of feminism, antifeminism, racism, and social media. Once again, we attend specifically to the affective dynamics of shame and ask how shamelessness, as a tactic of resistance, operates by cutting short the affective dynamics of online hate targeted against women and other others. Drawing on Facebook posts, blogs, and online discussion forums, we conceptualize the affective dynamics and intersectional nature of online hate. Our point of departure is that online misogyny cannot be understood in isolation from other trajectories of hate. Rather, it is steeped in and entangled with racism, homophobia, and transphobia in ways that require feminist analyses to zoom in on the interaction and interconnect-edness between power hierarchies (Collins 1990; Collins and Bilge 2016; Crenshaw 1991). All this entails bodies of flesh and viscera that are diversely marked by differences and mapped onto social hierarchies and power, but it equally concerns discursive bodies (rhetorical figures of a more fantastic kind that operate as grounds for contestation), as well as the smart devices, information networks, screens, and data archives that underpin and make possible the networked exchanges within which all this unfolds by con-necting and disconnecting bodies of flesh and language.

Despite the current high visibility of national populist politics, Islamo-phobic discourses, and the collaboration of anti-immigration and white supremacist activists across the Nordic countries, Swedish and Finnish contexts also come with notable historical differences. Unlike Sweden's traditionally lenient immigration policy (one that has become consider-ably less so during the past few years), Finland's policy long followed the principles of "Fortress Europe," and the country strictly patrols traffic at its borders. Populism, nationalism, and racism grew increasingly visible in Finnish mainstream politics in 2008 with the success of the Finns Party (Perussuomalaiset) (see Mäkinen 2016, 544). The focus on the control and management of immigration grew ever more articulate as a political agenda or imperative with the European refugee crisis, which brought over thirty thousand refugees into the country in 2015. In Sweden, the figure was as high as 156,000. The recent success in Sweden of the Sweden Democrats (Sverigedemokraterna) in 2014 and 2018, a party with racist and Neo-Nazi affiliations, in national politics has been partly attributed to tensions in immigration policy accompanied by rising nationalism and racism.

Furthermore, although both countries have long track records in gen-der equality, Swedish public discourse has involved much broader positive identifications with feminism than Finnish discourse does. In Sweden, leading politicians across the political spectrum have routinely identified as feminist, independent of their gender. In Finland, feminism has regularly failed to be similarly understood as an issue of gender equality—although the women-lead cabinet at the time of this writing marks a departure from this. Our Finnish examples of shaming and resistance focus on anti-immigration and multiculturalism, but our Swedish ones are more con-cerned with expanding the unruly agency of those deviating from white, straight cis-male norms. In analyzing their tactics, we argue that the interlaced dynamics of gender and whiteness remain key to understanding the forms that these instances of online hate, shaming, and resistance take.

Naive and Risky Tolerance

In the 2000s, the gendered category of *kukkahattutäti*—literally, "aunt with a flower hat," "lady in a flower/flowery hat" (Keskinen 2013; Petterson 2017), or "flower hat auntie" (Nikunen 2015)—emerged on Finnish-language anti-immigration discussion forums as a figure connoting simultaneous naiveté and moralistic disapproval. In its context of emergence, the flower-hat auntie was a figure to oppose, ridicule, and undermine as one willing to teach others how to live. As a rhetorical figure, the flower-hat auntie can battle against violent media entertainment, work for human or animal welfare, ask for tighter safety regulations, or express moral disapproval over the actions of others, yet she has been predominantly associated with women who support cultural diversity, gender equality, and social justice. Within the figure, a sense of moral superiority meets a patronizing (or more aptly, matronizing) outlook and a liberal, pro-multicultural agenda, hence conflating the two as an object of ridicule.

The flower-hat auntie stands in opposition to the rise of populist nationalist anti-immigration policies, wants to protect the cultural and educational sectors from governmental budget cuts, welcomes refugees, and waves the rainbow flag during Pride week (see Nikunen 2015). As such, these aunties belong to a long transnational lineage of figures such as the "antiracist busybodies" and "loony leftists" who are seen as eroding the cohesive, standard fabrics of a given society (van Dijk 1993, 1, 262). Its closest kin is nevertheless the more gender-neutral English-language term *social justice warrior*, which has traveled from 4chan and Reddit to additional social media platforms "as a pejorative . . . to describe individuals who they claim are overly invested in identity politics and political correctness. The 'SJW' is a humorless shrill who takes pleasure in demonstrating their superiority by policing the behavior of others" (Massanari and Chess 2018, 256). The flower-hat auntie, like the SJW, is a pedantic feminist killjoy with a strict pedagogical outlook. Generally, the flower-hat auntie connotes well-educated, liberal, middle-aged women who are engaged in humanitarian efforts and who are no longer young or conventionally sexy. At the same time, the term has been appropriated and embraced by people of diverse ages and genders as a flexible, resistant, and positive point of identification, and it is used as a self-definition in social media profiles and on pins proudly worn on coats.

Within the Finnish-language social media sphere, the flower-hat auntie is also closely connected to *suvakki*, a derogatory term combining *suvait-sevainen* (tolerant) with *vajakki*, which is the schoolyard variation of *vajaa-mielinen* (the retrograde term for people with mental impairments). The term *suvakki* (for people who are overtly tolerant and thus presumably impaired) was first introduced in 2012 in an anti-immigration blog detailing sexual crimes committed by foreign men against Finnish women and the ways in which "pathologically tolerant" women actively censor news of such incidents and accuse those who do circulate them of racism without understanding their own good (Xeima 2012). These women are seen to shame and silence people who disagree with their own liberal, presumably morally superior stances while also failing to see themselves as targets and potential victims of alien rape. Anti-immigration politician James Hirvisaari, a one-term member of the Finnish Parliament fined for hate speech and expelled from the populist Finns Party after hosting a guest who did a Nazi salute in the House of Parliament, coined the term *suvakkihuora*, which combines *suvakki* (pathologically tolerant) with *huora* (whore) in his widely read blog. According to Hirvisaari's own clarification, the term is not gender specific but refers to "infidelity toward one's own people" and is to be applied to people who label anti-immigration activists as racists.

The "tolerance whore," like the flower-hat auntie, is nevertheless strikingly and explicitly gendered in its focus. Effectively feminizing the people to which they are applied, both notions perform something of a gender binary in how anti-immigration activists and those opposing their views become hierarchically positioned. In doing so, the notions help to imagine anti-immigration activists as homosocially male even as women are highly visible within such political organizations. The term *tolerance whore* is a slur used by both women and men, yet it sticks particularly to bodies gendered as female—as well as to those marked as white. The aggressively gendered overtones of tolerance whore clearly differ from those of the desexualized flower-hat auntie. The slur builds on perennial anti-immigration fantasies of foreign men "taking our women" (either with or without consent) but also, in convoluted ways, on the figure of the Muslim rapist that resurfaced during the refugee crisis (Horsti 2017). Tolerance whores fail to understand the aggressive misogyny of foreign men because, like flower-hat aunties, they are too naive to accept the efforts of the men who want to protect them, such as the vigilante group Soldiers of Odin, which patrols city streets in order to keep them safe for women. Infidels to their own people, tolerance whores and flower-hat aunties fail to see white Finnish men as their true allies and protectors but rather accuse them of racism—and in doing so, both shame them and put everyone at risk of an alien invasion.

Writing of the Swedish context, Karina Horsti (2017, 1440–1441) argues that anti-Islamic bloggers operate with and create an imaginary of unified transnational whiteness that is seen to be under threat from both liberal feminism and Islam. Although the figure of the Nordic woman remains an object to be protected, her independent, headstrong, and possibly irresponsible tendencies are also seen to pose a risk to white masculinity. It then follows that hate speech targeted against women "polluted by multiculturalism" regularly takes the shape of rape fantasies: since these women do not understand the risks involved and ignore efforts made to protect innocent others, it would serve them right to be raped by immigrants (Horsti 2017, 1451).

Flower-hat aunties and tolerance whores are explicitly gendered figures implying liberal association. They may bleed into one another, yet they also come with different connotations. Flower-hat aunties are likely to be middle-aged, middle-class, and well educated, but tolerance whores can be either young or old and need not occupy any specific position within the social strata. Given their positioning as "race traitor" infidels to their own people, both categories are nevertheless construed as white and ethnically Finnish (a highly contested and politicized notion as such), despite the factual diversity among people resistant to anti-immigration activism. In these figures, misogynistic notions of female naiveté and obstinate simple-mindedness grow a dangerous edge connected to a desire to open up national borders and to open up national culture for multicultural resonances.

Sexual associations with male refugees and other immigrants generate particular stickiness to tolerance whores. These women are seen as being drawn to the laps of alien, non-Christian men, and by aiming to open national borders, they simultaneously and willingly open their own bodies to foreign embrace. According to this line of thinking, the foreign men in question are firmly heterosexual, predatory, and ready to abuse the helpfulness of their host country for personal financial gain and sexual gratification. Meanwhile, the "tyrannical" and "pathologically tolerant" women in question are driven by a "narcissistic desire" to improve the world. They are dangerous because they censor open debate and oppress the majority of the population through their claims to moral superiority. Consequently, the term suvakki has been associated with a disease that spreads through liberal media outlets and threatens national well-being ever since it was first coined (Xeima 2012).

These examples speak to how racist online hate encompasses and sticks to both the bodies marked as "non-us" and the bodies of white antiracist women who are seen as letting down their own kind. Hate sticks to bodies marked as other: it circulates and becomes amplified in ways that both efface and highlight the mutual differences among the bodies involved (Ahmed 2001; Tyler 2006). Although the targets of online "webs of hate" (Kuntsman 2010) include women, refugees, members of sexual minorities, and people of nonbinary gender identifications, these webs are deeply entwined with a widespread cultural contempt for feminine and racialized bodies. They assemble individuals and groups in temporary and more lingering alliances and conflicts where the intersecting categories of bodily difference and differentiation meet political stances and activist agendas. They are thread together and driven by affective intensities and investments, whose articulations stick to bodies representative of both "us" and "them" and occasionally fuel ambivalent movement between seemingly opposed identity positions. Misogynistic hate resonates differently with bodies distinctly marked in terms of ethnicity, nationality, sexuality, gender, size, religion, or race. At the same time, as Adrienne Shaw (2014, 273) points out, violent sexism and misogyny online are "compounded with racism, homophobia, ableism, and all other forms of hate." This means that intersectional forms of hate feed on and amplify one another (Lähdesmäki and Saresma 2014).

Like the more benign figure of the flower-hat auntie, the tolerance whore has become appropriated as a point of self-identification by many, including a feminist author and newspaper columnist (Talvitie 2016). The female artist duo Tärähtäneet ämmät (Nutty Tarts) has designed tolerance whore T-shirts for Amnesty Finland, which were launched at the 2016 Helsinki World Village Festival, an annual event advocating for global justice and multiculturalism. Nutty Tarts contextualized the design process by explaining that "Hate speech has increased in different media. We have also been called tolerance whores. There are many ways to approach hate speech—ours has been to take into our own use the labels of both tarts and whores" (Amnesty Finland n.d.). The anti-immigration group Soldiers of Odin has been linguistically and symbolically appropriated by the "Loldiers of Odin," who have dressed in clown gear and followed the vigilantes around during their street patrols since 2015 with the explicit aim to mock and ridicule. The first actions were covered internationally by the BBC, CBC, *The Guardian*, and the *New York Times*, and the news spread quickly via social media shares and online discussions threads, pointing out the ways that the divisions between online and offline that once were constitutive to internet research inquiry are now far less distinct. Through the casual yet knowing display of tolerance whore T-shirts or the in-your-face clownery performed by the Loldiers of Odin, linguistic appropriation enters public spaces as forms of performative, mundane, and embodied resistance. At the same time, the force and impact of such resistance is drastically expanded and amplified through social media coverage and circulation that allow for international visibility extending well beyond any singular place and time.

The group Soldiers of Odin was founded in Kemi, Finland, in 2015, when this small northern city received a large number of refugees through the Swedish border. The name Odin refers to a Norse deity, and the organization's logo—a bearded head wearing a horned Viking helmet—similarly gestures toward a heroic, mythical, Nordic past. This is not void of irony, given that there never were any Finnish Vikings and that Finnish and Norse folk mythologies do not share roots. Perhaps fittingly in terms of this ambiguity of belonging, Soldiers of Odin operate internationally, with groups in at least Australia, Belgium, Canada, Estonia, Germany, Sweden, and the United States. The organization has denied racist affiliation, but its founder has a conviction for racist violence and ties to the Nordic Resistance Movement, a neo-Nazi organization banned in Finland. The group's Twitter account, @soldiersofodin, has been suspended, yet many of the regional organizations are present on Facebook as both private and public groups, some with tens of thousands of followers. In addition, an alternative Soldiers of Odin account was present on both platforms from 2016 until 2019, with the following description (@soldiersofodin_):

> Hello likers of the page! Welcome! We are a group of people who like cats, pink, glitter and unicorns, and we think that there can never be too much of these things!

Suvakkihuora (2016)

"Suvakkihuora" is a negative term used by the right wing extremists in Finland for describing liberal, anti-racist women. We reclaimed the term by designing a T-Shirt for Amnesty Finland with the print of "Suvakkihuora". The term Suvakkihuora has also been reclaimed not only by the liberal women but also by the LGTQ community and liberal, anti-racist men.

Suvakkihuora T-shirts could be purchased from Amnesty Finland's online store.

Nutty Tarts design for a tolerance whore T-shirt, http://www.shaken-not-blurred .com/suvakkihuora.

Soldiers of Odin is a trademark for charity and solidarity, and in the future we will be selling patches, clothes, tote bags and other cool stuff! We are a counterforce to racism and discrimination, and we want to spread the message of love, tenderness and acceptance.

As its profile image, these Soldiers of Odin used an image of a pink unicorn surrounded by rainbow-colored hearts, and the account's cover image consisted of two words written in runes—letters used in several German languages before the adaptation of the Latin alphabet that gesture toward a mythic, Nordic past. When deciphered, these pink letters nevertheless read as two Finnish words, *natsit vittuun* (which can be translated as "fuck Nazis" but reads more literally as "Nazis to the cunt" or "Nazis up the cunt"). Following the operating principles of tactical media (Boler 2008a),

Alternative Soldiers of Odin Facebook page, 2019.

the accounts @soldiersofodin_ (Twitter) and @soldiersofodin.fi (Facebook) aimed to block and disturb the activities of the organization by celebrating a set of alternative values and selling sleeve and back patches decorated with an explicit runic message.

The strategies and registers of online hate aim both to shame and to create fear. Resorting to combinations of verbal abuse, death threats, rape threats, and body-shaming, online hate is oriented toward frightening, intimidating, and silencing the people it targets (Megarry 2014). To engage in debate or to defend oneself may translate as feeding the trolls, and since this is not a recommended policy, those under attack are left with the default choice of silence, and their voices remain unheard (Lumsden and Morgan 2017). In thinking through the affective politics of fear, Sara Ahmed (2004, 68) poses the question, "which bodies fear which bodies?" Fear operates in hateful encounters online in (at least) two interrelated ways: as fear of the other and as a silencing strategy. Attempts to silence, distance, intimidate, and mark apart the other can be seen as motivated by fear that is unequally distributed due to how it intersects with violence and its threat. The cold, sharp intensities of fear connected to online hate have the power to diminish the ability of women and other others to act, speak, challenge, engage, and take up space.

Online hate can be understood as a disruptive force aiming to modulate and control the capacities of bodies to act and move, to affect and to be affected by one another. As such, it impacts not only certain representational politics but also affective registers and capacities. If power within intersectional theorizing is usually something that links and organizes identity categories, power here becomes something that moves between bodies. Power comes to work relationally in a different sense as an affective force that can be restraining as well as enabling, rather than only determining (cf. Sundén 2013). Power—much like the online hate that it intermeshes with—comes to consist of affective circuits that tie subjects and objects together and make their mutual connections shift and change, possibly violently so. It then means that these affective circuits are the core terrain of resistance and jamming.

Alongside the possibly chilling effects of fear, online hate efficiently silences and otherwise incapacitates the bodies of others through shaming. By violently threatening, exposing, and sexualizing the bodies of female, feminine, and racialized subjects—whose bodies are already at the risk of being addressed in unwanted manners—misogynistic online hate has an intricate relation with shame. Not unlike fear, shame works on and through bodies by shaping and reshaping the social spaces in which they may move. When animated by shame, bodies turn away and inward in ways that imply their shrinking of sorts as well as the shrinking of spaces in which they move (Probyn 2005). For Silvan Tomkins (2008, 687), shame is "the affect of indignity, of defeat, of transgression, and of alienation, striking deep into the heart of the human being and felt as an inner torment, a sickness of the soul." As such, it operates as a circuit breaker, a disruption in sociability that is nevertheless fundamentally social. Understood in this vein, shame does not result from repression or internalization of "bad" behavior inasmuch as from a fundamental interruption in relational identity (Tomkins 1995b, 399–400; also Ahmed 2004, 103–105; Sedgwick 2003, 37). Shame makes identity by orienting and rerouting relational strategies toward oneself and others in ways that connect affect with cultural politics.

There are those, as Eve Sedgwick (2003, 63) notes, "whose sense of identity is for some reason tuned most durably to the note of shame." To Sedgwick, the question of shame-prone identities is intimately—although not exclusively—linked to queer shame, whereas others have emphasized intersections of women and queers (Dahl 2014; Munt 2007; Probyn 2005) and of "black" and "queer" (Stockton 2006) in the circuits of shame. Such identities and their overlaps take shape through experiences of being cast as social inferiors and misfits, for having been publicly marked as failed and degraded. Conceptualized in this vein, shame-prone identities take shape unevenly due to their proximity to and failure to embody white, straight, male norms and to be recognized and valued in relation to them.

There is, however, a risk in ascribing fear and shame as default affective currents connected to particular identity positions or to the dynamics of online hate and, consequently, in fixing their interconnections as something to be anticipated and known beforehand. Despite their sticking and layering, affective intensities remain unpredictable and in constant flux—in a process of being partly transformed into different qualities. The resistance to and the reworking of shame make evident that the currents of fear and shame ripple, stick, and slide differently in relation to different bodies while equally varying according to moment, context, and connection. There is no one singular affective dynamic that operates to uniform effect on either the individual or collective level. As Tomkins points out, "We may feel shame for many things for which no one has shamed us. We may not feel shame though another tries to make one feel ashamed. We may be shamed by another, though the other does not intend we should feel ashamed. We may be shamed because the other expresses negative affect toward us, though he does not wish to shame us as such. Finally, we may be shamed only because another tries to shame us" (Tomkins 2008, 370). Shaming and shame are not causal or simple dynamics: they involve what Tomkins identifies as "independent variability" within which shame is regularly both delayed and indirect.

As specifically labeled points of reference, fear, shame, and shamelessness need to be seen as parts of a mutable field of forces that impacts bodies and moves them from one state to another. These directions may be surprising. The recipient of hate speech—or one studying it—may for example burst out in laughter over its absurdity, failing to register any of the intended fear, anxiety, or insecurity (Mäkinen 2016). Online hate truncates the spaces of agency but may equally mobilize bodies into action in unpredictable ways. Feelings of shame and victimization can turn the shamed into a shamer who overturns or refuses the burning sensation of shame by searching for someone else to shame or who shames the one doing the intended shaming. In such instances, shame moves toward and between bodies, ripples, and layers (Stein 2006).

One key feminist countertactic is to turn shame on its head and to use "shamelessness" as a tactic of resistance. As a calculated response to condescension or mockery, shamelessness is a way to "demonstrate that I care as little for you as you do for me" (Tomkins 2008, 537). Queer and feminist voices on shame often have in common an interest in political tactics to brave or overcome shame (e.g., Bouson 2009; Burrus 2008; Munt 2007; Stockton 2006). Making use of anger as a way of breaking out from the circuits of shame and fear was an early feminist tactic, and the affiliate move from shame into pride was in line with the tactics of the gay pride and the black power movements. This tactic of turning assumed shame into pride has long involved the appropriation of hateful terminology. Cultural feminists reclaimed the notions of *hag* and *crone* for gynocentric purposes (e.g., Daly 1990/1978, 1994/1987), lesbian and gay activists repurposed terms such as *queer* and *dyke* as sources of pride (Bianchi 2014; Brontsema 2004), and fourth-wave feminists have organized SlutWalks to oppose slut-shaming and gendered victim-blaming in incidents of sexual crime since 2011 (Ringrose and Renold 2012). Appropriation has been broadly recognized as a tactic of the subaltern to turn the strategies of shaming and ridicule into potential sources of empowerment and to confuse the hierarchies of difference that their rhetorical force has relied on (Popa 2018). As Jo Reger (2015) notes when writing on SlutWalks in the United States, such points of identification are nevertheless not similarly accessible to all. Here, as in so many other contexts, derogatory labels intended to shame stick less firmly to bodies marked as white—which, consequently, are less confined by them.

The labels of naive *flower-hat aunties* and out-of-control *tolerance whores*, coined by Finnish anti-immigration activists, come attached to bodies that are assumedly white yet are inappropriately intimate with bodies that are not. As strategies of shaming, they set out to ridicule, undermine, and humiliate. They can be seen to emerge from a sense of hurt and shame caused by accusations of racism made against anti-immigration activists, as well as from being overlooked and resented by members of a higher socioeconomic group (Mäkinen 2016, 552). Flower-hat aunties and tolerance whores earn their titles by accusing anti-immigration activists of racism, redneckish ignorance, and prejudice. Within this dynamic, a perceived sense of being shamed triggers the necessity to shame and humiliate others in return. The affective reverb continues when these others embrace rather than recoil from the labels intended to shame, not through the tactic of shamelessness per se inasmuch as through an acceptance of sorts of being thus singled out. If the shamed desires no recognition or acceptance from the party doing the shaming, the affective circuits of shame, inferiority, and failure fail to be animated, and the interpellation of shame as a particular social relation falls short. As Tomkins (2008, 361) puts it, "Unless there has been interest in or enjoyment of the other person, or the anticipation of such positive feelings about the other, contempt from the other may activate surprise or distress or fear or anger, rather than shame." If you do not crave recognition from or connection with a member of a vigilante group with neo-Nazi ties that calls you a tolerance whore, shame may not automatically emerge.

Digital Intersections

As a feminist analytical tool, intersectionality examines power relations as constituted in and through a range of identity categories that coconstruct one another in multiple ways. Intersectionality challenges additive models of oppression (Collins 1990; Crenshaw 1991) and focuses instead on the interaction and interconnectedness between power hierarchies, and it has grown key to feminist inquiry since the 1990s. A question remains whether, as Nina Lykke (2004) argues, it is of strategic importance for feminist scholars to retain the category of gender and its analytical and political meanings, even if gender can never be the most important factor from an intersectional standpoint. The privileging of gender nevertheless sits uneasily with how intersectionality emerged from the struggles of black feminists as an intervention at the core of identity politics to challenge white feminist frameworks (Collins and Bilge 2016). Jasbir Puar (2011) argues that performances of intersectionality produce an ironic reification of gender as the foundational one that needs to be disrupted: "Despite decades of feminist theorizing on the question of difference, difference continues to be 'difference from,' that is, the difference from 'white woman.'" This dynamic is strikingly visible in the various feminist social media tactics examined in this book.

In their edited volume, *The Intersectional Internet: Race, Sex, Class, and Culture Online*, Safiya Umoja Noble and Brendesha M. Tynes (2016) extend the discussion of intersectionality and explore how social categories and relations of power are embedded in and organized through digital technologies. Intersectional analysis always involves a focus on the continuous production of social categories and their hierarchical organization. Intersectional analysis in digital media studies also adds a dimension of human/nonhuman intersections in networked formations. The feminist movements and tactics that we address are similarly fundamentally dependent on and crafted within networked exchanges bound to specific platforms and their affordances. Consider, for example, the functionality of the hashtag (discussed in chapters 2 and 3) and the ways that it allows for connective affiliation via Twitter and Facebook and enables political initiatives across temporal and physical distances. In the incidents of reframing, outing, and countershaming examined in chapter 4, feminist tactics are inseparable from the affordances of social media platforms—and are, in fact, primarily conditioned by them. In the examples of linguistic appropriation discussed in this chapter, the issue concerns the fluid boundaries of the online and the offline in a context of ubiquitous high-speed network connectivity that is something of the default within the Nordic countries. In a context involving heavy mobile internet use where social media smoothly permeates everyday life, terms coined on online platforms seldom remain confined to such settings but rather leak to quotidian language as something to be embraced, resisted, and worked with. There is a more-than-human dimension or constituent to how feminist tactics take shape within this context and how intersectionality may be understood.

Feminist Politics of Shamelessness

We have thus far focused on linguistic appropriation as a way to fight back against online hate and shaming by reinterpreting the pejorative as positive or at least as potentially productive. In what follows, we zoom in more closely on the forms and functions of shamelessness as a feminist countertactic through Swedish case studies involving affective retuning connected to nonmale agency. The first concerns the recent appropriation of the term *hagga* (the word *hag* is often used in connection with problematic indulgence in food, sex, and alcohol, as in the notion of the "wine hag") on social media platforms and elsewhere and the ways it resonates with the political tactics of moving through and reworking shame. In an article that was shared over 6,400 times on Facebook, the Swedish author Elin Grelsson Almestad (2016) traces what she—not entirely correctly—regards as a new feminist tendency driven by a desire to embrace shamelessness. She refers to an excerpt of Aase Berg's (2019, 7) at the time future novel *Haggan* (*The Hag*): "I'm in the trap for women. Hell now I'm getting out. I bring hag as my weapon. I now become a hag. And hag is also a verb. To hag. It is an action. A fucking active action." Based on a long line of excessive hags in literature and popular culture that connect Chris Kraus's (2015/1997) novel *I Love Dick* (in which the "I" describes herself as a money-swindling hag) with the "arch hags" Patsy and Edina of the TV series *Absolutely Fabulous*, Almestad visualizes a feminist movement that takes inspiration from women deemed "too old" to be rebellious and certainly too tired to please (straight men).

Berg's (2015) poetry collection *Hackers*, which spurred a fair amount of celebratory feminist media commentary, is another key reference in recent Swedish feminist hagging. "This is a threat," *Hackers* begins, and it continues with a furious form of feminist hacking, a poetic reprogramming of heteropatriarchy from within (Berg 2015, 5). In response to male violence, Berg (2015, 25) offers angry, raging resistance:

She hits back:
piercing fatso,
grog hag,
self-harm slur.

The well behaved woman
never raises
a hand.

In contrast to well-educated, self-composed, middle-class women, Berg delineates someone much more fleshy, damaged, violent, and considerably white trash. She makes the case that the hag is a much better feminist companion than the harmless *kulturtanten* (culture auntie), an obvious, liberal kin to the flower-hat aunties of the neighboring country. Hags in these depictions are aging, boozy, and less than considerate, at least when it comes to the feelings of men. In a podcast partly dedicated to the hag, the journalists Kristin Nord and Maria G. Francke (2016) point at the importance of alcohol for the hag (obvious in compounds such as "wine hag" and "grog hag") as something that lubricates her shamelessness, and they urge their listeners to engage in hagging also during the more sober office hours.

Counter to Almestad's claim, to use the hag as an oppositional feminist figure is not something entirely new. Writing on solidarity between women, hags, and other inappropriate female subjects in the spirit of 1970s cultural feminism, Mary Daly (1990/1978, xlvi) argues that the "primary intent of women who choose to be present to each other . . . is not an invitation to men. It is an invitation to our Selves. The Spinsters, Lesbians, Hags, Harpies, Crones, Furies who are the Voyagers of Gyn/Ecology know that we choose to accept this invitation for our Selves. This, our Self-acceptance, is in no way contingent upon male approval. Nor is it stopped by (realistic) fear of brutal acts of male revenge." In this densely written radical feminist project of linguistic appropriation, the hag harks back to an archaic female demon, "a Witch, Fury, Harpy, who haunts the Hedges/Boundaries of patriarchy, frightening fools and summoning Wired Wandering Women into the Wild" (Daly 1990/1978, 137). Originally coined in the late 1970s, Daly's gynocentric definition of female unruliness—premised on a clear, binary, and essentialized gender difference— reverberates with the current Swedish rediscovery of the hag and her potential feminist shamelessness. As discussed above (in chapters 2 and 4) in connection with feminist activist tactics and cunt art, feminist tactics of the 2010s and early 2020s have partly drawn from and blended into those of the 1970s. Again, the most visible successes of social media initiatives tend to come with a reiteration of a binary gender difference while obscuring the reverberations of race, sexuality, age, or class.

Our second Swedish example unfolded as a Facebook event, *Skam-lös utsläckning* (shameless extinction) that formed in late spring 2016 as a feminist guerrilla movement of sorts. In behavioral psychology, extinction is a gradual weakening of a conditioned response that results in the decrease or disappearance of the behavior. The name of the event thus alludes to an effort of making shame extinct through a feminist tactic of shamelessness. It involves a gradual weakening to the point of extinction of shame responses to male domination and ultimately an eradication of patriarchal power. The initiative came from Alice Kassius Eggers, a Swedish author, journalist, and literary critic, and her colleague Elliot Lundegård.

Attendance was cautious at first, but over the course of a few days, the event attracted more than six thousand attendants, many of whom were well-known public figures. The invitation included a call for "a wave of half-assed but genius artistic expressions on the internet and irl, in the city and on the countryside, outside of theatres and in stairwells"—an appeal involving the intent to redirect and redistribute the unequal circulation of gendered shame.

Their idea was as simple as it was seductive. Based on a deep frustration with how white cis men tend to support and promote other white cis men (even when charisma, uniqueness, nerve, and talent are missing), while at the same time shaming women, the event wanted to provide a space of "shamelessness" for nonmen where this dynamic could be turned on its head. The term *nonmen* has remained something of a battleground within feminist theory and practice for quite some time as a label built on a negation and hence as always reactive towards what is being negated—which, in turn, remains the norm as what is being resisted. The term also makes explicit the painful friction between woman-centered feminism and trans-inclusive feminism, in relation to which binary gender has never made sense. As a point of departure for a political movement or event, the category aims to include not only cis women but equally trans and nonbinary bodies positioned as other in relation to the white, straight male norm.

The Facebook event "Shameless Extinction" involved taking up space in innovative ways, playing with social norms and expectations, and dreaming and fantasizing collectively and shamelessly, with the purpose of making room for more and other bodies and voices. The emphasis was primarily on thought experiments rather than direct action. At the same time, such collective thinking, playing, joking, and fantasizing may well be elementary to how bodies can be set in motion or become reoriented. Eventually, the event was dissolved and was divided into two closed groups. The group for shameless feminist imagination—*Skamlös utsläckning: Fantastisk fantasi* (Shameless extinction: Fantastic imagination)—soon changed its name to *Gränslös, skamlös, hejdlös* (Boundless, shameless, unstoppable). The group for direct action was *Aktioner i skamlös utsläckning* (Direct actions in shameless extinction). During the event, people wrote about grandiose projects, some of them factual and many not. Many spoke about their experiences as nonmen but from a reverse perspective by casting themselves in the role of the shameless oppressor:

I will write editorials again, but stop proofreading my texts (both facts
   and language) before going home, one hour too early, every day. Then
   the guys at the newsroom who dutifully stay on get to save my texts.
   Because it's my brilliant thoughts that are important, and obviously I
   can only take them down quickly before I have to do something else,
   more importantly. Like moderating a panel by winging it, or participating in a debate program delivering sweeping truths about the state of the
   nation/USA/the universe. (April 28, 72 likes)

I'm in the mood for directing a theatre performance and hit on half of the
   artistic team, ignore the rest, and let all my anxiety flood everybody.
   Then I will claim that we have worked in a horizontal organization and
   take credit for all the work. (April 28, 162 likes)

In part due to the specificity of the semiclosed world facilitated by the
Facebook event function, a sense of belonging to a secret society was established, which afforded the occasion with a particular temporal dynamic
feeding an affective intensity. Through the logics of a carnivalesque, trans-
gressive upside-down world (Bakhtin 1968), the event gave rise to a temporal feminist comedic sphere densely populated by womansplainers,
woman spreaders, cuntblockers, absent mothers, female stalkers, middle-
aged women with a taste for fresh meat, lesbophobia, old-girl networks, and
the occasional "good" meninist girl. These are no feminist killjoys. This is
feminist comedy:

Sometimes I get a bit offended and send pictures of my cunt. It's after all a
   fucking good looking cunt. (April 29, 65 likes)

It's so boring that you can't have an intellectual conversation anymore
   without being accused of "woman-splaining" or "girl-guessing" as soon
   as you try to inform others about something and happen to be a woman.
   (May 1, 35 likes)

The day my sons bring home girlfriends, then I'll fucking pull out the gun.
   No chick will ever put her filthy hands on my princes. I'm a girl myself,
   so I know how girls work. (May 1, 253 likes)

Sometimes when men speak to me I don't answer. I need to think for a good
   long while and sort of don't arrive at an answer. The strange thing is that
   it only happens with guys, never with girls. Just saw a guy at the subway
   who was stressed and asked his girl if she had packed their passports, and

she didn't reply, just stared emptily in front of her and put in some snuff. I could totally relate! (May 3, 64 likes)

Within this comedy, gynocentric feminist tactics of the 1970s and 1980s reemerge and become revisited, possibly in an unacknowledged fashion. Daly's (1994/1987) "dicks," "dickspeakers," "tomfools," "snot boys," "sniv-elards," and their affiliate army of disappointing, sexist male figures blind to their own privilege make a return—both direct and not—onto the stage of a Swedish Facebook event as ironic masks and positions to be played with. As the event weaves in and out of histories of feminist countertactics, it leaves an underlining gender binary untouched in the firmness of which it structures the relations and connections between different bodies.

The Affective Boundaries of Shamelessness

Online misogyny violently targets nonmen, nonwhite and nonstraight sub-jects who make noise and manifest embodied differences on public online platforms. Public figures such as politicians and journalists inhabit particu-larly vulnerable positions, as do authors, artists, and musicians who stand up for feminism and antiracism. The Swedish author Maria Sveland (2013) argues that although public feminists and antiracists are disproportionally targeted by haters, it is often enough to merely be visible and audible as a woman on online platforms and elsewhere (without expressing any feminist standpoints) to unleash ripples and waves of hate. Wendy Chun (2016) con-ceptualizes online slut-shaming as displacement of fear cultivated via leaky digital technologies onto the bodies of women and their allegedly shame-ful acts. Although not dealing explicitly with online hate, the activities of "Shameless Extinction" formed a space from which to resist it by providing a platform for feminist counterimaginaries. In this respect, the event contrib-uted toward affective publics premised on female shamelessness:

Overwhelmed by guerilla feelings. Goodnight lovelies. Remember, bad is the new political. (April 27, 93 likes)

One gets completely breathless of all these thoughts and ideas, when one imagines the practice of a completely different order, a different world. (April 28, 24 likes)

Do you understand how many we are? (May 2, 118 likes)

Alexander Cho (2015) discusses reverb as a temporal metaphor for understanding the force, intensity, and flow of affect online as it not merely becomes registered in its instantaneity but lingers on. A reverb is something that reverberates through something else, as a resounding or an echo, and as such becomes a form of vibratory repetition with a difference. The reverb of the humorous feminist upside-down world ran deep within the participants, carrying an echo in unpleasant past experiences that resounded in comical ways through the present while equally reverberating with decades-old feminist linguistic countertactics. Making use of discomfort, frustration, and anger as points of departure, the explosive quality of the event had everything to do with a particular and powerful kind of affective resonance or attunement between bodies that afforded a sense of sympathetic vibration through recognition (see Paasonen 2011). Additionally, a feeling of secrecy about belonging to a low-frequency subversion, if not revolution, from below afforded an intensely compressed sense of connectivity reminiscent of how Jodi Dean (2010) discusses the power of networked enjoyment and infectious capture within affective circuits of drive.

If we consider shame as something that makes identity, then there is no getting rid of it. Understood in this vein, shamelessness is not the opposite of shame, nor does it translate as the absence of shame. Rather, it is something that *plays with* shame and attempts at shaming by intervening in the affective dynamics of operation—turns them around and knowingly ignores or ridicules attempts to shame. In rewriting shame, Sally Munt (2007, 182) speaks of the subject who "has been shamed, who has turned away and been released, whose gaze is momentarily free to look around and make new, propitious connections." "Shameless Extinction" can be seen as a space of such discharge, where gazes are free to wander, and auspicious novel connections can be established.

There is also a flipside to the political uses of shamelessness because taking up space always happens at the expense of someone else. Who, then, gets to be shameless? Whose space may be taken over? And who may still be bound by shame? A few Facebook event participants were concerned about how these bold feminist fantasies take shape at the expense of men, only to be schooled at length on the explosive political potential of parody and the rightful practice of the oppressed to kick back or to kick up. By explicitly inviting nonmen, "Shameless Extinction" gathered a diverse crowd of people—women, racial others, queers, trans, and nonbinary people. Their mutual differences were not rendered particularly visible or operative in the performative aspects of the posts, however, given how the event came together around a critique and mockery of a set of exclusive white straight male norms. Precisely by playing with and performing white straight masculinity (even through the gendered logic of a complete role reversal), the event mostly concealed how the contributors themselves were differently positioned in relation to such norms. This concealment then worked to obscure the ways in which a politics of shamelessness is linked to both class and race privilege.

Within the gender flip that occurs when white straight male norms are turned on their head and performed by female bodies in the feminist imaginary of the upside-down world, the shameless hag takes center stage. "She" takes the liberty to move through the world "like a man," serving defiance of shame tied to those norms that guard and envelop respectable white bourgeois femininity. Whiteness comes across not only as an assumed part of masculine privilege but also as a central axis of difference playing into the event. It figures simultaneously as part of the norms that guarantee respectable femininity and to which the shameless hag poses a threat. But to be able to resist or play with the norms of respectable femininity, one needs access to respectability in the first place (see Dobson 2013, 2014; Skeggs 1997). The shameless hag and her white working-class trashiness may seem liberating from the vantage point of middle-class sensibility, just as "tolerance whore" T-shirts may more snugly adorn lean white middle-class bodies than those diversely marginalized in terms of education, race, size, social class, occupation, income, or citizenship. It can be argued that such a play with shame and respectability is inaccessible to or at least much more cumbersome to achieve for nonwhite women and other racially marked subjects who may already be cast as shameful or sexually deviant (Perry 2015). While resisting or working through the gendered politics of shame, the turn to shamelessness in "Shameless Extinction" was underpinned by middle-class, white privilege.

Reanimating Hags and Whores

The feminist forms of resistance to online silencing, ridicule, shaming, and hate discussed in this chapter work in somewhat fantastic political registers of appropriation, imagination, and affective reattunement through shamelessness. Rather than merely being reactive in the face of online misogyny, they are productive in providing a space for feminist counter-imaginaries—as white and middle-class as their core may be—within an otherwise rather depressive contemporary Nordic political climate. As Lauren Berlant argues, "as a political tactic, shamelessness is the performative act of refusing the foreclosure on action that a shamer tries to induce" (in Najafi, Serlin, and Berlant 2008). Explicit or "shameless" forms of shamelessness may nevertheless fold back into shame rather than rupture its affective circuits. To be out and proudly shameless may come with a wish to be shamed in the sense of daring others to do so. Berlant uses the political shamelessness of the right-wing media as an example of such hyperbolic performative instances: "Bring shame on, they say. We're shameless, so give us your best shot!" But as Berlant notes, performative acts of shamelessness need not be confrontational. They may involve composure or self-control in unexpected places.

Understated performances of shamelessness have the potential to undo normative defenses in that they fail and actually refuse to tap into the affective registers that shamers require in order to be in control of the exchange. As such, they point to the failure in the dynamic of shaming, which, following Tomkins, requires desire to be accepted and recognized by those doing the shaming. If such desire is absent, the affective circuits are cut short, and no sense of failure is likely to emerge. In instances where one does not care or need to comply with the norms according to which the labels of tolerance whores, flower-hat aunties, or shameless hags are articulated, the hurtful stickiness of derogatory labels thins away. As we have argued, such spaces of distance, disinterest, and disavowal are more easily available to those not positioned through inferiority, failure, and shame by default. Affective distance and the possibility to play with speech intended to hurt speak of privilege (Mäkinen 2016, 548).

A kindred way of relieving the pressure of derogatory labels is, again, to reappropriate or reclaim the terms used to shame or injure. In their discussion of the animacy of language—what makes language lively and lends it affective force—Mel Y. Chen (2012) considers how linguistic insults contain hierarchies of matter in that they refer to some humans as less than human. Fueled by its capacity to enliven matter, language works in such instances (perhaps paradoxically) as deanimating and dehumanizing: "Insults, shaming language, slurs, and injurious speech can be thought of as tools of objectification, but these also, in crucial ways, paradoxically rely on animacy as they objectify, thereby providing possibilities for reanimation" (Chen 2012, 30). Due to the vibrant affectivity of language, acts of reclaiming or reanimating certain labels aim at seizing their affective power in a move toward political agency. Shameless hags and tolerance whores can thus be understood as linguistic and affective turning points, as instances in which the object making of slurs is redirected into practices of subject making. Hags and whores are in a sense abject subjects (or perhaps object subjects) aware of their objectification, yet they rework this objectness in the direction of subjectness in ways that mix shame with pride and poise. In doing so, they play at what Chen (2012, 35) identifies as "the dizzying is-and-is-not politics of the reclaiming of insults."

Given that acts of reanimation and reclaiming are based on the volatility of affect, however, their outcomes are always less than certain. The power of reclaiming lies in the affective stickiness of labels—the fact that the very force of objectification is somehow operative in the new use, although in a different way (as something that "is and is not"). This also means that the boundary between reclaiming and objectifying remains unpredictable and unstable. Although tolerance whores provide an explicit link between deanimation and reanimation, the work of the hag remains more subtle in that her recent upsurge does not correspond to a rise in deanimation but rather builds on a long history of derogatory labeling (and its radical and gynocentric feminist appropriations). It should also be noted that the effects of acts of reclaiming are unevenly distributed both within and beyond the group that performs these acts. The affective work of labels such as *aunties*, *hags*, and *whores* in our examples has clear ties to and possibly resonances with the group reclaiming the label. It is nevertheless much more uncertain whether this affective work shifts the simultaneous heaviness and sharpness of the terms for those who use them to injure and whether such linguistic labor has effects on how this terminology plays out in the society at large.

In reclaiming shameless hags and tolerance whores, something is nevertheless put in motion and amplified through posts, likes, and shares. Social media plays an obvious and key role in contemporary projects of linguistic reclaiming. The viral stickiness and instant appeal of "weaponized memes" deployed in US politics would be one of its more powerful forms (see Zannettou et al. 2018). Flower-hat aunties, hags, and tolerance whores populate the same social media landscape as the "nasty woman," "bad hombres," and those grabbed by the pussy (or wearing pussy hats)—all figures that were quickly picked up and reanimated in resistance to Trump after his presidential election in 2016. These models of resistance and reanimation add a new stitch to the memetic logics of online humor. In a similar vein, Carrie A. Rentschler and Samantha C. Thrift (2015, 340) show how feminist memes create a particular "feeling of community" through cheeky laughter, a rather transitory formation that does not necessarily build on ideological or identificatory similarity. This chapter is yet another testimony to how such fleeting forms of networked feminist politics take shape by using collective imagination, humor, and wit to refuel feminist connective practices.

6 Manels, Dadpreneurs, and the Allure of Binary Gender

Frustrated with the recurring all-male panels in her field of international relations, postdoctoral scholar Saara Särmä set up the Tumblr blog "Congrats, you have an all male panel!" in February 2015. According to its straightforward rationale, the tumblr consists of photographs of all-male panels in conferences, symposia, and other expert meetings with academics, officials, and politicians, with the additional visual pleasure of a small picture of David Hasselhoff of the 1980s *Knight Rider* era lifting his thumb in a gesture of solemn approval.

The tumblr soon attracted contributions from readers, and international media attention gave the project a viral lift that made *manel* something of an academic household word. By November 2015, "Congrats, you have an all male panel!" had gained over 100,000 visits, more than 8,000 followers, and some 83,000 reactions on Facebook and been addressed in more than 9,000 tweets. *Time* magazine framed the initiative as "a hilarious takedown of everyday sexism" by "brilliantly shaming" those organizing and participating in all-male panels (Toppa 2015), and *The Guardian* had high hopes for how the tumblr "shakes up status quo" (Locker 2015). Writing for *The Telegraph*, Robert Tait (2015) commented on the use of Hasselhoff's photo: "Once the face of hedonistic masculinity on *Baywatch* . . . now the handsome features of David Hasselhoff are being used to ironically expose a less seductive aspect of maleness—plain old-fashioned sexism." For Särmä (2016), it is the younger Hasselhoff as the lone male hero Michael Knight who has the most appeal: "the Hoff" provides the project with a quickly recognizable, humorous incarnation of white, straight masculinity of the pronouncedly virile sort.

On the one hand, the "Congrats, you have an all male panel!" tumblr and its binary gender logic make strikingly evident the virility of the

Translation: joining efforts for breastfeeding.

https://www.reporteindigo.com/reporte/ausencia-mujeres-en-panel-lactancia-materna-genera-indignacion/

NOVEMBER 28, 2018 (8:00 AM)   37 NOTES

"Congrats, you have an all male panel!" tumblr (translation: "Joining efforts for breastfeeding").

"malestream" in how expertise and leadership continue to be articulated and embodied and in how nonmen continue to be excluded from their realm. On the other hand, this logic renders invisible other intersecting variables of difference and axes of power, such as race, nationality, age, and class. For example, it took another tumblr to address the dominant position of whiteness. Following the success of "Congrats, you have an all male panel!," Särmä launched two other tumblrs—"Congrats, you have an all white panel!" and "Congrats, you did not cite any feminist work!"—yet neither of them has gone viral. As we have argued throughout this book, feminist tactics in social media—from the #MeToo movement to the shaming of male harassers—regularly operate within the framework of binary gender. They critique the ways in which gender binaries structure relations of power in particular ways, but the logic of these projects seems to resist more intersectional takes on other differences that matter. In this sense, feminist social media tactics become invested in the reductive logic of binary difference that they question.

This chapter proposes that rather than repeatedly pointing out such flattening out of differences through intersectional critique, it is necessary to take seriously the appeal—or indeed the seduction—of gender binaries in feminist social media tactics. Although such an appeal may seem counterintuitive, both feminist activism and feminist humor—brought together in the materials explored in this book—are embedded in a logic where gender can be discussed as a system consisting of two mutually opposing poles, one of which holds power over the other. In this logic, differences within gender categories are easily effaced, while differences between them become constitutive to the whole. Binary gender provides much of feminist humor with its punch, even when this humor may be questioning the very logic within which differences become established and social hierarchies are drawn. There is a seductive simplicity to binaries, which also fuels comic interventions and attempts to turn the tables. Operating within the binaries that are being critiqued involves default degrees of ambiguity where spaces of critique and laughter are opened up at the expense of differences irreducible to a binary logic.

In order to address the pleasures and transformative potential that all this may entail, we examine both the tumblr "Congrats, you have an all male panel!" and the Twitter and Facebook accounts of "Man who has it all" by an anonymous "working dad" or "dadpreneur" who serves "top tips for men juggling a successful career and fatherhood." As feminist parody and satire, "Man who has it all" exposes the absurdities of male domination and sexism by imagining a world of gender reversal, including workplace equality, beauty regimes, and body normativity concerning men only. According to its Facebook page, "Man who has it all" highlights "the sexism, stereotypes and bias women experience everyday by imagining a world where men are treated in the same way society treats women." Our analysis of these two initiatives extends to the rhythms and temporalities of social media platforms, from the archival functions of Tumblr to the participatory impulses of Twitter and Facebook, and the different scenes that they afford for feminist humor.

Feminist Tumblr Logics

In addition to the tumblr "Congrats, you have an all male panel!," a number of social media initiatives point to the problem of letting men embody expertise in a compulsory fashion. The Twitter accounts of @genderavenger (also GenderAvenger.com) and @eupanelwatch call out "pale, male and stale panels," and websites urge male experts to take a pledge not to participate in all-male panels. Owen Barder is a development economist and director for Europe at the Center for Global Development. On his website Owen.org, people can take the following pledge: "At a public conference I won't serve on a panel of two people or more unless there is at least one woman on the panel, not including the Chair." Similar to Särmä's tumblr, these projects draw attention to how the quantifiable problem of representation is linked to structural issues concerning gender and power. They argue for the importance of diversity, and as they strive to ensure that women are always part of public discussions, they reduce it to the question of gender balance.

The success of "Congrats, you have an all male panel!" has likely been fueled by its combination of a simple yet striking visual technique and its use of humor in tackling a topic as dismal as sexism. In writing for *Bustle*, Anjali Patel (2015) argues that the tumblr brilliantly illustrates the lack of visual evidence of women in important public spaces in a way that is both funny and poignant and adds: "The other best part? The posts are badged with images of David Hasselhoff. Why? I don't know, but it's excellent. Hasselhoff's gloriously blue-eyed stares and approving thumbs up just adds an extra punch to the joke." Having Hasselhoff "congratulate" the panel members on a job well done in the name of male dominance is a pitch-perfect take on a form of masculinity dating back to an earlier time—the gym-conscious masculine ideal of 1980s popular culture—that is repurposed as an ironic figure of feminist critique some thirty-five years later.

This is not the only instance where Tumblr has been deployed as a site of subversive feminist humor (Ringrose and Lawrence 2018). Before being purged of sexual content in 2018, the platform was known as a significant hub for alternative and subcultural content (see Cho 2015; Fink and Miller 2014; Renninger 2015; Tiidenberg 2015). Individual Tumblr blogs may consist of original user-generated content, but people usually reblog content from other tumblrs or share content harvested from across the web. A tumblr assembles this content into a novel thematic whole that can in return feed into other blogs. Within the endless circulation or "tumbling" that is characteristic of the platform, focus is, as Alexander Cho (2015, 46) points out, much less on authorship and original content than on the processes of selection and curation connected to a user's personalized stream. The tumblrs resulting from selection and circulation may combine surprising and apparently incompatible elements or bring together similar images from diverse sources into a new whole—as is the case of "Congrats, you have an all male panel!"

For Cho (2015, 46–47), Tumblr operates with a nonlinear "queer reverb" of "repeat and repeat" that entails the potential for community, kinship, and intimacy outside of heteronormative arrangements. In addition to images or entire tumblrs resonating with their users and becoming affectively charged, the repetitive reblogging involves a temporal element of reverb "that has the additional quality of amplification or diminishment (intensity) through echo or refrain; in this sense, it can be modulated to serve a purpose. Reverb is a quality and a process, a way to understand the direction and intensity of the flows of affect. It has been startling to watch this pattern over the years: a post lingers until it hits a popular Tumblr, then takes off, dies down again, and takes off again, almost like a breathing thing" (Cho 2015, 53). Extending focus beyond the queer ecosystems that Cho addresses, we wonder whether his conceptualization of affective rhythms, modulations, and reverbs can be adapted to understanding the potentialities and attractions of Tumblr more generally—or to more specific instances, such as that of feminist humor.

Tumblr can be bewildering for the uninitiated in its pulsing jumble of images and links. Research on Tumblr feminism has emphasized how the relatively low traffic in direct comments on posts, in combination with a flexible structure of discrete modes of following and the use of pseudonymous identities (as opposed to real-name policies) make for a relatively safe and feminist friendly environment (Kanai 2015; Renninger 2015; Ringrose and Lawrence 2018; Thelandersson 2014). Pseudonymous identification safeguards sensitive identities from nonconsensual outing while having the potential to facilitate recognition in collective terms (Cho 2018). As Bryce Renninger (2015, 1523) puts it, "Identities on Tumblr are often closeted, collective, obscured, or evanescent." Other obvious points of contact or recognition consist of the naming of individual tumblrs and the use of hashtags. In times of violent backlash against feminist politics and practices, it may be risky to self-identify as feminist. In that sense, the disconnect with real-life identities can provide a respite from antifeminist antagonism and open up spaces in which to breathe—and laugh—more easily.

Most of the interaction with posts across the site consists of likes and reblogs, sometimes with added commentary (as part of reblogging a post on one's own tumblr). Likes and reblogs are embedded in notes linked to posts, which further deemphasize comments as a form of public engagement. These subtle or soft affective structures of interaction amplify curatorial visual practices while downplaying heated public debate, and they shape spaces that are relatively protected from the snarkiness, hostile flaming, and trolling occurring elsewhere online—and on social media platforms such as Twitter (also Tiidenberg 2015). The platform architecture of Tumblr does not, however, seem to free these spaces from internal tension or drama. As Fredrika Thelandersson (2014, 528) argues, feminist debates on Tumblr involve calling others out and blaming them in abundance for being ignorant or downright offensive: "Sometimes it's just as disheartening as the toxic Twitter climate. . . . Much of the discussion is based around 'policing' other participants about what they're doing wrong instead of encouraging them for what is being done right." In other words, the kind of feminist humor that may flourish on Tumblr comes vested in a protective shell of sorts toward outer hostility and the muddy, ubiquitous terrain of sexist online humor. At the same time, the platform is internally troubled by the same tensions that haunt feminisms in general, whether they are drawn along the axes of sexuality, race, or class—or even gender itself, as made evident by queer and trans-feminist critiques.

Cho's queer reverb senses and makes sense of Tumblr as a pulse, a rhythm, and an affective temporality entailing variations in intensity. In addition to posts that grow more or less visible and engagements with them that grow more or less intense over time, a tumblr involves a different kind of temporality tied to a thematic archive that displays the posted items as a gallery. On the "Congrats, you have an all male panel!" tumblr, this gallery appears endless, and it assembles images of expert meetings from across the globe and from various professional and disciplinary strata. The panels are firmly male and focus on topics such as education, electoral policies, digital transformation, campus sustainability, gender equality, abortion, and reproductive rights. The captions are generally matter-of-fact and often sarcastic, as in "Men talk about Descartes," "Translation: joining efforts for breastfeeding," "A workshop with a goal of inspiring more women to pursue careers in tech has an all-male panel," or "The pope and his all-male panel!"

"Congrats, you have an all male panel!" builds on irony by saying the opposite of what is meant for critical effect. Its congratulatory gesture in the name of sexism uses irony to make visible the practices of exclusion or the people who are not part of the picture—women. The logics of Tumblr assemble separate elements into thematic galleries that then become archives and more than the sum of their parts. As Särmä (2016, 473) herself notes, "When you scroll through a conference website listing all-male panels, and you keep scrolling and scrolling, yet they never seem to end, it is quite difficult to argue that the issue does not exist." The tumblr brings together user submissions from different professional fields while remaining under Särmä's editorial control. In doing so, it results in a seemingly paradoxical mix of viral visibility and curatorial containment. This combination of visual repetition, irony, and curatorial control makes for its own form of feminist, humorous reverb—of "repeat and repeat"—because the farther down you scroll in the archive of all-male panels, the weirder or more absurd these images start to look. The absurdity of this seemingly endless scroll of images is not without its own form of humor. It creates a particular form of feminist cringe comedy. What at first glance (sadly) comes across as completely unremarkable quickly becomes quite strange and notable due to the high volume of images and the "Hoffsome" ironic overlay. It may also seem as though the Hoffsome badge begs to become a reaction GIF, especially considering how reaction GIFs are a kind of lingua franca on Tumblr, yet the very stillness of the thumb exerts power precisely for remaining immobile, understated, and resisting resolution.

This feminist "repeat and repeat" reverb may be completely void of the erotic qualities of the kind that Cho examines as queer reverberations throbbing within and tying certain queer Tumblr communities together (although this is less the case since December 2018). Instead, this feminist reverb is more static as a steady repeat and repeat of more of the same.

Through the destabilizing quality of irony, it inserts a certain affective disturbance within this very sameness. As an echo of sorts, irony in these image galleries affords a repetition with a difference, which in turn introduces a difference to the issue at hand. The farther down you scroll, the more the male panel participants start to look uncongenial, out of place, sometimes hilarious, and plain absurd.

Risky Embarrassment and Cringe Criticism

Media coverage of "Congrats, you have an all male panel!" and its success have repeatedly drawn attention to its ability to shame the men involved (Crellin 2015; Toppa 2015). As with many other feminist social media initiatives addressed in this book, it operates within the affective registers of shame in calling out male panels and the men making them happen. More specifically, the type of shame operative in the tumblr entails embarrassment over being called out for having put together or having participated in yet another all-male panel and hence being complicit in the reproduction of gendered patterns of discrimination and exclusion. After *male panel* and *manel* grew into broadly recognizable terms with the high visibility of Särmä's tumblr, potential participation in them quickly grew into a reputational risk, at least in many academic settings. It then follows that people invited to all-male panels may refuse such requests or propose gendered amendments to them in order to avoid reputational damage. The potential embarrassment involved thus comes with risks and possibly something of a sharp edge.

In comparison to #MeToo and @assholesonline, which operate within the registers of shame and humiliation, the dynamics of embarrassment involve less affective intensity or an intensity of a different sorts. "Congrats, you have an all male panel!" may not be benign, yet its bite is less sharp than that of many other feminist social media projects calling out men on their disappointing behavior. Practices of shaming operate on a scale of variable affective sharpness that makes a difference to the kind of intensity that may take hold of the body and affect its capacities to act. To be inconvenienced by embarrassment differs from the loops of shaming operative in sexually aggressive online hate, which ultimately aims to frighten, control, and shrink the body and the spaces in which it can move. "Congrats, you have an all male panel!" observes, witnesses, and renders the state of affairs visible for future visiting. In this sense, the social embarrassment it entails comes with a persistent reverb: a manel of some years past may never quite go away, resisting removal like a particularly difficult and unfortunate stain ghosting as a persistent refrain.

In his theatrical understanding of social interaction, Erving Goffman (1956) frames embarrassment as something densely social and as such always present in human encounters. Embarrassment threatens to disrupt the flow of the situation and to turn social comfort into awkward discomfort—or in his terms, "discomfiture." Goffman analyzes the fragility of social situations and relations, as well as their scales of intensity and rhythm: "Abrupt embarrassment may often be intense, while sustained uneasiness is more commonly mild, involving barely apparent flusterings" (Goffman 1956, 265). The initial viral breakthrough of "Congrats, you have an all male panel!" may have been due to its suddenly introduced disturbance in somewhat routine social arrangements and the experiential spike of embarrassment that it affords. The tumblr's continuing appeal or life nevertheless builds on embarrassment entailing a more even and sustained sense of discomfort irreducible to a singular affective spike or event.

Goffman argues that it is not always or perhaps even typically the case that one person is both the cause of embarrassing social dissonance, the one for whom things are embarrassing, and the one for whom the embarrassment is felt. Rather, when some people find themselves in a situation that should render them embarrassed yet have little reaction, others may blush instead. Embarrassment, then, can potentially shuttle among three parties: those causing the embarrassing situation, those for whom the situation is or should be embarrassing, and those who feel embarrassment. Embarrassment is therefore difficult to contain: "This is why embarrassment seems to be contagious, spreading, once started, in ever widening circles of discomfiture" (Goffman 1956, 268). "Congrats, you have an all male panel!" operates with embarrassment variably distributed across those who ought to feel embarrassed, a logic that rapidly spread in widening circles as the tumblr went viral. Some have felt and continue to feel the "mild discomfiture" and its "flustering syndrome" (Goffman 1956, 264), judging from the number of men taking a pledge to avoid all-male panels. Meanwhile, others are more immune to such social nervousness and unease. The ones taking a pledge may even feel embarrassed on behalf of the ones who remain seemingly unrattled.

Due to the contagious nature of embarrassment, it also threatens to spill over onto those pointing out the embarrassing behavior: in this case, onto everybody contributing to the steadily growing tumblr. Goffman points out that embarrassment is about unfulfilled expectations and that being the one causing the embarrassment can be embarrassing in and of itself, given that the one bringing attention to something embarrassing is the one who simultaneously disrupts the social comfort of others. This is part of the affective dynamic of making use of embarrassment and the social shaming this entails as a feminist tactic. Pointing to an injustice disturbs the fun of others, in this case the fun in constantly being in the company of other men, who perhaps up until this point have been unaware that there was something problematic in such ways of conducting themselves. Goffman does not engage much with considerations of power (other than loosely referencing social hierarchies), and he certainly does not engage with the topic of gender. But we do because it is a disruption of the homosocial comfort and ease of male dominance that "Congrats, you have an all male panel!" causes, an attempt to insert a low-frequency form of continuous embarrassment and awkwardness to fluster participants in all-male panels.

Luna Dolezal (2015, 9) regards "shame and embarrassment to be variations of the same affect, with perhaps varying antecedents, where embarrassment can be considered to be merely a milder, or less intense, form of shame." Due to the ambiguity and unpredictability of affect and its oscillating intensities, the differences or distinctions between shame and embarrassment are not altogether clear, just as shame may intensify into a sense of humiliation. These experiences are bound to vary both from one temporal instance to another and within the affective registers of any singular person. Something that makes me mildly embarrassed may make someone else feel a deep sense of shame, and a social event that haunts me as persistently shameful could well fail to be registered by someone else similarly positioned. There is also the unpredictable sliding between and intermeshing of affective registers. In Silvan Tomkins's affect theory, embarrassment is a weaker and possibly fleeting expression of shame that may, however, change its shapes and forms if "what might have been a momentary distress is transformed into an enduring mood of sadness or, rather than becoming attenuated with time, they grow in intensity, so that a momentary uneasiness grows into overwhelming panic or embarrassment is transformed into humiliation" (Tomkins 2008, 362). Although embarrassment marks a weak sense of coming short, self-disgust and contempt mark intensity comparable to humiliation.

Shame, then, lingers, and shame felt for another involves affective connectivity. Shame makes identity in a fundamental sense by orienting, reorienting, and disrupting one's sense of self in social relations (Sedgwick 2003, 36–37). In delineating a "cringe criticism," Nick Salvato (2013) identifies embarrassment not as a version or subspecies of shame but as something distinct. As much as shame disrupts what it shapes and is integral to the processes of self-formation, embarrassment can be understood as a situational sense of identity connected to social failure (Salvato 2013, 682). Shame operates within the core of self-formation, and embarrassment traffics in social anxiety, awkwardness, and a disruption of particular social norms as tied to a sense of having disappointed and failed. "Congrats, you have an all male panel!" works precisely in such registers of disappointment and social failure, aiming to induce enough anxiety for men to withdraw from manels in an effort to, if nothing else, look better in the eyes of others. This may take the shape of mild embarrassment or, when it involves a realization that one has violated shared values and modes of conduct, guilt—which for Tomkins (2008, 361) is yet another dimension of shame-humiliation.

Salvato writes of a feeling of embarrassment arising when the performative self is exposed in a social situation (real or imagined) as undesirably divided. The sensation can be physically manifested as blushing or cringing. He argues that what is missing from most accounts of embarrassment, including Goffman's, "is just how powerfully the cringe, as well as or even in place of the blush, may connote the production of embarrassment . . . that distinctive flavor or range of shrinking and flinching and shivering" (Salvato 2013, 687). The reason for this oversight, he believes, is that although studies of embarrassment mention the capacity to feel embarrassed by or for someone else, they focus primarily on self-embarrassment, as manifested by the blush: "Conversely, the cringe, a mode of contracting and thus withdrawing, is likelier to be associated with a withdrawal from another and thus with embarrassment on that other's behalf" (Salvato 2013, 687). Such cringe is encapsulated in the Finnish term *myötähäpeä* (coshame): a prickly, yet potentially titillating sense of unease caused by the social failures of others.

The cringe has been abundantly used within the world of comedy, even as its own comedic subgenre of "cringe comedy," including sitcoms such as *Seinfeld, Parks and Recreation, Mr. Bean,* and *Veep* and dramedies like *Girls* and *Insecure.* Cringe comedy derives its sense of humor and pleasure from social awkwardness, audience discomfort, and the possibly politically incorrect breaking of social norms. As Lori Marso (2019) shows in her analysis, feminist cringe comedy pulls or turns the body inward, whereas laughter opens up the body toward others. Marso treats the cringe and the laughter as two separate things. What may at first sight present itself as a paradoxical bodily response that both fuels and interrupts laughter is on second thought a laughter of a particular kind because cringe comedy elicits discomforting laughter that has its own pleasures. "Congrats, you have an all male panel!" can be thought of as feminist cringe comedy of sorts because the tumblr creates sociability among both those engaged in embarrassing others and also those cringing on behalf of those who ought to feel embarrassed. The cringe can be thought of as an affective glue that joins together people who follow or visit the tumblr. It is a particular mixture of embarrassment that entails even potential pity for the long line of men gathered around rectangular tables to discuss topics that matter. As viewers scroll through the archive of all-male panels seemingly without end, they may find it both awkwardly embarrassing on the behalf of these men and also weirdly funny. A particularly cringeworthy tweet at the Twitter account @allmalepanels (September 19, 2018) reads: "Congrats to . . . and . . . for responding to criticism of their manels by adding a woman to each of them . . . and then complaining about it at the event."

Into the Binary

"Congrats, you have an all male panel!" tackles sexism and male domination by playing with what provides sexism with its toxicity: the oppositional hierarchy of binary gender. As such, it has the potential to speak to a wide range of women and other nonmen variously positioned in relation to heterosexist norms. The tumblr provides striking visual evidence of how supposedly neutral expert knowledge, as displayed on all-male panels, is a particular construct embodied by mostly white, able-bodied, and cisgender men in ways that make invisible a multiplicity of other bodies. These others, however, have one thing in common: they are not part of the picture. When worked over by the cogs and cogwheels of binary gender, this complexity in terms of, for example, race, ability, and gender itself has to give way to a far more simple logic—that of a binary that assumes and erases much more than it shows. The simplicity of binary gender, we argue, affords it a compelling quality—a kind of seduction that, paradoxically, comes to fuel humorous feminist interventions. The reductionism of gender binaries is infuriating, yet this reductionist simplicity seems to have made the feminist social media initiatives discussed in this book go viral.

There are different ways of playing the binary. The strategy used in "Congrats, you have an all male panel!" is additive rather than more radically transformative in that it asks for a correction: add women (or at least one woman). This demand can be highly efficient due to its seeming modesty. All you have to do is add a woman. How hard can it be? As Särmä (2016) points out, the success of the tumblr has functioned as a conversation starter while simultaneously marking the beginning of a much larger conversation. This larger debate needs to engage with questions of power and privilege and to inquire into whose voices are being heard publicly, whose voices are considered to count, and whose voices remain inaudible. The tumblr nevertheless seems to suggest that, in order to have this larger discussion and to challenge, open up, or even overthrow the binary, we need a binary to begin with—not a false pairing that builds on the effacement of women and other nonmen under the guise of supposedly neutral knowledge production.

This binary that is no binary resonates with the work of Luce Irigaray, where the language of gender, as a binary relation, assumes two terms: male and female, masculine and feminine. For Irigaray, one of these poles—the feminine—is virtually unrepresentable within the hegemonic, masculine order. Irigaray (1993/1977, 26) performs a familiar mathematical operation in considering the relationship between man and woman as based on the contrast between the one: "The *one* of form, of the individual, of the (male) sex organ, of the proper name, of the proper meaning," and the *not* one: "The negative, the underside, the reverse." Such a binary is no binary because the dominance of the one over the not one is powerful to the point of obliteration: "The 'feminine' is always described in terms of deficiency or atrophy, as the other side of the sex that alone holds a monopoly on value: the male sex. Hence the all too well-known 'penis envy'" (Irigaray 1993, 69).

"Congrats, you have an all male panel!" has everything to do with the presence of the one (of the penis, of the proper meaning) and the paradoxical absence of the not one. How can something that is not even part of the picture form an actual absence? The tumblr, moreover, has everything to do with the monopoly of the male sex in what matters and how it matters, while also managing to illustrate what the very absence of women in various fields of knowledge actually looks like. Following Irigaray, making a negative signify may seem a virtually impossible task, but the tumblr succeeds in rendering visible such an absence with the help of ironic juxtaposition. The absence and silence are made ever louder and all the more absurd by the themes examined by some of these panels, from gender equality to reproductive rights. When an all-male panel takes on the topics of abortion, breastfeeding, and women's rights to their own bodies, the absence of nonmen in the room becomes a presence of sorts that loudly calls for gender diversity at the table. To the extent that the tumblr can be seen to play with the notion of penis envy, it does so with a humorous backspin that throws the question of the proper meaning of the male organ back onto the penis holders themselves by repeatedly referring to all-male panels as "sausage fests."

A quite different way of making fun of binary gender is manifested in the popular Twitter and Facebook accounts of "Man who has it all," composed by a fictitious, anonymous "working dad" who juggles fatherhood, work outside the home, "me time," and looking good by making comedic use of the advice in women's magazines and self-help literature. This is feminist parody that sometimes moves into the more biting satirical terrain of mockery and sarcasm. "Man who has it all" flips the switch on binary gender as a way to reimagine everything from workplace discrimination and sexual harassment to normative advice on beauty, staying sexy, and maintaining a healthy marriage while being a parent. It turns the tables on everyday heterosexism, and in no more than the 140 (which in 2018 was expanded to 280) characters of a tweet—or as catchy meme templates on Facebook—it manages to expose its absurd dimensions. "Man who has it all" uses terms like "male chairwomen" and "gentlemen doctors" as a means of countering the gendering of professional women, plays with the idea of hiring men as workplace eye-candy, and calls them overtly sensitive, hormonal, or "testoric" (that is, male hysteric) if they complain about gender-based discrimination and exclusion.

Tweets include sage advice from "Claire, CEO" ("Some men complain when you call them boys while others see it as a compliment, making it

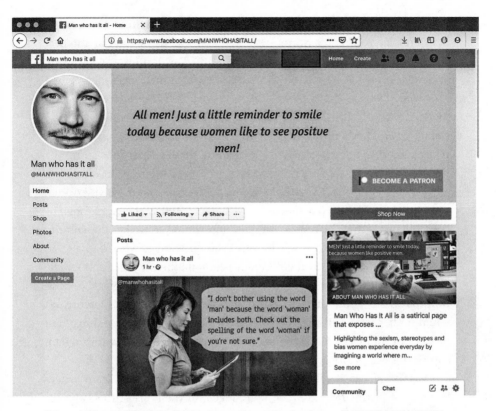

"Man who has it all" Facebook page, https://www.facebook.com/MANWHOHASITALL.

impossible to know whether to infantilize boys or not. You just can't win," April 22, 2018), statements on the inclusivity of professional titles ("'Man scientist' is NOT an offensive term. It is simply a way to differentiate them from proper scientists. End of story," November 17, 2018), and vital beauty routine tips ("PENIS STEAMING. To achieve a clean & balanced penis, squat over steaming water containing herbs such as cumin, cayenne pepper and chilli," July 7, 2017). In some instances, the point of the critique concerns sexist attitudes that are markedly vintage (as in debates over women's abilities to participate in the labor force), and some are more specific to the contemporary moment (as in the gender reversal of tips on "vaginal steaming" offered on Gwyneth Paltrow's lifestyle site, Goop, in 2016, to much social media contestation and merriment).

The foundational strategy of "Man who has it all" involves reading binary gender in reverse. By overturning and switching its two poles, it is as simple as it is efficient: "ALL MEN! You can be anything you want to be. Don't let your crazy hormones, irrational moods or inferior intellect hold you back" (Twitter, November 13, 2018). The Twitter and Facebook accounts, as well as a book providing self-help in a more extended format (*The Man Who Has It All: A Patronizing Parody of Self-Help Books for Women* by @ManWhoHasItAll, 2016), dig into the absurdity of gendered beauty standards and body norms and, in doing so, comment on the ubiquity of sexism. Yet it may be precisely in performing these gender flips along the lines of "reverse sexism" (or "reverse objectification") that "Man who has it all" also loses some of its critical edge. When sexism is reverse engineered through the oppositional hierarchy of binary gender, the most obvious consequence is that the notions of male and female, as well as masculinity and femininity, appear to switch seats. The question is what happens to relations of power and to the different positionalities of male and female subjects in this reversal, given that the binary is one of hierarchical opposition that holds bodies in place with considerable force. Put differently, as a humorous tactic, this play with binary gender through reversal may fail to account for or challenge the heterosexist power relations within which something like the logic of objectification comes about.

"Man who has it all" explicitly comments on objectification where women (or in this reversal, men) are judged on the basis of their appearance and attractiveness—for example, by sharing tweets covering the television appearances of male British politicians with comments such as "Mr Blair, 65, flashes his slender ankles in perilously short trousers and matching jacket, proving older men can still be relevant." A key term in feminist critiques of media and the beauty industry for some four decades, the notion of objectification presumes a dynamic where women are perceived as and are rendered into objects to be gazed at or even consumed for instrumental value, whereas men are afforded the status of subjects who do the gazing and consuming. Understood in this vein, the process of objectification requires a subject, an object, and a relational power asymmetry. An object—for all practical, linguistic, and philosophical purposes—is what is being acted on (by a subject). As such, it lacks autonomy. An object can be anything that is visible or tangible and relatively stable in form: a thing, a person, or a matter in relation to which thought or action is directed. In arguments over objectification, the model of binary gender meets a binary conception of agency where the positions of objects and subjects are mutually exclusive inasmuch as they are hierarchical. While helping to illustrate unequal social relations, the notion of objectification also congeals them and, in doing so, may reify the model of binary gender that is being critiqued. This, however, is not the only framework for understanding the processes of object making.

Mel Chen (2012), in examining the hierarchical structure of "animacy" (or affective liveliness, agency, and mobility) as a kind of political grammar, considers the slippage between persons and things as objects. Objectification, then, happens when some humans—such as women, racial others, or queers—are referred to as less than human. When humans are mixed with objects, they move "down" on the animacy hierarchy, becoming dehumanized and desubjectified. Chen is quick to "rescue" such abject subjects, however, by exploring how they may "kick back" in ways that turn object making into subject making. The question is whether the logic of gender reversal in "Man who has it all" is animate or agential to the point where the object (the female as well as femininity) can be turned into a subject. A reversal in gender does not automatically lead to a reversal in power, but can it afford spaces for kicking back? If understood as a binary formation, gender builds on both separation and unity as compulsory heterosexuality in violent and oppressive ways shapes gender as bipolar opposites (Butler 1999, 30). Here, binary gender is completely dependent on heterosexuality to function *as* a binary. "Man who has it all" intervenes in binary gender arrangements and heterosexual desire by reversing positions and by pointing out their absurdity. In doing so, it reperforms the power asymmetry of the binary in question, drawing its appeal from the very logic that it critiques while also opening up spaces for laughter.

Playing with Sexism, at Different Speeds

When browsing through the "Man who has it all" Twitter and Facebook accounts, its one-liners soon grow repetitive and thus possibly less funny than when consumed at the pace at which they are published (a few tweets and posts per day that may or may not appear in one's social media feeds). Furthermore, focusing on the posts alone provides a partial understanding of "Man who has it all" as a social media phenomenon, given that its sound bites take off in a different way in the comment sections, where followers collectively investigate the alternate universe imagined, dig deeper into its dimensions of parody, and amp up the sarcasm. One of the tweets that took on a life of its own, partly since it was pinned and hence highlighted in its visibility, reads: "My friend is a history teacher. She's compiling a list of great historical figures and she needs a male to add to the list. Suggestions?" This binary gender play clearly hit a nerve among the followers and proved to be the ignition to feverish activity as the tweet gained some 3,000 comments, 11,000 retweets, and 35,000 heart-shaped likes. One of the top comments reads, "not a lot of people know, but Mark Twain was actually a man," which got the response "I think that's been debunked though. How could that wonderful writing be done by a man?" And off it went. Many tried to think of that handsome husband of a well-known and outstanding historical female figure, without much luck. Others went on a bender by reimagining the science lab of the famous Rosalind Franklin, where there could have been a man or two who did something useful with DNA, but they just could not quite remember their names. This exchange quickly escalated into snarky comments over men's bodies working in labs:

They're terribly dowdy a lot of these fellas, aren't they? One suspects the lab
   is a bit of a refuge for the plain boys.

Boys are terrible in the lab: they fall in love with you, then they cry . . .

I half wonder whether men should be allowed in labs. Could be a distraction to hard working women. They at least need to dress appropriately

What's proper attire?
well skirts instead of those ridiculous tight 'pantaloon' things . . . we get it,
   fellas

The pace and feel of the "Man who has it all" comment sections are similar to the contagious intensity of the Facebook event "Shameless Extinction" (discussed in chapter 5) that equally thrives in parodic and imaginative world making where gender binaries are turned on their head for critical, comical effect. But there are also differences. "Shameless Extinction" exploded over a period of just a couple of weeks, produced by a collaborative activity on overdrive that was difficult to keep up with in real time. In a Facebook event that you had to sign up for, the participants' passionate engagement created a sense of belonging to a secret society of a feminist underworld, coining subversion from below. As such, it was community driven, shaped by collaborative fantasies of what a world could look like where women conducted themselves shamelessly. This universe of shameless, fleshy, damaged, egotistical hags provided the foundation for contagious, networked laughter, seemingly releasing some of the tensions created by lifelong habits of embodying shame and sober, white, middle-class moderation.

The feel and rhythm of "Man who has it all" provide more of a slow, simmering, steady flow, which has endured. Launched in the spring of 2015, its base of followers has grown steadily for several years. Sociability among followers thrives in the comment sections that regularly return to references to genital steaming and the indulgence of snacking on almonds (but not too many) as in-group jokes of sorts, but these accounts are not only public in a different way from the closed Facebook event but also produced by a single—if yet anonymous and fictitious—author. This gives these accounts a noticeably top-down feel, amplified by the discursive echoes in "men's magazines" and the growing volume of posts containing merchandise, such as T-shirts with quotes from "Man who has it all." The accounts are editorial inasmuch as commercial as a social media brand that one can support via Patreon. Followers who are not active coproducers of content get a slow-paced stream of "advice" for men who, indeed, can have it all, bent around a twist in gender. Some days, these snippets pass by unnoticed. Other times, the gender twist turns into the absurd and becomes compelling indeed. Consider the following "Man who has it all" tweet that one of us sent the other when preparing this chapter: "Working husband? How do you protect your hair from Autumn? John, age 46, 'I apply yoghurt to my penis.' Inspirational." Followers not only liked the tweet 1,600 times but engaged with the tip:

Not just any yoghurt, Jesus—only artisinal (sic) blended Greek yoghurt with activated almonds, I'm not a fucking savage #blessed #naturalman

Autumn seems to be a really tough time for some men's locks. But what do the lactose-intolerant put on their penises? Is a tepid soy-milk immersion bath for three hours an acceptable alternative? Husband really struggling here.

I prefer a man who goes completely natural. Why is it ok for them to do all this stuff??? It's just a trick to get our attention and then one morning we have to see the truth. . . . HE DOES NOT wake up looking like that. It's deceitful.

And can I just add . . . it seems a bit selfish to be wasting my hard earned money on yogurt for your beauty regime.

They should do all their me time beauty stuff in private. Women don't want to hear about it. Ruins the magic.

There is also something to be said about social media research methods here, given how different an account appears when analyzed systematically in its entirety and when encountered within its mundane flows and rhythms. Our means of sampling and analysis transform the objects of study in how they become experienced and possibly enjoyed. All this ties in with the particularity of social media platforms—and in fact, speaks of the difficulty of tackling the instances and dynamics of laughter in academic inquiry. Studying these accounts can somewhat kill the joy, as began to happen during our analysis of "Man who has it all." It may be the case that when studying humor in general, things can become rather flat and that a joke, once explained, fails to amuse. As Tomkins (2008, 1965) points out, the excitement connected to laughing at a joke grows paler in the course of repetition. When the form of humor or the shape of the joke is repetitive and variation narrow, a novel post is similar to those already read. A variation of the tweet on applying yoghurt on a penis for autumnal hair protection, cited above, for example, reemerged some months later as another seasonal tip: "Working husband? How do you protect your hair from Spring? John, age 46, 'I apply almond milk to my testicles.' Inspirational." Four years earlier, in September 2015, the variation was "Working husband? How do you protect your hair from getting dehydrated? John, age 58, 'I work yoghurt into the roots.' What an inspiration." There can be enjoyment to the joke as it gets recycled or reiterated—after all, repetition, in connection with variation, often is key for amplifying the punch and hilarity of a joke. There is nevertheless also the risk of a feminist reverb—of "repeat and repeat"—ending up sounding much like an old record, spinning round and round.

Sexism can certainly feel like an old vinyl with deep scratches where the record needle gets repeatedly and frustratingly stuck. Within such a reverb, the flipping of the gender switch grows less funny when the same stifling restrictions of bodies and spaces are replayed for comic effect. Such repetition curbs the ripples of laughter that individual posts, with their rich comment sections, evoke. The "repeat and repeat" of "Man who has it all" both plays with and reiterates a binary: in its realm, men are driven to "testeria" and steal precious "me time" away from housework and for the beauty routines necessary for keeping their wives sexually interested. When read in a bulk, the posts gain a quality of repetition that eventually appears to make little difference. This reverb seems to be different than that of "Congrats, you have an all male panel!," which equally gains its vitality and virality from repetition. Consumed individually, tweets and Facebook posts on manels are considerably much less sticky or affective. In other words, the archival function of Tumblr is quintessential to "Congrats, you have an all male panel!," whereas the appeal of "Man who has it all" is more dependent on the serendipitous trickle of individual posts, some of which strike a nerve and others fail to.

At the same time, with 235,000 Twitter followers and over 440,000 follows to its Facebook page, "Man who has it all" points at how broad and deep its feminist reverb runs. No matter how differently positioned people may be in relation to heterosexist norms and normality, they can easily recognize the dynamics that its twisted mirror displays. The clarity of its gender switch is well attuned with the affective attention economy of social media built on fast reactions, likes, and shares, yet the length of many of the comment threads also speaks of attraction and engagement exceeding the instantaneous and the fleeting. There is stickiness to the binary play catered, while its repetitions afford mundane affective releases within social media feeds.

Feminism as Satirical Fabulation

On its Patreon page, "Man who has it all" is defined as mocking the patriarchy by creating "a wonderful satirical world, where women tell and own the jokes" (Patreon 2019). At least three things are noteworthy here. First, the framework of patriarchy situates the initiative firmly within a binary gender dynamic premised on the politics of patrilinear male domination where women are excluded from the realm of power and are possibly objectified in the process. Second, the initiative is presented as one of feminist world making through women's own jokes, despite the number of followers and commentators with male-presenting user accounts. In this framing, "Man who has it all" becomes a site of fabulation that, like documentary cinema in Ilona Hongisto's (2015, 21) analysis, "can create resistance to actual circumstances and envision new ways of being in the world." For Hongisto (2015, 67), fabulation entails acts of invention, composition, and storytelling through which alternative lives and worlds can be imagined. The participatory fabulation emerging in Twitter and Facebook comment threads speaks of the affective appeal, stickiness, and force that all this may entail.

Third, "Man who has it all" is defined as satire—that is, as a form of humor making use of irony, parody, hyperbole, and ridicule in order to critique the existing state of affairs, often entailing a subversive edge. As an affective genre, satire thus comes with a fair degree of aggression, armed with humor and wit. "Most importantly," Lisa Colletta (2009, 860) argues, "satire's efficacy relies on the ability of the audience to recognize the irony that is at the heart of its humor . . . If the irony is missed, or the better moral standard is also ironically presented as just another construction, then satire is no longer an effective social critique and may even be misunderstood as an example of the very thing it sets out to critique." According to Linda Hutcheon (1985), satire addresses the social world and its norms, whereas parody, as a closely interconnected form of humor, imitates artistic productions or genres. The two seem to intermesh in "Man who has it all," which both presents "facts" about men and also provides elaborate parodies of the repertoires of women's magazines and their genre of how-to tips, as in these select tweets from October–November 2018:

Working husband? How do you stay hydrated? Barry, age 59, "I keep a spare cherry tomato in my hand." Inspirational.

MEN! Is having it all REALLY possible? Kids, wife, work outside the home, a bright complexion, guilty pleasures and soft, silky elbows?

"Man writer" is NOT an offensive term. It is simply a way to differentiate them from good writers. End of story.

TODAY'S FACT: All penises are beautiful, but some are more fashionable than others.

The conflation of sarcasm and parody entails a conflation in the lines of critique, from the social world to the conventions of women's magazines, while the comment threads further blur the lines between the contemporary moment and those of decades past. References to "pantaloons" worn by suffragettes merge with critiques of social media lifestyle tips into a manifold entity that is both layered in its absurdity and seemingly coherent as a construction based on binary gender. In critiquing sexism, "Man who has it all" fabulates an alternative world of reversal and hyperbole that has lightness to it, while individual posts grow heavy and even airless when consumed *en masse*.

Writing on parody, Marta Dynel (2014, 629) argues that "the parodist aims to imitate and poke fun at, ridicule, or mock an individual (an event, or another entity). Therefore, like irony, parody conveys a negative evaluative attitude." This is certainly evident in the tweets addressed above. A similar tactic of parodic reversal and exaggeration is also in use in feminist online initiatives such as *Reductress* (established in 2013), defined as a satirical women's magazine with the mission of taking "on the outdated perspectives and condescending tone of popular women's media, through the eyes of the funniest women in comedy today" (*Reductress* 2019). The mood of *Reductress* is more blunt and angry than that of "Man who has it all," and although its posts are often retweeted, comments remain fewer. Perhaps the most notable difference between these two accounts, despite their similarities, lies less in the narrator—the fictitious "working dad" versus the fictitious editorial team of a woman's magazine—than it does in their degrees of absurdity and the lightness they entail.

In thinking through the differences and similarities between the feminist social media tactics examined in this book, we return to what we proposed in the introduction—the centrality of the absurd in disrupting the operations of binary gender that lend these initiatives with much of their appeal. Both projects discussed in this chapters, in zooming in on the binary operations of gender through repetition and reversal, turn attention away from the diversity among the men gathered in manels and the specificities of white middle-class privilege among "dadpreneurs." At the same time, we argue that absurdity, similarly to surprise-startle in Tomkins's affect theory, resets focus, reroutes attention, and simply renders things ridiculous. As such, it helps to point out the ridiculousness of social hierarchies—possibly for productive, critical effect.

7 Conclusion: Laughter and Networked Absurdism

On February 10, 2019, *The Guardian* tweeted a link to its article "Me and My Vulva: 100 Women Reveal All" on a new book of "vulva portraits" by the photographer Laura Dodsworth. A Twitter user with the first name of Paul commented, "The correct word is vagina." In the active interaction that followed, another user replied with "No it's not. But thanks for the mansplaining on something you obvs know nothing about," provoking Paul to critique this use of the notion of mansplaining, as others enthusiastically chimed in:

That's an incorrect use of the word mansplaining. :-). Not that I want to legitimize the term, but by its own definition it requires more than just having just a man who is explaining something. Even if some in the audience are women.

Never thought I'd see the day when a guy would try to correct women on what to call a part of their body.

It is neither polite nor respectful to correct erroneously how someone refers to their own genitalia.

Vulva was used because it is vulvas that have been photographed and it is vulvas that are being discussed in the article/photography piece. It's that simple. Vagina is not the correct word. Vulva, Paul, vulva.

It's probably best for you not to "correct" someone when they aren't wrong. But to correct you, this is indeed #mansplaining

A physiotherapy PhD responded with an anatomical diagram, and a gynecologist sent a Venn diagram illustrating the difference between a vagina and a vulva. "Paul" responded with five interconnected tweets arguing that the term *vagina*, in its current everyday use, refers to something broader than the strictly anatomical notion and that his empirical claim cannot be countered with expert knowledge in too narrow and technical a manner. The thread grew, fueled by clickbait headlines and Facebook shares as an example of epically failed mansplaining and hilarious feminist trolling, soon attracting some fifteen hundred comments and ironic reaction GIFs. The short-lived viral Twitter incident drew its comic effect from absurdist, theatrical incongruity: a man erroneously yet vigorously and with dogged, grim persistence insisted on the correctness of his own opinion, unfazed by ridicule or alternative views posed by female experts. As an incident of mansplaining, the exchange was rather meta: a man tells women what a vagina means, dictates what terminology is appropriate, and mansplains what *mansplaining* actually means. Soon flaring up into social theater, the incident was absurd and yet pointed to the constant production of gendered hierarchies in knowledge production. Commenters aimed to shame "Paul," who nevertheless refused to be shamed and did not, for example, remove the Twitter thread.

Like many of the other social media incidents addressed in this book, the debate operated fully in a binary gender model: a man mansplains vaginas as others insist that women choose the terms used to describe their genitalia, foregrounding embodied knowledge. In writing this book, we have often felt stuck in a similar gender binary as it reemerges time and time again as a hegemonic understanding or as a frame of intelligibility for thinking about similarity and difference. Dick pics are countered with v-pics; men are called out as assholesonline and manelists; the "Man who has it all" mirrors sexist stereotypes in reverse; women embrace the labels of *sluts, tolerance whores, flower-hat aunties,* and *hags* that are targeted against them; and women mobilize against sexual harassment practiced by men under the #MeToo hashtag that has proved resistant to the experiences of nonfemale identifying, queer, and transgender people. #MeToo seems similarly disconnected from harassment practiced by women, despite such accusations being targeted, for example, against the actor Asia Argento, a key figure within the movement.

Binary gender is a ubiquitous, immensely powerful, and largely taken-for-granted framework for organizing individual, social, and collective lives. As such, it is no laughing matter. Some of the feminist tactics discussed

← **Tweet**

Jennifer Gunter ✓ @DrJenGunter · Feb 10 ⌄
Replying to and @guardian
Hi, I am a gynecologist and an international expert on both the vagina and vulva. These are vulvas. I wrote this post with a handy Venn diagram to help people separate the two! Enjoy 😉

Vulva/Vagina Venn Diagram
I'm sick of people forgetting the poor vulva and referring to everything in the female lower reproductive tract as vagina. To help ...
🔗 drjengunter.com

💬 130   🔁 495   ♡ 4.8K   ⬆️

A Venn diagram illustrating the difference between vulva and vagina in a Twitter thread, February 12, 2019.

in this book are hilarious, others are angry and not very funny at all, yet they all revolve around binary gender as both a point of identification and a logic of critique to the degree that there may seem no way out. Stuckness in binary gender comes with a sinking, claustrophobic feeling that instances of absurdity, in the affective dynamics of surprise and startle that they entail, can momentarily reset. The vagina/vulva Twitter debate, randomly spinning out of control from a newspaper's promotional tweet, is an example of a binary logic gone absurd, allowing for laughter evoked by incongruity, possibly combined with a sense of superiority toward the man being mocked and critiqued. This laughter may also be connected to a sense of relief in that it disrupts the stuckness of mundane gender logic by playing it *ad absurdum* in both serious registers and those of tongue-in-cheek trolling.

To reiterate the issue: once gender is made sense of as a binary involving two opposing and hierarchically differentiated poles, the differences within the categories of women and men become effaced while the differences between them are highlighted. An activist tactic operating within this logic can be efficient in tapping into dynamics and power differentials that are instantaneously recognizable. At the same time, as we have argued throughout this book, it comes with the risk of turning attention away from different ways of acting or doing gender; relating sexually to others; being racialized, exoticized, or comfortably resembling a norm; being singled out or shamed on the basis of body size, shape, ability, or neurodiversity; moving from age and degree of autonomy to another; belonging to political, occupational, religious, or ethnic communities; having a particular level of income; speaking a language; and having citizenship status or political rights.

The reiteration of binary gender in the social media tactics we address gets repeatedly mapped onto and articulated through normative whiteness, in particular. White subjects are foregrounded in discussions on #MeToo in North America and Europe, rendering opaque other social differences contributing to harassment and violence. The "Man who has it all" is white and middle-class as he emulates the model subject of women's magazines. Hannah Gadsby's zeitgeist standup comedy is butch lesbian but also white. SlutWalks tend to be attended by those who are afforded respectability—mostly white and middle-class young women (Skeggs 1997)—while Stormy Daniels's tactic of shamelessness comes embedded in whiteness, sexual desirability, occupational and financial success, and celebrity status.

Laughter is a means of bringing bodies together and pulling them apart depending on what or who is the butt of the joke, who finds things funny, and who gets to tell the joke. Laughing at, with, or along creates lines of connection and disconnection that may contribute to or be drawn in accordance with affective homophily—the love of feeling the same. This, however, does not apply to absurdity, the form of humor foregrounded in this book. For us, absurd instances are the ones that afford the most joy and affective release precisely due to the unpredictability and surprise that they entail. By turning things nonsensical, absurd humor refuses to operate within a preset logic, whether one of binary gender, heteronormativity, or something else. There is volatile vibrancy to the absurd, and as we have argued, it can function similarly to the resetting affect of startle-surprise in Silvan Tomkins's conceptualization as a rupture that brings forth a change in focus, attention, or affective state and that can tilt toward positive, negative, or ambiguous intensities. Our book can be read as an answer to Sarah Kember's (2015) call for an antagonistic feminist political theory of humor—one based on rebellious laughter in the face of ridicule within sexist social media theaters of the absurd. Such laughter is not merely reactive and does not merely assert what was previously critiqued or negated. Instead, it is about letting bodies experience the force of ambivalence. As Kember (2015, 117) puts it, "laughter is, more specifically, antagonism in action, a tension un-held, ex-pressed in the space-time of the laugh."

Online humor is rife with absurdism, including the most popular videos of the social media app, TikTok, and a broad range of quirky memes and animated GIFs. Writing for *The Medium*, Megan Hoins (2016) characterizes such humor as specific to millennials and as drawing from the legacy of dadaism: "This generation is fueled by a similar desire to that of the Dadaists: to address the disillusionment of our generation in relation to all of the current events we are witnessing, particularly within the United States." In this framing, absurdism, as "deliberate confusion and nonsense," becomes an aesthetic expressive of the woke generation: "Past generations have enjoyed family sitcoms as their sources for humor, for example, implicitly identifying their cultural values as having to do with family and spending time with them to connect and form lasting bonds. The millennial generation, in contrast, enjoys the absurd and the weird, implying that they may value the willingness to profess one's viewpoint, or perhaps the ironic or satiric approach to viewing life and the problems we all face on a daily basis" (Hoins 2016). We remain highly resistant to such a simplified account of generation, humor, and critical outlook. Furthermore, our interest in the absurd is situated within the much more specific political context of resistance to sexism—from its mundane, routine forms to the aggressive edges and violent flares of misogynistic hate. Within such contexts, instances of nonsense are much less expressions of nihilism or cynicism than openings for critical distance and affective rerouting.

In studies of humor operating within an easy gender binary, women have been seen to enjoy absurd jokes, and men have had a preference for hostile humor. In summing up some of these findings, Helga Kotthoff (2006, 15) argues that "absurd humor threatens no one"—possibly since the butt of its joke is by no means easy to identify. We, again, are much less willing to make such a claim, arguing instead that the unpredictability of absurdity invests it with volatility and energy that can come across as threatening as it refuses and makes fun of the assumedly self-evident state of the social world. Absurdity is a tactic for rupturing things and opening them up. It is not easily aligned with the heavy, lingering stickiness of shame in that it turns things around, inside-out and upside down, without being confined to the affective dynamics from which it emerges.

Back to the Future?

> Things look different after #MeToo. And not just after #MeToo, but after several years of a surging fourth wave of feminism. There has been fury against patriarchy—with the term itself, after decades of dormancy, surging back into use to explain everything from the rise of Donald Trump to sexual violence in India to pay inequality in western Europe.
>
> Everywhere, dams of silence and fear are bursting, as women speak out about wrongs committed by men whose powerful positions once rendered them unassailable. Women have also rewritten the private stories they have told themselves (or buried) about their lives, from family relationships to workplace troubles to sexual encounters. In this atmosphere of revisionism, new stories have been needed. Kristen Roupenian's "Cat Person," published at the end of 2017 in *The New Yorker*, owed its viral success to a wave of recognition from female readers. It told a story about dating and sex that seemed intensely true but, till then, barely told.

In this excerpt from her *Guardian* article, the journalist Charlotte Higgins (2019) identifies #MeToo as a watershed moment that revitalized feminist activism, allowing for women's experiences and resentments to be voiced and heard and inspiring a return to the feminist concepts and concerns of decades past. The notion of patriarchy, as evoked here, refers to a system of domination where men hold political and religious power and authority over women, and, as an ideology, it naturalizes these inequalities. The concept remained virtually absent from feminist terminology for two decades, having been broadly critiqued as ahistorical, generalizing, and not allowing for contextual nuance across time and space (see Walby 1989). As Vrushali Patil (2013, 847) points out, patriarchy results in and represents "homogenous, monolithic accounts of gender oppression." Patriarchy has nevertheless made a high-profile comeback as common shorthand for gendered inequalities on personal, social, and political levels—in academia, activism, and beyond.

As the reemergence of the notion of patriarchy suggests, movements such as #MeToo witness a return of sorts to 1970s feminist tactics that highlight women's shared experiences, collectivity, and even separatism in ways that efface differences within the category of women. This is the case despite the centrality of inclusive and intersectional understandings of gender, sexuality, and difference in contemporary feminist theory and activism. In fact, although the feminism involved in the initiatives discussed in this book may be "fourth wave," its tactics bear an uncanny resemblance to those of the second. Clare Hemmings (2011) argues that stories of feminism's recent past are easily cast as stories of progress, loss, or return. As we argue in chapter 2, the wave metaphor is a powerful narrative device in shaping such stories of progress and loss in particular, but it is less effective for showing how multiple stories may run in parallel or overlap (as the past perhaps becomes a wave that folds back on or breaks into the present). Similarly, although queer theory—as something that destabilizes identities, norms, and normalcy—has played a key part in academic feminist work for three decades, many of these social media initiatives build on heteronormativity.

Jack Halberstam (2016) addresses the question of generations, as broadly connected to the waves of feminism, through the forms and presence of humor, arguing that "Recent controversies within queer communities around language, slang, satirical or ironic representation and perceptions of harm or offense have created much controversy with very little humor recently, leading to demands for bans, censorship and name changes." Halberstam sketches out a trajectory from 1970s cultural feminism and lesbian separatism characterized by the perpetual presence of hurt and trauma resulting in "a messy, unappealing morass of weepy, hypo-allergic, psychosomatic, anti-sex, anti-fun, anti-porn, pro-drama, pro-processing postpolitical subjects." This is contrasted with the 1990s where "weepy white lady feminism gave way to reveal a multiracial, poststructuralist, intersectional feminism of much longer provenance" and where "people began to laugh." Finally, Halberstam seems to argue that members of the current younger generation are returning to weepiness in their willing readiness to take offense. This also involves a focus on language that highlights its

potential to shame and offend over the possibilities of linguistic appropriation as a tactic of resistance. For Halberstam, the issue boils down to
snowflakes who are "too vulnerable to take a joke, too damaged to make
one." Despite the seduction of this story about how ready offense springs
from and reproduces a default fragility of the self, we would like to propose
a slightly different take on humor and generation.

Radical and cultural feminisms were certainly concerned with experiences of trauma and harm, yet they were not void of humor. Humor was
a tactic of intervention in the 1968 "No More Miss America" protest in
Atlantic City, where, in an act of ironic parody, a sheep was crowned as
beauty queen; in the theatrical activities of the organization Women's
International Terrorist Conspiracy from Hell (aka W.I.T.C.H.) since the late
1960s; and in Mary Daly's elaborate gynocentric reworking of the English
language. Meanwhile, SlutWalks are organized and attended by people in
their twenties who are completely capable of playing with offensive language. Seriousness connected to offense, hurt, and anger can be seen as an
affective dynamic that drives and fuels activist projects across decades and
generations. #MeToo is a ready contemporary example of such affective
homophily. This, however, is not the whole story, for absurdity and affective heterophily equally contribute to the dynamics of surprise and possibly
even to those of startle.

Rather than discussing such differences in feminist politics in terms of
"waves" or "generations," it is more productive to frame them through
overlapping and at times contradictory temporalities. Hemmings (2011,
132) recognizes how there commonly is "a feminist desire to distance ourselves from uses of gender or feminism within which we do not recognise
ourselves . . . and in so doing [we are] likely to miss important points of
overlap that link a range of narratives about the feminist past and present."
These moments of misrecognition have provided us with productive analytical friction as we have distanced ourselves from some of the current
tendencies in networked digital feminism. Then again, this may also mean
that we overlook valuable moments of overlap that tie together different
timelines. The history of feminist theory and practice is hardly a linear
story. It consists instead of parallel and sometimes anachronistic timelines
better understood as modes of turning to the past in order to make sense of
the present and for reimagining the future. This is evident in the contemporary takes on vaginal imagery harking back to 1970s feminist cunt art

(as discussed in chapter 4) and in tactics of linguistic appropriation where hags make their comeback as feminist figures (chapter 5). As discussed in chapters 2 and 3, the tactics of making the personal political loudly resonate with second-wave feminist activism and consciousness raising. In considering both the complexity of contemporary networked media environments and the diverse scales and shapes that feminist initiatives take, it would nevertheless be erroneous to consider them simply as variations of the same. The current feminist uses of *slut*, *whore*, and *hag* also bring something new to the table in the sexual agencies they address, in the refusal of confining to the rules of shame that they communicate, and in the sociotechnical assemblages that they operate as.

Rhythms of Laughter

The social media projects discussed in this book return back to and create variations of past feminist tactics, remaking them as networked, affective publics on social media platforms dependent on their social and technological affordances, rhythms, and modes of engagement. These rhythms are generally fast as user attention gets geared toward the trending and the most novel. An amusing post may not amuse twice, just as a news item grows old in the course of its reading. Flame wars, offenses, and memes all have limited, generally short lifespans because the affective intensities driving them flare up and fade. Pew Research Center's analysis of the 19 million English-language tweets using the hashtag #MeToo between October 2017 and September 2018 illustrates the oscillations in intensity, as implied by the volume of tweets. Harvey Weinstein's resignation from the board of his company, *Time* magazine's Person of the Year article focusing on #MeToo, the Golden Globes, International Women's Day, Leslie Moonves's resignation from his executive position at CBS, and Brett Kavanaugh's and Christine Blasey Ford's hearings in the US Senate all mark peaks in hashtag activity. There was an average of 55,319 tweets per day using the hashtag during the period analyzed, but the number jumped past 800,000 as the news on Moonves broke (Anderson and Toor 2018).

As Zizi Papacharissi (2016) points out, the viral speeds of social media may not be compatible with the much slower tempo of social transformation: social change is gradual and possibly frustratingly slow. Kaarina Nikunen (2019, 3) similarly argues that affective energy mobilized through media "does not necessarily lead to significant social change" as its intensities fade away. For Nikunen (2019, 5), the issue is one of sustainability as "ideas, forms, and productions that last and that can be created in a fair way with practices of listening and cooperation." Affective publics and social media campaigns and movements are not necessarily sustainable in this sense: in addition to activities fizzling out after the initial heat precipitates, the platforms on which they operate can change their content policies (for example, by banning sexual content as Tumblr did), content may simply disappear (in 2019, MySpace reported it lost or removed all data uploaded before 2016), and services can simply be closed down (as happened with the Twitter-owned Vine in 2017). In such instances, archives disappear, and social connections established through user names and other aliases become severed, possibly permanently so. Commercial social media platforms are precarious bases for social activism and cultural resistance. It can be argued that these platforms—which are geared toward monetary profit in the data economy they operate in and impacting users' possible ways of acting—cannot be sustainable in the sense discussed by Nikunen.

All social media initiatives are bound up in the speeds of online attention economy, yet they involve different temporalities and rhythms. Both Instagram and Tumblr allow for the creation of accumulating galleries where creative projects (such as Stephanie Sarley's "Crotch Monsters") coexist with the public display of online harassment and hate (as in the case of @byefelipe and @assholesonline). Over time, such galleries grow in bulk and gravity, some of them becoming phenomena in themselves. As discussed in the context of "Congrats, you have an all male panel!," the archival functions of a Tumblr blog afford a sense of repetition, both astonishing and numbing, that helps to connect individual images of manels into a cross-cultural spectacle of gender exclusion. Although tweets remain available unless deliberately removed, they are buried low in the linearity of a feed or a profile. The same applies to Facebook, where the newest and the most popular content gets seen first and selectively. Heated exchanges, such as those connected to the terminology of vulvas and vaginas, remain accessible but are also soon forgotten because the platforms' dynamics are driven by nuggets of novelty catered as a perpetual, steady flow. A Facebook event, such as "Shameless Extinction," is temporarily bound, while closed and secret groups facilitate slower, long-term exchanges and community building. An initiative operating as a Facebook, Twitter, or Instagram account remains present to its followers as posts sprinkled in news feeds, fighting for attention with sponsored content, advertising, updates, and shared links. Projects gain visibility through likes, comments, and shares, occasionally expanding into a social theater.

The heated waves of #MeToo are good business for Twitter and Facebook, just as hate campaigns fuel the exchange and circulation of data that is key to value generation in social media. As Alison Harvey points out, "Hate—like sex—sells, and that is not a problem when those who are hurt are those who have always suffered in capitalism . . . intensification and expansion of hate online, as with #GamerGate, is revealed to be not a problem but a profitable development for those who manage the software and services designed to police online vitriol in light of legal limitations" (in Shepherd et al. 2015, 5). Hate fits in and helps to generate value within the online attention economy. Tactics of feminist resistance operate under the same rules and constraints.

A Politics of Pleasure and Difference

In exploring a range of feminist social media tactics, we have engaged with what Carrie Rentschler and Samantha Thrift (2015) call "networked laughter" as something that refuels contemporary forms of feminist critique and political agency. We have investigated how ripples of laughter intensify digital connectivity and how the experience of laughing together—even if physically apart—pulls bodies closer together. But we have also analyzed how the contagious qualities of the cheeky, derisive laugh draw lines between those who are "like us" and those who are not. How those lines are drawn vary, and yet in the context of viral feminist tactics operating within a default framework of whiteness and heterosexuality, it is much easier for some to laugh than it is for others. Along the lines of a networked logic of affective homophily, of being interlinked through a love of feeling the same, a feminist "we" is formed in both powerful and particular ways. Networked laughter may electrify connections while cutting off power elsewhere, forging a blank disconnect. Feminist solidarity and the joy of "having a good laugh" are thus differently distributed on social media platforms, invoking a pleasure of recognition while fostering exclusion. We have contrasted such bonds of affective similarity with a different kind of pleasure tied to the more unpredictable terrain of feminist absurdism, which by indulging in the illogical and the inappropriate risks disrupting a sociality based on sameness.

The politics of joy and pleasure seem to have recently made a comeback within feminist theory and practice. In *Radical Happiness: Moments of Collective Joy*, Lynne Segal (2018) writes about what she sees as the lost art of "radical happiness," an antidote to both individualist isolation and public feelings of pain and sadness. Against the backdrop of her experiences of the 1970s women's movement, this radical happiness is deeply linked to the pleasure of collective joy, a transformative sense of being part of a political movement within which the future can be imagined otherwise. "Such joy may be fleeting," she argues, but "sometimes, the strength, confidence and sense of purpose we gain from moments of joyful solidarity lasts a very long time" (Segal 2018, 260). Even if something like #MeToo is not primarily a movement based on a joyful solidarity (but rather based on outrage, anger, pain, and sadness), there can doubtlessly be a discernible joy in coming together in this way, in the sense of direction and gravity of the moment. Such joy stems not from the root cause of the action but from the shared experience of taking action.

In a more popular call for pleasure and joy in politics, or pleasure *as* politics, adrienne maree brown's *Pleasure Activism: The Politics of Feeling Good* (2019, 3) turns our attention to how pleasure may be essential to social justice since pleasure, as she puts it, "is a measure of freedom." Building on a black feminist tradition and on Audre Lorde's 1978 essay "Uses of the Erotic," in particular, brown urges her readers to make happiness, joy, and desire central in organizing against oppression and provides a range of embodied tactics that make pleasure a central practice of liberation. Throughout the book, she provides assignments that invite the reader to explore erotic and emotional possibilities, such as exercises in masturbation, taking sexy selfies, or negotiating sexual consent. She also emphasizes the many ways in which people of color, sex workers, and queer, trans, and nonbinary people have been denied joy and the reasons it is necessary to focus on their pleasure as a principle of political organization and mobilization.

Our book similarly links the joy and pleasure of laughter to the realm of feminist politics, as pleasure of laughing at power, at inequality, at injustice. The darker the overall political climate turns, the more necessary it is to provide spaces for shared laughter, as a mode of survival. Then again, such politics of feeling good together may not be as liberating as they first might seem because some will feel better and laugh harder than others. And as we have showed, to laugh is not merely a joyful or pleasurable experience. In our focus on the affective volatility of absurdist humor and laughter, we emphasize the political potential in networked laughter to feel differently together. As remedy to affective homophily, or uniformity of feeling as a way of feeling good together, affective heterophily allows for degrees of freedom in feeling differently. When feminist communities are construed only around similarity in opinion (are you the right kind of feminist?) and similarity in feeling (are you feeling the right kind of feminist feelings?), our spaces shrink as we run out of air. The kind of laughter that disrupts the dividing lines of these communities is risky because it may disrupt the sociality on which these spaces build: it may well offend. But such disruptions are also vital in that they make room for curiosity and difference by centering affective ambivalence. Our networked feminist absurdism builds a politics and a critique that is not merely reactive but, by shamelessly playing up the nonsensical along with the unseemly, reimagines feminist world making.

References

Adut, Ari. 2008. *On Scandal: Moral Disturbances in Society, Politics, and Art*. New York: Cambridge University Press.

Ahmed, Sara. 2001. "The Organisation of Hate." *Law and Critique* 12(3): 345–365.

Ahmed, Sara. 2004. *The Cultural Politics of Emotion*. Edinburgh: Edinburgh University Press.

Ahmed, Sara. 2010. *The Promise of Happiness*. Durham: Duke University Press.

Ahmed, Sara. 2015. "Introduction: Sexism—A Problem with a Name." *New Formations* 86: 5–13.

Almestad, Elin Grelsson. 2016. "Att hagga sig ur kvinnofällan." Sveriges Radio, September 26. http://sverigesradio.se/sida/avsnitt/794894?programid=503.

Amnesty Finland. n.d. "Suvakkihuora-paita." http://www.amnestystore.fi/product/360/suvakkihuora-paita-kapea-malli.

Anderson, Christina. 2018. "In Nobel Scandal, a Man Is Accused of Sexual Misconduct. A Woman Takes the Fall." *New York Times*, April 12. https://www.nytimes.com/2018/04/12/world/europe/sara-danius-swedish-nobel-scandal.html.

Anderson, Monica, and Skye Toor. 2018. "How Social Media Users Have Discussed Sexual Harassment since #MeToo Went Viral." Pew Research Center, October 11. http://www.pewresearch.org/fact-tank/2018/10/11/how-social-media-users-have-discussed-sexual-harassment-since-metoo-went-viral.

Antonakis-Nashif, Anna. 2015. "Hashtagging the Invisible: Bringing Private Experiences into Public Debate: An #outcry against Sexism in Germany." In *#Hashtag Publics: The Power and Politics of Discursive Networks*, edited by Nathan Rambukkana, 101–114. New York: Peter Lang.

Apostolidis, Paul, and Juliet A. Williams. 2004. "Introduction: Sex Scandals and Discourses of Power." In *Public Affairs: Politics in the Age of Sex Scandals*, edited by Paul Apostolidis and Juliet A. Williams, 1–35. Durham: Duke University Press.

Atmore, Chris. 1999. "Victims, Backlash, and Radical Feminist Theory (or, The Morning after They Stole Feminism's Fire)." In *New Versions of Victims: Feminists Struggle with the Concept*, edited by Sharon Lamb, 183–212. New York: New York University Press.

Bailey, Moya, Sarah Jackson, and Brooke Foucault Welles. 2019. "Women Tweet on Violence: From #YesAllWomen to #MeToo." *Ada: A Journal of Gender, New Media, and Technology* 15. https://adanewmedia.org/2019/02/issue15-bailey-jackson-welles.

Bakhtin, Mikhail. 1984/1968. *Rabelais and His World*. Cambridge: MIT Press.

Banet-Weiser, Sarah. 2018. *Empowered: Popular Feminism and Popular Misogyny*. Durham: Duke University Press.

Barreca, Regina, ed. 1988. *Last Laughs: Perspectives on Women and Comedy*. New York: Gordon and Breach.

Bauer, Susan Wise. 2008. *The Art of the Public Grovel: Sexual Sin and Public Confession in America*. Princeton: Princeton University Press.

Bennett, Jessica. 2017. "With Her App, Women Are in Control." *New York Times*, March 18. https://www.nytimes.com/2017/03/18/fashion/bumble-feminist-dating -app-whitney-wolfe.html.

Berg, Aase. 2015. *Hackers*. Stockholm: Albert Bonniers Förlag.

Berg, Aase. 2019. *Haggan*. Stockholm: Aberg Bonniers Förlag.

Bergson, Henri. 1999/1911. *Laughter: An Essay on the Meaning of the Comic*. Translated by Cloudesley Brereton and Fred Rothwell. New York: Macmillan.

Berlant, Lauren. 2017. "Humorlessness (Three Monologues and a Hair Piece)." *Critical Inquiry* 43(2): 305–340.

Berlant, Laurent, and Sianne Ngai. 2017. "Comedy Has Issues." *Critical Inquiry* 43(2): 233–249.

Bianchi, Claudia. 2014. "Slurs and Appropriation: An Echoic Account." *Journal of Pragmatics* 66(1): 35–44.

Bivens, Rena, and Anna Shah Hoque. 2018. "Programming Sex, Gender, and Sexuality: Infrastructural Failures in the 'Feminist' Dating App Bumble." *Canadian Journal of Communication* 43(3): 441–459.

Bobker, Danielle. 2017. "Towards a Humor Positive Feminism: Lessons from the Sex Wars." *Los Angeles Review of Books*, December 17. https://lareviewofbooks.org/article/ toward-humor-positive-feminism-lessons-sex-wars.

Boler, Megan, ed. 2008a. *Digital Media and Democracy: Tactics in Hard Times*. Cambridge, MA: MIT Press.

Boler, Megan. 2008b. "Introduction." In *Digital Media and Democracy: Tactics in Hard Times*, edited by Megan Boler, 1–50. Cambridge, MA: MIT Press.

Bonello Rutter Giappone, Krista, Fred Francis, and Iain MacKenzie, eds. 2018. *Comedy and Critical Thought: Laughter as Resistance*. London: Rowman & Littlefield.

Bore, Inger-Lise Kalviknes, Anne Graefer, and Allaina Kilby. 2017. "This Pussy Grabs Back: Humour, Digital Affects and Women's Protest." *Open Cultural Studies* 1: 529–540.

Börjesson, Robert, and Karolina Skoglund. 2018. "Test av semlor och 'Gittan'— Så har Danius stil splittrat ledamöterna i Akademien!" *Expressen*, April 11. https://www.expressen.se/nyheter/det-tuffa-spelet-bakom-kriget-i-svenska-akademien.

Borrelli-Persson, Laird. 2018. "From the U.S. Presidential Race to Sweden's Literature Nobel Prize Organization: The Politicization of the Pussy Bow." *Vogue*, April 18. https://www.vogue.com/article/pussy-bow-symbol-political-protest-from-melania -trump-to-sara-danius.

Boryczka, Jocelyn M. 2017. "An Anatomy of Sexism: The Colonized Vagina." *New Political Science* 39(1): 36–57.

Bouson, J. Brooks. 2009. *Embodied Shame: Uncovering Female Shame in Contemporary Women's Writings*. New York: SUNY Press.

Boyd, Kealey. 2018. "Hannah Gadsby's Exquisite Performance in Calling Out Artists Who Abuse Their Power." *Hyperallergic*, August 16. https://hyperallergic.com/ 455340/hannah-gadsbys-exquisite-performance-in-calling-out-artists-who-abuse -their-power.

Boyle, Bridget. 2015. "Take Me Seriously. Now Laugh at Me! How Gender Influences the Creation of Contemporary Physical Comedy." *Comedy Studies* 6(1): 78–90.

Boyle, Karen. 2019. *#MeToo, Weinstein and Feminism*. London: Palgrave.

Brontsema, Robin. 2004. "A Queer Revolution: Reconceptualizing the Debate over Linguistic Reclamation." *Colorado Research in Linguistics* 17(1). http://citeseerx.ist.psu .edu/viewdoc/download?doi=10.1.1.582.8182&rep=rep1&type=pdf.

Broude, Norma, and Mary D. Garrard. 1994. "Introduction: Feminism and Art in the Twentieth Century." In *The Power of Feminist Art: The American Movement of the 1970s, History and Impact*, edited by Norma Broude and Mary D. Garrard, 10–29. New York: Abrams.

brown, adrienne maree. 2019. *Pleasure Activism: The Politics of Feeling Good*. Chico: AK Press.

Brown, Melissa, Rashawn Ray, Ed Summers, and Neil Fraistat. 2016. "#SayHerName: A Case Study of Intersectional Social Media Activism." *Ethnic and Racial Studies* 40(11): 1831–1846.

Bruns, Axel, and Jean Burgess. 2015. "Twitter Hashtags from Ad Hoc to Calculated Publics." In *#Hashtag Publics: The Power and Politics of Discursive Networks*, edited by Nathan Rambukkana, 13–28. New York: Peter Lang.

Burrus, Virginia. 2008. *Saving Shame: Martyrs, Saints, and Other Abject Subjects*. Philadelphia: University of Pennsylvania Press.

Butler, Judith. 1997. *Excitable Speech: A Politics of the Performative*. London: Routledge.

Butler, Judith. 1999. *Gender Trouble: Feminism and the Subversion of Identity*. New Edition. New York: Routledge.

Chakraborty, Arpita. 2019. "Politics of #LoSha: Using Naming and Shaming as a Feminist Tool on Facebook." In *Gender Hate Online: Understanding the New Anti-Feminism*, edited by Debbie Ging and Eigenia Siapera, 195–212. London: Palgrave.

Chamberlain, Prudence. 2017. *The Feminist Fourth Wave: Affective Temporality*. New York: Springer.

Chen, Mel Y. 2012. *Animacies: Biopolitics, Racial Mattering, and Queer Affect*. Durham: Duke University Press.

Chicago, Judy. 1996. *The Dinner Party*. London: Penguin.

Cho, Alexander. 2015. "Queer Reverb: Tumblr, Affect, Time." In *Networked Affect*, edited by Ken Hillis, Susanna Paasonen, and Michael Petit, 43–57. Cambridge, MA: MIT Press.

Cho, Alexander. 2018. "Default Publicness: Queer Youth of Color, Social Media, and Being Outed by the Machine." *New Media & Society* 20(9): 3183–3200.

Chun, Wendy Hui Kyong. 2016. *Updating to Remain the Same: Habitual New Media*. Cambridge, MA: MIT Press.

Chun, Wendy Hui Kyong. 2018. "Queering Homophily." In *Pattern Discrimination*, edited by Clemens Apprich, Wendy Hui Kyong Chun, Florian Cramer, and Hito Steyerl, 59–97. Minneapolis: Meson Press.

Cixous, Hélène. 1975. "Le rire de la Méduse." *L'arc* 61: 39–54.

Claeson, Linnéa. 2017. "Det är inte sex som står i fokus—Det är makt." *Aftonbladet*, August 26. https://www.aftonbladet.se/nyheter/kolumnister/a/wW3aA/det-ar-inte -sex-som-star-i-fokus-det-ar-makt.

Claeson, Linnéa. 2019. "Feminismen står inte och faller med mig." *Göteborgs-Posten*, November 21. https://www.gp.se/kultur/kultur/linnéa-claeson-feminismen-står-inte -och-faller-med-mig-1.20629629.

Clark, Rosemary. 2016. "'Hope in a Hashtag': The Discursive Activism of #WhyIStayed." *Feminist Media Studies* 16(5): 788–804.

Collectif. 2018. "Nous défendons une liberté d'importuner, indispensable à la liberté sexuelle." *Le Monde*, January 8. http://www.lemonde.fr/idees/article/2018/01/09/ nous-defendons-une-liberte-d-importuner-indispensable-a-la-liberte-sexuelle _5239134_3232.html.

Colletta, Lisa. 2009. "Political Satire and Postmodern Irony in the Age of Stephen Colbert and Jon Stewart." *Journal of Popular Culture* 42(5): 856–874.

Collins, Patricia Hill. 1990. *Black Feminist Thought: Knowledge, Consciousness, and the Politics of Empowerment*. Boston: Unwin Hyman.

Collins, Patricia Hill, and Sirma Bilge. 2016. *Intersectionality*. Cambridge: Polity.

Condon, Stephanie. 2010. "Former Porn Star Stormy Daniels: I'm a Republican." *CBS News*, April 6. https://www.cbsnews.com/news/former-porn-star-stormy-daniels -im-a-republican.

Consalvo, Mia. 2012. "Confronting Toxic Gamer Culture: A Challenge for Feminist Game Studies Scholars." *Ada: A Journal of Gender, New Media & Technology* 1(1). http://adanewmedia.org/2012/11/issue1-consalvo/?utm_source=rss&utm_medium =rss&utm_campaign=issue1-consalvo.

Crellin, Olivia. 2015. "Only Men at Your Event? This Blog Will Shame You." *BBC Trending*, May 27. https://www.bbc.com/news/blogs-trending-32789580.

Crenshaw, Kimberle. 1991. "Mapping the Margins: Intersectionality, Identity Politics, and Violence against Women of Color." *Stanford Law Review* 43(6): 1241–1299.

Dahl, Ulrika. 2014. *Skamgrepp: Femme-inistiska essäer*. Stockholm: Leopard förlag.

Dahl, Ulrika, Marianne Liljeström, and Ulla Manns. 2016. *The Geopolitics of Nordic and Russian Gender Research 1975–2005*. Huddinge: Södertörn University. http://urn .kb.se/resolve?urn=urn:nbn:se:sh:diva-30844.

Daly, Mary. 1990/1978. *Gyn/Ecology: The Metaethics of Radical Feminism*. Boston: Beacon Press.

Daly, Mary. 1994/1987. *Webster's First Intergalactic Wickedary of the English Language*. New York: HarperCollins.

Dean, Jodi. 2010. *Blog Theory: Feedback and Capture in the Circuits of Drive*. Cambridge: Polity.

Debord, Guy. 1967. *La société du spectacle*. Paris: Buchet-Chastel.

de Certeau, Michel. 2002/1984. *The Practice of Everyday Life*. Translated by Steven Rendall. Berkeley: University of California Press.

de la Cretaz, Britni. 2015. "When Women Send Unsolicited Naked Pictures, It Isn't Revenge: It's Harassment." *Washington Post*, December 1. https://www.washingtonpost

.com/news/soloish/wp/2015/12/01/when-women-send-unsolicited-naked-pictures
-it-isnt-revenge-its-harassment/?utm_term=.ed4388e39bad.

DiAngelo, Robin. 2011. "White Fragility." *International Journal of Critical Pedagogy* 3(3): 54–70.

DiAngelo, Robin. 2018. *White Fragility: Why It's So Hard for White People to Talk about Racism*. Boston: Beacon Press.

DiDomizio, Nicolas. 2016. "This Artist Is Fighting Unsolicited Dick Pics with Sassy, Smoking Vaginas on Instagram." *Mic*, March 17. https://mic.com/articles/138198/this-artist-is-fighting-unsolicited-dick-pics-with-sassy-smoking-vaginas-on-instagram#.uKmqmbffY.

Di Leo, Jeffrey R. 2018. "Philosophy without Apologies." *American Book Review* 39(6): 2.

Dobson, Amy Shields. 2014. "Laddishness Online: The Possible Significations and Significance of 'Performative Shamelessness' for Young Women in the Post-Feminist Context." *Cultural Studies* 28(1): 142–164.

Dobson, Amy Shields. 2013. "Performative Shamelessness on Young Women's Social Network Sites: Shielding the Self and Resisting Gender Melancholia." *Feminism & Psychology* 24(1): 97–114.

Dolezal, Luna. 2015. *The Body and Shame: Phenomenology, Feminism, and the Socially Shaped Body*. Lanham: Lexington Books.

Donegan, Moira. 2018. "The Comedian Forcing Standup to Confront the #MeToo Era." *The New Yorker*, June 28. https://www.newyorker.com/culture/culture-desk/the-comedian-forcing-stand-up-to-confront-the-metoo-era.

Dragotto, Francesca, Elisa Giomi, and Sonia Melchiorre. 2020. "Putting Women Back in Their Place: Reflections on Slut Shaming, the Case of Asia Argento and Twitter in Italy." *International Review of Sociology* 30(1): 46–70.

Dry, Jude. 2018. "'Nanette': Why Everyone Is Talking about Hannah Gadsby's Netflix Comedy Special." *IndieWire*, July 6. https://www.indiewire.com/2018/07/nanette-netflix-hannah-gadsby-lesbian-comedy-1201981484.

Duff, Seamus. 2017. "Harvey Weinstein 'Almost Died after Gastric Band Failed at Naomi Campbell's Party—and Was Nicknamed The Pig,' Ex Driver Reveals." *Mirror*, October 22. https://www.mirror.co.uk/3am/celebrity-news/harvey-weinsteins-ex-driver-recalls-11387121.

Dynel, Marta. 2014. "Isn't It Ironic? Defining the Scope of Humorous Irony." *Humor* 27(4): 619–639.

Eglington, James. 2018. "A 'New Puritanism'?" *ABC*, March 20. http://www.abc.net.au/religion/articles/2018/03/02/4811225.htm.

Elrick, Kathy. 2016. "Ironic Feminism: Rhetorical Critique in Satirical News." PhD diss., Clemson University. http://tigerprints.clemson.edu/all_dissertations/1847.

Enck, Suzanne Marie. 2018. "Accountability Amidst the 'Me Too' Reckoning: Kevin Spacey's Homopatriarchal Apologia." *QED: A Journal in GLBTQ Worldmaking* 5(2):80–86.

Fessenden, Tracy, Nicholas F. Radel, and Magdalena J. Zaborowska, eds. 2001. *The Puritan Origins of American Sex: Religion, Sexuality, and National Identity in America Literature*. New York: Routledge.

Fink, Marty, and Quinn Miller. 2014. "Trans Media Moments: Tumblr, 2011–2013." *Television & New Media* 15(7): 611–626.

Finney, Gail, ed. 1994. *Look Who's Laughing: Gender and Comedy*. Amsterdam: Gordon and Breach.

Flanagan, Caitlin. 2018. "The Humiliation of Aziz Ansari." *The Atlantic*, January 14. https://www.theatlantic.com/entertainment/archive/2018/01/the-humiliation-of -aziz-ansari/550541.

Flaxman, Seth, Sharad Goel, and Justin M. Rao. 2016. "Filter Bubbles, Echo Chambers, and Online News Consumption." *Public Opinion Quarterly* 80(1): 298–320.

Frank, Priscilla. 2016. "You Can Start a Small Revolution Just by Drawing a Vagina (NSFW)." *Huffington Post*, March 16. https://www.huffingtonpost.com/entry/ stephanie-sarley-vagina-drawings_us_56e8912fe4b0860f99dae1a2.

Freud, Sigmund. 1960/1905. *Jokes and Their Relation to the Unconscious*. Volume 8 of *The Standard Edition of the Complete Psychological of the Works of Sigmund Freud*. Translated and edited by James Strachey. London: Hogarth Press.

Gajanan, Mahita. 2018. "How Hannah Gadsby Channeled Her Own Trauma, Bill Cosby and Monica Lewinsky in the New Netflix Comedy Special *Nanette*." *Time*, June 18. http://time.com/5313575/hannah-gadsby-nanette-metoo.

Gemzöe, Lena, 2018. "Solidarity in Head-Scarf and Pussy Bow Blouse: Reflections on Feminist Activism and Knowledge Production." *Social Inclusion* 6(4): 67–81.

Gilbert, Joanne R. 2004. *Performing Marginality: Humor, Gender, and Cultural Critique*. Detroit: Wayne State University Press.

Gill, Rosalind, and Shani Orgad. 2018. "The Shifting Terrain of Sex and Power: From the 'Sexualization of Culture' to #MeToo." *Sexualities* 21(8): 1313–1132.

Goffman, Erving. 1956. "Embarrassment and Social Organization." *American Journal of Sociology* 62(3): 264–271.

Gray, Frances. 1994. *Women and Laughter*. Charlottesville: University Press of Virginia.

Griffith, James D., Sharon Mitchell, Christian L. Hart, Lea T. Adams, and Lucy L. Gu. 2013. "Pornography Actresses: An Assessment of the Damaged Goods Hypothesis." *Journal of Sex Research* 50(7): 621–632.

Groshek, Jacob, and Karolina Koc-Michalska. 2017. "Helping Populism Win? Social Media Use, Filter Bubbles, and Support for Populist Presidential Candidates in the 2016 US Presidential Election." *Information, Communication & Society* 20(9): 1389–1407.

Grosz, Elizabeth.1995. *Space, Time, Perversion*. London: Routledge.

Guha, Pallavi, Radhika Gajjala, and Carole Stabile. 2019. "Introduction: Sexual Violence, Social Movements, and Social Media." *Ada: A Journal of Gender, New Media, and Technology* 15. https://adanewmedia.org/2019/02/issue15-gajjala-guha-stabile.

Gunn, Caitlin. 2015. "Hashtagging from the Margins: Women of Color Engaged in Feminist Consciousness-Raising on Twitter." In *Women of Color and Social Media Multitasking: Blogs, Timelines, Feeds, and Community*, edited by Keisha Edwards Tassie and Sonja M. Brown Givens, 21–34. Lanham: Lexington Books.

Gustafsson, Hanna. 2019. "Därför har feminismen inte råd med fejkade fakta." *Arbetet*, November 22. https://arbetet.se/2019/11/19/darfor-har-feminismen-inte-rad -med-fejkade-fakta.

Gustavsson, Matilda. 2017. "18 Kvinnor: Kulturprofil har utsatt oss för övergrepp." *Dagens Nyheter*, November 21. https://www.dn.se/kultur-noje/18-kvinnor-kulturprofil -har-utsatt-oss-for-overgrepp.

Halberstam, Jack. 2016. "You Are Triggering Me! The Neo-Liberal Rhetoric of Harm, Danger and Trauma." *Bully Bloggers*, July 5. https://bullybloggers.wordpress.com/ 2014/07/05/you-are-triggering-me-the-neo-liberal-rhetoric-of-harm-danger-and -trauma.

Halberstam, Judith. 1998. *Female Masculinity*. Durham: Duke University Press.

Hanisch, Carol. 1970. "The Personal Is Political." In *Notes from the Second Year: Women's Liberation: Major Writings of the Radical Feminists*, edited by Shulamith Firestone and Anne Koedt, 76–78. New York: Radical Feminism. https://repository.duke.edu/ dc/wlmpc/wlmms01039.

Haraway, Donna. 1991. *Simians, Cyborgs, and Women: The Reinvention of Nature*. New York: Routledge,

Hayes, Rebecca M., and Molly Dragiewicz. 2018. "Unsolicited Dick Pics: Erotica, Exhibitionism or Entitlement?" *Women's Studies International Forum* 71(6): 114–120.

Helén, Ilpo, and Yesilova, Katja. 2006. "Shepherding Desire: Sexual Health Promotion in Finland from the 1940s to the 1990s." *Acta Sociologica* 49(3): 257–272.

Hemmings, Clare. 2011. *Why Stories Matter: The Political Grammar of Feminist Theory.* Durham: Duke University Press.

Hemmings, Clare. 2012. "Affective Solidarity: Feminist Reflexivity and Political Transformation." *Feminist Theory* 13(2): 147–161.

Hemmings, Clare. 2018. "Resisting Popular Feminism: Gender, Sexuality, and the Lure of the Modern." *Gender, Place and Culture* 25(7): 963–977. https://doi.org/10.1080/0966369X.2018.1433639.

Higgins, Charlotte. 2019. "Skin in the Game: Do We Need to Take Down Nudes—or Look at Them Harder?" *The Guardian*, February 27. https://www.theguardian.com/artanddesign/2019/feb/27/skin-renaissance-nude-royal-academy-naked-women-men.

Highfield, Tim. 2016. *Social Media and Everyday Politics.* Cambridge: Polity.

Hindes, Sophie, and Bianca Fileborn. 2019. "'Girl Power Gone Wrong': #MeToo, Aziz Ansari, and Media Reporting of (Grey Area) Sexual Violence." *Feminist Media Studies* (May 3). DOI:10.1080/14680777.2019.1606843.

Hird, Myra J. 2000. "Gender's Nature: Intersexuality, Transsexualism and the 'Sex'/'Gender' Binary." *Feminist Theory* 1(3): 347–364.

Hoins, Megan. 2016. "'Neo-Dadaism': Absurdist Humor and the Millennial Generation." *The Medium*, February 23. https://medium.com/@meganhoins/neo-dadaism-absurdist-humor-and-the-millennial-generation-f27a39bcf321.

Hongisto, Ilona. 2015. *Soul of the Documentary: Framing, Expression. Ethics.* Amsterdam: Amsterdam University Press

hooks, bell. 2015/1984. *Feminist Theory: From Margin to Center.* New York: Routledge.

Horeck, Tanya. 2014. "#AskThicke: 'Blurred Lines,' Rape Culture, and the Feminist Hashtag Takeover." *Feminist Media Studies* 14(6): 1105–1107.

Horsti, Karina. 2017. "Digital Islamophobia: The Swedish Woman as a Figure of Purity and Dangerous Whiteness." *New Media & Society* 19(9): 1440–1457.

Howard, Jane. 2018. "Hannah Gadsby's *Nanette* Dares to Dream of a Different Future—for Ourselves and for Comedy." *The Guardian*, June 26. https://www.theguardian.com/tv-and-radio/2018/jun/27/hannah-gadsbys-nanette-dares-to-dream-of-a-different-future-for-ourselves-and-for-comedy.

Hutcheon, Linda. 1985. *A Theory of Parody: The Teachings of Twentieth-Century Art Forms.* New York: Methuen.

Hutcheon, Linda. 1994. *Irony's Edge: The Theory and Politics of Irony.* London: Routledge.

Illouz, Eva. 2014. *Hard-Core Romance: "Fifty Shades of Grey," Best-Sellers, and Society.* Chicago: University of Chicago Press.

Irigaray, Luce. 1993/1977. *This Sex Which Is Not One.* Translated by Catherine Porter. Ithaca: Cornell University Press.

Isaak, Jo Anna. 1996. *Feminism and Contemporary Art: The Revolutionary Power of Women's Laughter.* London: Routledge.

Izadi, Elahe. 2018. "Why Hannah Gadsby's Netflix Special 'Nanette' Is So Remarkable." *Washington Post,* July 3. https://www.washingtonpost.com/news/arts-and -entertainment/wp/2018/07/03/why-hannah-gadsbys-netflix-special-nanette-is-so -remarkable/?utm_term=.2ada07a93625.

Jackson, Sarah J. 2016. "(Re)imagining Intersectional Democracy from Black Feminism to Hashtag Activism." *Women's Studies in Communication* 39(4): 375–379.

Jane, Emma Alice. 2014a. "'Back to the Kitchen, Cunt': Speaking the Unspeakable about Online Misogyny." *Continuum* 28(4): 558–570.

Jane, Emma Alice. 2014b. "Your a Ugly, Whorish, Slut." *Feminist Media Studies* 14(4): 531–546.

Jane, Emma Alice. 2016. *Misogyny Online: A Short (and Brutish) History.* London: Sage.

Jeshion, Robin. 2013. "Expressivism and the Offensiveness of Slurs." *Philosophical Perspectives* 27(1): 231–259.

Johnson, Katherine. 2015. *Sexuality: A Psychosocial Manifesto.* Cambridge: Polity.

Jones, Amelia. 1996. *Sexual Politics: Judy Chicago's* Dinner Party *in Feminist Art History.* Los Angeles: Hammer Museum of Art and University of California Press.

Jones, Amelia. 2012. *Seeing Differently: A History and Theory of Identification and the Visual Arts.* Abingdon: Routledge.

Kahn, Andrew. 2018. "Stand-Up Tragedy: Hannah Gadsby's *Nanette* Shows How Comedy Is Broken, and Leaves Us to Pick up the Pieces." *Slate,* July 11. https://slate .com/culture/2018/07/hannah-gadsbys-netflix-special-nanette-is-powerful-anti -comedy.html.

Kanai, Akane. 2015. "WhatShouldWeCallMe? Self-Branding, Individuality and Belonging in Youthful Femininities on Tumblr." *M/C Journal* 18(1). http://www .journal.media-culture.org.au/index.php/mcjournal/article/viewArticle/936/0.

Kanai, Akane. 2016. "Sociality and Classification: Reading Gender, Race, and Class in a Humorous Meme." *Social Media+ Society* 2(4). https://journals.sagepub.com/doi/ full/10.1177/2056305116672884.

Karatzogianni, Athina. 2012. "Epilogue: The Politics of the Affective Digital." In *Digital Cultures and the Politics of Emotion*, edited by Adi Kuntsman and Athina Karatzogianni, 245–249. London: Palgrave Macmillan.

Kelly, Daniel. 2011. *Yuck! The Nature and Moral Significance of Disgust*. Cambridge, MA: MIT Press.

Kember, Sarah, 2015. "Uncloaking Humour: Ironic-Parodic Sexism and Smart Media." *New Formations* 86: 113–117.

Kennelly, Jacqueline. 2014. "'It's This Pain in My Heart That Won't Let Me Stop': Gendered Affect, Webs of Relations, and Young Women's Activism." *Feminist Theory* 15(3): 241–260.

Keskinen, Suvi. 2013. "Antifeminism and White Identity Politics: Political Antagonisms in Radical Right-Wing Populist and Anti-Immigration Rhetoric in Finland." *Nordic Journal of Migration Research* 3(4): 225–232.

Khazan, Olga. 2017. "A Viral Short Story for the #MeToo Moment." *The Atlantic*, December 11. https://www.theatlantic.com/technology/archive/2017/12/a-viral-short-story-for-the-metoo-moment/548009.

Khoja-Moolji, Shenila. 2015. "Becoming an 'Intimate Publics': Exploring the Affective Intensities of Hashtag Feminism." *Feminist Media Studies* 15(2): 347–350.

Knudsen, Britta Timm, and Karsten Stage. 2012. "Contagious Bodies. An Investigation of Affective and Discursive Strategies in Contemporary Online Activism." *Emotion, Space and Society* 5(3): 148–155.

Koivunen, Anu, Katariina Kyrölä, and Ingrid Ryberg. 2018. "Vulnerability as a Political Language." In *The Power of Vulnerability: Mobilising Affect in Feminist, Queer and Anti-Racist Media Cultures*, edited by Anu Koivunen, Katriina Kyrölä, and Ingrid Ryberg, 1–26. Manchester: Manchester University Press

Kokoli, Alexandra M. 2016. *The Feminist Uncanny in Theory and Art Practice*. London: Bloomsbury Academic.

Kolnai, Aurel. 2004. *On Disgust*. Translated and edited by Barry Smith and Carolyn Korsmeyer. Chicago: Open Court.

Korn, Jenny Ungbha. 2015. "#FuckProp8: How Temporary Virtual Communities around Politics and Sexuality Pop Up, Come Out, Provide Support, and Taper Off." In *#Hashtag Publics: The Power and Politics of Discursive Networks*, edited by Nathan Rambukkana, 127–138. New York: Peter Lang.

Kotthoff, Helga. 2006. "Gender and Humor: The State of the Art." *Journal of Pragmatics* 1: 4–26.

Kraus, Chris. 2015/1997. *I Love Dick*. London: Tuskar Rock.

Krefting, Rebecca. 2014. *All Joking Aside: American Humor and Its Discontents*. Baltimore: Johns Hopkins University Press.

Krefting, Rebecca, and Rebecca Baruc. 2015. "A New Economy of Jokes? #Socialmedia #Comedy." *Comedy Studies* 6(2): 129–140.

Kulick, Don. 2005. "Four Hundred Thousand Swedish Perverts." *Journal of Lesbian and Gay Studies* 11(2): 205–235.

Kulick, Don. 2014. "Humorless Lesbians." In *Gender and Humor: Interdisciplinary and International Perspectives*, edited by Delia Chiaro and Raffaella Baccolini, 99–113. New York: Routledge.

Kuntsman, Adi. 2010. "Webs of Hate in Diasporic Cyberspaces: The Gaza War in the Russian-Language Blogosphere." *Media, War and Conflict* 3(3): 299–313.

Kuo, Rachel. 2019. "Animating Feminist Anger: Economies of Race and Gender in Reaction GIFs." In *Gender Hate Online: Understanding the New Anti-Feminism*, edited by Debbie Ging and Eugenia Siapera, 173–194. London: Palgrave.

Kyrölä, Katariina. 2010. "Expanding Laughter: Affective Viewing, Body Image Incongruity and Fat Actress." In *Working with Affect in Feminist Readings: Disturbing Differences*, edited by Marianne Liljeström and Susanna Paasonen, 72–84. London: Routledge.

Lähdesmäki, Tuuli, and Tuija Saresma. 2014. "The Intersections of Sexuality and Religion in the Anti-Interculturalist Rhetoric in Finnish Internet Discussion on Muslim Homosexuals in Amsterdam." In *Building Barriers and Bridges: Interculturalism in the 21st Century*, edited by Jonathan Gourlay and Gabriele Strohschen, 35–48. Oxford: Inter-Disciplinary Press.

Lamb, Sharon. 1999. "Constructing the Victim: Popular Images and Lasting Labels." In *New Versions of Victims: Feminists Struggle with the Concept*, edited by Sharon Lamb, 108–138. New York: New York University Press.

Lazarsfeld, Paul, and Robert K. Merton. 1954. "Friendship as a Social Process: A Substantive and Methodological Analysis." In *Freedom and Control in Modern Society*, edited by Morroe Berger, Theodore Abel, and Charles H. Page, 18–66. New York: Van Nostrand.

Leeker, Martina. 2017. "Intervening in Habits and Homophily: Make a Difference! An Interview with Wendy Hui Kyong Chun by Martina Leeker." In *Interventions in Digital Cultures: Technology, the Political, Methods*, edited by Howard Caygill, Martina Leeker, and Tobias Schulze, 75–85. Lüneburg: Meson Press.

Lefebvre, Sam. 2016. "Forbidden Fruit: Why Provocative Art and Instagram Don't Mix." *The Guardian*, March 10. https://www.theguardian.com/artanddesign/2016/mar/10/stephanie-sarley-provocative-art-instagram-blood-oranges-feminism-sexuality.

Lejon, Johanna. 2018. "Så gick knytblusen från tråkig och gammaldags—Till att bli en symbol för kvinnokamp." *Elle*, April 13. https://www.elle.se/sara-danius -knytblus.

Lille, Karl. 2018. "Jag kan inte se något tecken på förnyelse." *Ekot*, Sveriges Radio, April 19. https://sverigesradio.se/sida/artikel.aspx?programid=478&artikel=6934290.

Ljung, Susanne. 2018. "Knytblusen är smått genialisk." *Dagens Nyheter*, April 13. https://www.dn.se/livsstil/susanne-ljung-knytblusen-ar-smatt-genialisk.

Locker, Melissa. 2015. "Congrats, You Have an All-Male Panel! How One Tumblr Shakes Up Status Quo." *The Guardian*, May 28. https://www.theguardian.com/world/ 2015/may/28/congrats-you-have-an-all-male-panel-creator-viral-tumblr.

Lockyer, Sharon, and Michael Pickering, eds. 2005. *Behind a Joke: The Limits of Humour*. New York: Palgrave Macmillan.

Lorde, Audre. 1978. *Uses of the Erotic: The Erotic as Power*. Brooklyn: Out & Out Books.

Lott-Lavigna, Ruby. 2015. "Bumble Is Tinder's New Feminist Competitor: Does It Work?" *Wired*, September 11. https://www.wired.co.uk/article/bumble-feminist -dating-app.

Lumsden, Karen, and Heather May Morgan. 2017. "Media Framing of Trolling and Online Abuse: Silencing Strategies, Symbolic Violence, and Victim Blaming." *Feminist Media Studies* 17(6): 926–940.

Lundberg, Anna. 2008. *Allt annat än allvar: Den komiska kvinnliga grotesken i svensk samtida skrattkultur*. Göteborg: Makadam.

Lykke, Nina. 2004. "Between Particularism, Universalism and Transversalism: Reflections on the Politics of Location of European Feminist Research and Education." *Nora: Nordic Journal of Women's Studies* 12(2): 72–82.

MacLeod, Caitlin, and Victoria McArthur. 2018. "The Construction of Gender in Dating Apps: An Interface Analysis of Tinder and Bumble." *Feminist Media Studies* 19(6): 822–840.

Mäkinen, Katariina. 2016. "Uneasy Laughter: Encountering the Anti-Immigration Debate." *Qualitative Research* 16(5): 541–556.

Marks, Laura Helen. 2020. "Stormy Daniels: All-American Hero." *Adult DVD Talk*, March 3. https://interviews.adultdvdtalk.com/stormy-daniels-comedy.

Marshall, William P. 1991. "The Concept of Offensiveness in Establishment and Free Exercise Jurisprudence." *Indiana Law Journal* 66: 351–377.

Marso, Lori. 2019. "Feminist Cringe Comedy: Dear Dick, the Joke Is on You." *Politics & Gender* 15(1): 1–23.

Martinsson, Lena, Gabriele Griffin, and Katarina Giritli Nygren, eds. 2016. *Challenging the Myth of Gender Equality in Sweden*. Bristol: Policy Press.

Marwick, Alice. 2013. "Memes." *Contexts* 12(4): 12–13.

Marwick, Alice. 2014. "Gender, Sexuality, and Social Media." In *The Social Media Handbook*, edited by Jeremy Hunsinger and Theresa M. Senft, 59–75. New York: Routledge.

Marwick, Alice. 2019. "None of This Is New (Media): Feminisms in the Social Media Age." In *The Routledge Handbook of Contemporary Feminism*, edited by Tasha Oren and Andrea L. Press, 309–331. New York: Routledge.

Marwick, Alice, and Robyn Caplan. 2018. "Drinking Male Tears: Language, the Manosphere, and Networked Harassment." *Feminist Media Studies* 18(4): 543–559.

Massanari, Adrienne. 2015. *Participatory Culture, Community, and Play: Learning from Reddit*. New York: Peter Lang.

Massanari, Adrienne. 2019. "'Come for the Period Comics. Stay for the Cultural Awareness': Reclaiming the Troll Identity through Feminist Humor on Reddit's /r/TrollXChromosomes." *Feminist Media Studies* 19(1): 19–37.

Massanari, Adrienne L., and Shira Chess. 2018. "Attack of the 50-Foot Social Justice Warrior: The Discursive Construction of SJW Memes as the Monstrous Feminine." *Feminist Media Studies* 18(4): 525–542.

Måwe, Ida. 2018. "Swedish Metoo Movement Greatest Impact amongst the Nordic Countries." *Swedish Secretariat for Gender Research*, March 8. https://www.genus.se/en/newspost/swedish-metoo-movement-greatest-impact-amongst-the-nordic-countries.

May, Vivian M. 2014. "'Speaking into the Void?' Intersectionality Critiques and Epistemic Backlash." *Hypatia* 29(1): 94–112.

McPherson, Miller, Lynn Smith-Lovin, and James M Cook. 2001. "Birds of a Feather: Homophily in Social Networks." *Annual Review of Sociology* 27: 415–444.

Megarry, Jessica. 2014. "Online Incivility or Sexual Harassment? Conceptualising Women's Experiences in the Digital Age." *Women's Studies International Forum* 47(1): 46–55.

Mendes, Kaitlynn, Jessica Ringrose, and Jessalynn Keller. 2019. *Digital Feminist Activism: Girls and Women Fight Back against Rape Culture*. Oxford: Oxford University Press.

Meyer, John C. 2000. "Humor as a Double-Edged Sword: Four Functions of Humor in Communication." *Communication Theory* 10(3): 310–331.

Miller, Carl. 2014. "Women Use Misogynistic Terms on Twitter Almost as Often as Men." *Wired*, May 15. https://www.wired.co.uk/article/women-abuse-online.

Miller, William Ian. 1997. *The Anatomy of Disgust*. Cambridge, MA: Harvard University Press.

Milner, Ryan M. 2014. "Hacking the Social: Internet Memes, Identity Antagonism, and the Logic of Lulz." *Fibreculture Journal* 22. http://twentytwo.fibreculturejournal.org/fcj-156-hacking-the-social-internet-memes-identity-antago-nism-and-the-logic-of-lulz.

Milner, Ryan M. 2016. *The World Made Meme: Public Conversations and Participatory Media*. Cambridge, MA: MIT Press.

Miltner, Kate. 2014 "'There's No Place for Lulz on LOLCats': The Role of Genre, Gender, and Group Identity in the Interpretation and Enjoyment of an Internet Meme." *First Monday* 19(8). http://pear.accc.uic.edu/ojs/index.php/fm/article/view/5391/4103.

Mitchell, Kimberly J., Michele L. Ybarra, and Josephine D. Korchmaros. 2014. "Sexual Harassment among Adolescents of Different Sexual Orientations and Gender Identities." *Child Abuse & Neglect* 38(2): 280–295.

Moskowitz, Peter. 2018. "The *Nanette* Problem." *The Outline*, August 20. https://theoutline.com/post/5962/the-nanette-problem-hannah-gadsby-netflix-review?zd=1&zi=p4tjrrba.

Mühleisen, Wencke. 2007. "Mainstream Sexualization and the Potential for Nordic New Feminism." *Nora: Nordic Journal of Women's Studies* 15(2–3): 172–189.

Munt, Sally R. 2007. *Queer Attachments: The Cultural Politics of Shame*. Aldershot: Ashgate.

Najafi, Sina, David Serlin, and Lauren Berlant. 2008. "The Broken Circuit: An Interview with Lauren Berlant." *Cabinet* 31. http://www.cabinetmagazine.org/issues/31/najafi_serlin.php.

Nash, Jennifer C. 2008. "Re-Thinking Intersectionality." *Feminist Review* 89(1): 1–15.

Nikunen, Kaarina. 2015. "Politics of Irony as the Emerging Sensibility of the Anti-Immigrant Debate." In *Affectivity and Race: Studies from the Nordic Context*, edited by Rikke Andreassen and Katherine Vitus, 21–42. Farnham: Ashgate.

Nikunen, Kaarina. 2019. *Media Solidarities: Emotions, Power and Justice in the Digital Age*. Los Angeles: Sage.

Noble, Safiya Umoja, and Brendesha M. Tynes, eds. 2016. *The Intersectional Internet: Race, Sex, Class, and Culture Online*. New York: Peter Lang.

Noonan, Will. 2014. "Absurdist Humor." In *The Encyclopedia of Humor Studies*, edited by Salvatore Attardo, 1–4. Thousand Oaks: Sage.

Nord, Kristin, and Maria G. Francke. 2016. "Att även på kontorstid hagga runt lite." *Nord & Francke* podcast, part 20, September 29. http://www.sydsvenskan.se/2016-09-29/att-aven-pa-kontorstid-hagga-runt-lite.

Nuzzi, Olivia. 2018. "Stormy Daniels Didn't Want to Be Anybody's Hero." *The Cut*, October 14. https://www.thecut.com/2018/10/women-and-power-stormy-daniels.html.

Nyren, Erin. 2018. "Michael Haneke Says #MeToo Movement Leads to 'Man-Hating Puritanism.'" *The Variety*, February 11. http://variety.com/2018/biz/news/michael-haneke-metoo-backlash-puritanism-1202694779.

NZ Herald. 2020. "Harvey Weinstein's Disgusting Deformity Revealed." *NZ Herald*, February 7. https://www.nzherald.co.nz/entertainment/news/article.cfm?c_id=1501119&objectid=12306654.

Orgad, Shani, and Rosalind Gill. 2019. "Safety Valves for Mediated Female Rage in the #MeToo Era." *Feminist Media Studies* 19(4): 596–603. https://doi.org/10.1080/14680777.2019.1609198.

Oring, Elliott. 2003. *Engaging Humor*. Urbana: University of Illinois Press.

Paasonen, Susanna. 2011. *Carnal Resonance: Affect and Online Pornography*. Cambridge, MA: MIT Press.

Paasonen, Susanna. 2017. "Smutty Swedes: Sex Films, Pornography and the Figure of Good Sex." In *Tainted Love: Screening Sexual Perversities*, edited by Darren Kerr and Donna Peberdy, 120–136. London: I. B. Tauris.

Paasonen, Susanna, Kylie Jarrett, and Ben Light. 2019. *NSFW: Sex, Humor, and Risk in Social Media*. Cambridge, MA: MIT Press.

Paasonen, Susanna, Ben Light, and Kylie Jarrett. 2019. "The Dick Pic: Harassment, Curation, and Desire." *Social Media + Society* (April 3). Doi: 10.1177/2056305119826126.

Palmer, Jerry. 1994. *Taking Humor Seriously*. London: Routledge.

Papacharissi, Zizi. 2014. *Affective Publics: Sentiment, Technology, and Politics*. New York: Oxford University Press.

Papacharissi, Zizi. 2016. "Affective Publics and Structures of Storytelling: Sentiment, Events and Mediality." *Information, Communication & Society* 19(3): 307–324.

Parvulescu, Anca. 2010. *Laughter: Notes on a Passion*. Cambridge, MA: MIT Press.

Patel, Anjali. 2015. "The 'All Male Panel' Tumblr Calls Out Everyday Sexism, and Is Every Bit as Hilarious as It Is Bleak—PHOTOS." *Bustle*, May 13. https://www.bustle.com/articles/82900-the-all-male-panel-tumblr-calls-out-everyday-sexism-and-is-every-bit-as-hilarious-as.

Patil, Vrushali. 2013. "From Patriarchy to Intersectionality: A Transnational Feminist Assessment of How Far We've Really Come." *Signs: Journal of Women in Culture and Society* 38(4): 847–867.

Patreon. 2019. "Manwhohasitall Is Creating a Satirical World Where Women Rule." https://www.patreon.com/manwhohasitall.

Pellegrini, Ann. 2018. "#MeToo: Before and After." *Studies in Gender and Sexuality* 19(4): 262–264.

Penny, Laurie. 2013. *Cybersexism: Sex, Gender and Power on the Internet*. London: A&C Black.

Perry, Leah. 2015. "I Can Sell My Body If I Wanna: Riot Grrrl Body Writing and Performing Shameless Feminist Resistance." *Lateral* 4. http://csalateral.org/issue/4/i-can-sell-my-body-if-i-wanna-riot-grrrl-body.

Persson, Cecilia. 2018. "Om knytblusar och klass." *Författaren* (April 18). https://www.forfattaren.se/l/knytblusar-och-klass/

Petterson, Katarina. 2017. "Ideological Dilemmas of Female Populist Radical Right Politicians." *European Journal of Women's Studies* 24(1): 7–22.

Phillips, Whitney. 2015. *This Is Why We Can't Have Nice Things: Mapping the Relationship between Online Trolling and Mainstream Culture*. Cambridge, MA: MIT Press.

Phillips, Whitney, and Ryan Milner. 2017. *The Ambivalent Internet: Mischief, Oddity, and Antagonism Online*. Cambridge: Polity.

Popa, Bogdan. 2017. *Shame: A Genealogy of Queer Practices in the 19th Century*. Edinburgh: Edinburgh University Press.

Powell, Anastasia, and Nicola Henry. 2017. *Sexual Violence in a Digital Age*. Basingstoke: Palgrave Macmillan.

Probyn, Elspeth. 2000. *Carnal Appetites: FoodSexIdentities*. London: Routledge.

Probyn, Elspeth. 2005. *Blush: Faces of Shame*. Minneapolis: University of Minnesota Press.

Protevi, John. 2009. *Political Affect: Connecting the Social and the Somatic*. Minneapolis: Minnesota University Press.

Puar, Jasbir. 2011. "'I Would Rather Be a Cyborg Than a Goddess': Intersectionality, Assemblage, and Affective Politics." *Transversal* 8(2). http://eipcp.net/transversal/0811/puar/en.

Quinn, Kerry. 2015. "Here's What Happens When You Send 40 Unsuspecting Guys a Preemptive V-Pic." *Thrillist*, November 18. https://www.thrillist.com/sex-dating/

los-angeles/we-sent-a-preemptive-v-pic-before-dudes-could-send-dick-pics-heres
-what-happened.

Rambukkana, Nathan. 2015. "#Introduction: Hashtags as Technosocial Events." In
#Hashtag Publics: The Power and Politics of Discursive Networks, edited by Nathan Rambukkana, 1–10. New York: Peter Lang.

Reductress. N.d. "About". http://reductress.com/about.

Reed, Jennifer. 2011. "Sexual Outlaws: Queer in a Funny Way." *Women's Studies*
40(6): 762–777.

Reger, Jo. 2015. "The Story of a Slut Walk: Sexuality, Race, and Generational Divisions in Contemporary Feminist Activism." *Journal of Contemporary Ethnography*
44(1): 84–112.

Reilly, Ian. 2015. "The Comedian, the Cat, and the Activist: The Politics of Light
Seriousness and the (Un)Serious Work of Contemporary Laughter." *Comedy Studies*
6(1): 49–62.

Renninger, Bryce. 2015. "'Where I Can Be Myself . . . Where I Can Speak My Mind':
Networked Counterpublics in a Polymedia Environment." *New Media & Society*
17(9): 1513–1529.

Rentschler, Carrie A. 2015. "#Safetytipsforladies: Feminist Twitter Takedowns of
Victim Blaming." *Feminist Media Studies* 15(2): 353–56.

Rentschler, Carrie A. 2017. "Bystander Intervention, Feminist Hashtag Activism, and
the Anti-Carceral Politics of Care." *Feminist Media Studies* 17(4): 565–584.

Rentschler, Carrie A., and Samantha C. Thrift. 2015. "Doing Feminism in the Network: Networked Laughter and the 'Binders Full of Women' Meme." *Feminist Theory*
16(3): 329–359.

Resick, Patricia A., and Monica K. Schnicke. 1992. "Cognitive Processing Therapy
for Sexual Assault Victims." *Journal of Consulting and Clinical Psychology* 60(5):
748–756.

Ringrose, Jessica, and Emily Lawrence. 2018. "Remixing Misandry, Manspreading,
and Dick Pics: Networked Feminist Humour on Tumblr." *Feminist Media Studies*
18(4): 686–704.

Ringrose, Jessica, and Emma Renold. 2012. "Slut-Shaming, Girl Power, and 'Sexu-
alisation': Thinking through the Politics of the International 'SlutWalks' with Teen
Girls." *Gender and Education* 24(3): 333–343.

Rofel, Lisa. 2007. *Desiring China: Experiments in Neoliberalism, Sexuality, and Public
Culture*. Durham: Duke University Press.

Roslund, Emilie. 2019. "Med offerskapet som inkomstkälla." *Göteborgs-Posten,* November 15. https://www.gp.se/kultur/kultur/med-offerskapet-som-inkomstskälla -1.20349737.

Roupenian, Kristen. 2017. "Cat Person." *The New Yorker,* December 4. https://www .newyorker.com/magazine/2017/12/11/cat-person.

Rowe, Kathleen Rowe. 1995. *The Unruly Woman: Gender and the Genres of Laughter.* Austin: University of Texas Press.

Rubin, Gayle. 1984. "Thinking Sex: Notes for a Radical Theory of the Politics of Sexuality." In *Pleasure and Danger: Exploring Female Sexuality,* edited by Carole S. Vance, 267–319. Boston: Routledge & Kegan Paul.

Russo, Mary. 1994. *The Female Grotesque. Risk, Excess, and Modernity.* London: Routledge.

Ryzik, Melena. 2018. "The Comedy-Destroying, Soul-Affirming Art of Hannah Gadsby." *New York Times,* July 24. https://www.nytimes.com/2018/07/24/arts/Nanett -gadsby-comedy-nanette.html.

Sable, Marjorie R., Fran Danis, Denise L. Mauzy, and Sarah K. Gallagher. 2006. "Barriers to Reporting Sexual Assault for Women and Men: Perspectives of College Students." *Journal of American College Health* 55(3): 157–162.

Sadowski, Helga. 2016. "From #aufschrei to hatr.org: Digital-Material Entanglements in the Context of German Digital Feminist Activisms." *Feminist Media Studies* 16(1): 55–69.

Salter, Anastasia, and Bridget Marie Blodgett. 2012. "Hypermasculinity and Dickwolves: The Contentious Role of Women in the New Gaming Public." *Journal of Broadcasting and Electronic Media* 56(3): 401–416.

Salter, Michael. 2015. "Privates in the Online Public: Sex(ting) and Reputation on Social Media." *New Media & Society* 18(11): 2723–2739.

Salter, Michael. 2019. "Online Justice in the Circuit of Capital: #MeToo, Marketization and the Deformation of Sexual Ethics." In *#MeToo and the Politics of Social Change,* edited by Bianca Fileborn and Rachel Loney-Howes, 317–334. Basingstoke: Palgrave Macmillan.

Salvato, Nick. 2013. "Cringe Criticism: On Embarrassment and Tori Amos." *Critical Inquiry* 39(4): 676–702.

Sampson, Tony D. 2012. *Virality: Contagion Theory in the Age of Networks.* Minneapolis: University of Minnesota Press.

Sanders, Barry. 1995. *Sudden Glory: Laughter as Subversive History.* Boston: Beacon Press.

Särmä, Saara. 2016. "Congrats, You Have an All-Male Panel!" *International Feminist Journal of Politics* 18(3): 470–476.

Scherer, Jenna. 2018. "'Nanette': Hannah Gadsby on Her Gamechanging Stand-Up Special." *Rolling Stone*, July 9. https://www.rollingstone.com/tv/tv-features/Nanette -hannah-gadsby-on-her-gamechanging-stand-up-special-696354.

Schwartz, Drew. 2002. "Jurors in the Harvey Weinstein Trial Had to See Photos of His 'Deformed' Penis." *Vice*, February 5. https://www.vice.com/en_us/article/y3m3qg/ jurors-in-the-harvey-weinstein-trial-had-to-see-nude-photos-of-his-deformed-penis.

Sedgwick, Eve Kosofsky. 2003. *Touching Feeling: Affect, Pedagogy, Performativity.* Durham: Duke University Press.

Sedgwick, Eve Kosofsky, and Adam Frank. 1995. *Shame and Its Sisters: A Silvan Tomkins Reader.* Durham: Duke University Press.

Segal, Lynne. 2018. *Radical Happiness: Moments of Collective Joy.* London: Verso Books.

Senft, Theresa M. 2008. *Celebrity and Community in the Age of Social Networks.* New York: Peter Lang.

Shah, Nishant. 2015. "Sluts 'r' Us: Intersections of Gender, Protocol and Agency in the Digital Age." *First Monday* 20(4–6). http://firstmonday.org/ojs/index.php/fm/ article/view/5463.

Shaw, Adrienne. 2014. "The Internet Is Full of Jerks, Because the World Is Full of Jerks: What Feminist Theory Teaches Us about the Internet." *Communication and Critical/Cultural Studies* 11(3): 273–277.

Shaw, Frances. 2016. "'Bitch I Said Hi': The Bye Felipe Campaign and Discursive Activism in Mobile Dating Apps." *Social Media + Society* (October–December): 1–10. doi: 10.1177/2056305116672889.

Shepherd, Tamara, Alison Harvey, Tim Jordan, Sam Srauy, and Kate Miltner. 2015. "Histories of Hating." *Social Media+ Society* 1(2): doi: 10.1177/2056305115603997.

Shifman, Limor, and Menahem Blondheim. 2010. "The Medium Is the Joke: Online Humor about and by Networked Computers." *New Media & Society* 12(8): 1348–1367.

Shulman, George. 2004. "Narrating Clinton's Impeachment: Race, the Right, and Allegories of the Sixties." In *Public Affairs: Politics in the Age of Sex Scandals,* edited by Paul Apostolidis and Juliet A. Williams, 167–184. Durham: Duke University Press.

Sisley, Dominique. 2016. "How Finger-Fucking Fruit Became an Act of Protest." *Dazed*, June 13. http://www.dazeddigital.com/artsandculture/article/31497/1/how -finger-fucking-fruit-became-an-act-of-protest.

Skeggs, Beverley. 1997. *Formations of Class and Gender: Becoming Respectable*. London: Sage.

Stache, Lara C. 2015. "Advocacy and Political Potential at the Convergence of Hashtag Activism and Commerce." *Feminist Media Studies* 15(1): 162–164.

Stein, Arlene. 2006. *Shameless: Sexual Dissidence in American Culture*. New York: New York University Press.

Stensrud, Rockwell. 2015. "What's the Difference between a Pilgrim and a Puritan?" *Newsweek*, November 26. http://www.newsweek.com/whats-difference-between-pilgrim -and-puritan-397974.

Stockton, Kathryn Bond. 2006. *Beautiful Bottom, Beautiful Shame: Where "Black" Meets "Queer."* Durham: Duke University Press.

Strömquist, Susanna. 2015. "Sara Danius: Jag är alltid på jakt efter en snygg knytblus." *Elle*, December 12. https://www.elle.se/sara-danius-jag-ar-alltid-pa-jakt-efter-en -snygg-knytblus.

Sundén, Jenny. 2012. "Desires at Play: On Closeness and Epistemological Uncertainty." *Games and Culture* 7(2): 164–184.

Sundén, Jenny. 2013. "Corporeal Anachronisms: Notes on Affect, Relationality, and Power in Steampunk." *Somatechnics* 3(2): 369–386.

Sundén, Jenny. 2015. "On Trans-, Glitch, and Gender as Machinery of Failure." *First Monday* 20(4). http://firstmonday.org/ojs/index.php/fm/article/view/5895/4416.

Sveland, Maria. 2013. *Hatet: En bok om antifeminism*. Stockholm: Leopard.

Tagg, Caroline, P. Seargent, and Amy Aisha Brown. 2017. *Taking Offence on Social Media: Conviviality and Communication on Facebook*. New York: Springer.

Tait, Amelia. 2017. "Swipe Right for Equality: How Bumble Is Taking on Sexism." *Wired*, August 30. https://www.wired.co.uk/article/bumble-whitney-wolfe-sexism -tinder-app.

Tait, Robert. 2016. "David Hasselhoff Becomes the Unlikely Face of Campaign against All-Male Panels." *The Telegraph*, May 24. https://www.telegraph.co.uk/news/2016/ 05/24/david-hasselhoff-becomes-the-unlikely-face-of-campaign-against-a.

Talvitie, Eveliina. 2016. "Ylpeästi Suvakkihuora." *Satakunnan kansa*, March 24. https://www.satakunnankansa.fi/kotimaa/ylpeasti-suvakkihuora-13754462.

Tambe, Ashwini. 2018. "Reckoning with the Silences of #MeToo." *Feminist Studies* 44(1): 197–203.

Thelandersson, Fredrika. 2014. "A Less Toxic Feminism: Can the Internet Solve the Age Old Question of How to Put Intersectional Theory into Practice?" *Feminist Media Studies* 14(3): 527–530.

Tiidenberg, Katrin. 2015. "Boundaries and Conflict in a NSFW Community on Tumblr: The Meanings and Uses of Selfies." *New Media & Society* 18(8): 1563–1578.

Tomkins, Silvan S. 1995a. *Exploring Affect: The Selected Writings of Silvan S. Tomkins.* Edited by E. Virginia Demos. Cambridge: Cambridge University Press.

Tomkins, Silvan S. 1995b. *Shame and Its Sisters: A Silvan Tomkins Reader.* Edited by Eve Kosofsky Sedgwick and Adam Frank. Durham: Duke University Press.

Tomkins, Silvan S. 2008. *Affect Imagery Consciousness: The Complete Edition.* New York: Springer.

Toppa, Sabrina. 2015. "'Congrats! You Have and All-Male Panel' Is a Hilarious Takedown of Everyday Sexism." *Time*, May 15. http://time.com/3859765/congrats-all-male-panel-tumblr-women-sexism-feminism-discrimination-gender.

Tyler, Imogen. 2006. "Chav Scum: The Filthy Politics of Social Class in Contemporary Britain." *M/C Journal* 9(5). http://journal.media-culture.org.au/0610/09-tyler.php.

van der Nagel, Emilie. 2016. "Harassment and High Fives: The Many Victims of Shaming Culture." *Medium*, October 10. https://medium.com/@emily.vdn/harassment-and-high-fives-the-many-victims-of-shaming-culture-c83437eed7f2#.4vvhgial4.

van Dijk, Teun A. 1993. *Elite Discourse and Racism.* Newbury Park: Sage.

Verduin, Kathleen. 1983. "'Our Cursed Natures': Sexuality and the Puritan Conscience." *New England Quarterly* 56(2): 220–237.

Vidal, Maria Elena, and Jenny Petrak. 2007. "Shame and Adult Sexual Assault: A Study with a Group of Female Survivors Recruited from an East London Population." *Sexual and Relationship Therapy* 22(2): 159–171.

Vitis, Laura, and Fairleigh Gilmore. 2016. "Dick Pics on Blast: A Woman's Resistance to Online Sexual Harassment Using Humour, Art and Instagram." *Crime, Media, Culture* 13(3): 335–355.

Walby, Sylvia. 1989. "Theorising Patriarchy." *Sociology* 23(2): 213–234.

Waling, Andrea, and Tinonee Pym. 2019. "'C'mon, No One Wants a Dick Pic': Exploring the Cultural Framings of the 'Dick Pic' in Contemporary Online Publics." *Journal of Gender Studies* 28(1): 70–85.

Warner, Michael. 2000. *The Trouble with Normal: Sex, Politics, and the Ethics of Queer Life.* Cambridge, MA: Harvard University Press.

Webb, Lewis. 2015. "Shame Transfigured: Slut-Shaming from Rome to Cyberspace." *First Monday* 20(4). https://firstmonday.org/ojs/index.php/fm/article/view/5464/4419

Williams, Raymond. 1977. *Marxism and Literature.* Oxford: Oxford University Press.

Williams, Sherri. 2015. "Digital Defense: Black Feminists Resists Violence with Hashtag Activism." *Feminist Media Studies* 15(2): 341–344.

Williams, Sherri. 2016. "#SayHerName: Using Digital Activism to Document Violence against Black Women." *Feminist Media Studies* 16(5): 922–925.

Willsher, Kim. 2018. "Catherine Deneuve's Claim of #MeToo Witch-Hunt Sparks Backlash." *The Guardian*, January 10. https://www.theguardian.com/film/2018/jan/10/catherine-deneuve-claim-metoo-witch-hunt-backlash.

Wolf, Naomi. 1993. *Fire with Fire: The New Female Power and How It Will Change the 21st Century.* London: Vintage.

Wood, Elizabeth Anne. 2008. "Consciousness-Raising 2.0: Sex Blogging and the Creation of a Feminist Sex Commons." *Feminism & Psychology* 18(4): 480–487.

Xeima. 2012. "Aikamme Kuva: Mediasensuuri, Vähemmistötyrannia ja 2 Somaliraiskaajaa." *Fundamentti*, February 23. https://web.archive.org/web/20160110224139/http://fundamentti.blogspot.fi/2012/04/aikamme-kuva-mediasensuuri.html.

Zannettou, Savvas, Tristan Caulfield, Jeremy Blackburn, Emiliano De Cristofaro, Michael Sirivianos, Gianluca Stringhini, and Guillermo Suarez-Tangil. 2018. "On the Origins of Memes by Means of Fringe Web Communities." In *Proceedings of IMC '18.* New York: ACM. https://doi.org/10.1145/3278532.3278550.

Zarkov, Dubravka, and Kathy Davis. 2018. "Ambiguities and Dilemmas around #MeToo: #ForHowLong and #WhereTo?" *European Journal of Women's Studies* 25(1): 3–9.

Index